The Paths to Domination, Resistance, and Terror

The Paths to Domination, Resistance, and Terror

EDITED BY

Carolyn Nordstrom

AND

JoAnn Martin

UNIVERSITY OF CALIFORNIA PRESS
Berkeley   Los Angeles   Oxford

University of California Press
Berkeley and Los Angeles, California
University of California Press
Oxford, England
Copyright © 1992 by
The Regents of the University of California
Printed in the United States of America

1   2   3   4   5   6   7   8   9

**Library of Congress
Cataloging-in-Publication Data**

The Paths to Domination, Resistance, and
 Terror / edited by Carolyn
Nordstrom and JoAnn Martin.
     p.   cm.
   Includes bibliographical references and
index.
     ISBN 0–520–07315–0 (cloth)
     ISBN 0–520–07316–9 (paper)
   1. Social conflict—Cross-cultural studies.
2. Violence—Cross-cultural studies. 3. Government, Resistance to—Cross-cultural studies.
4. Terrorism—Cross-cultural studies.
5. Social movements—Cross-cultural studies.
I. Nordstrom, Carolyn, 1953–
II. Martin, JoAnn, 1955–
HN17.5.D647   1992
303.6—dc20   91–4767
                                         CIP

CONTENTS

ILLUSTRATIONS

ACKNOWLEDGMENTS

Many people have helped and supported us in the process of writing this book. We want to thank Laura Nader for her critical comments on the introduction and Elizabeth Colson and Burton Benedict for their advice and encouragement throughout the process of writing and editing. The chapters in this volume were presented at the 1988 American Anthropology Association Meetings and have benefited from the critical comments of the discussants Leith Mullings and Laura Nader. Keith Gohsler and Wenyi Wu, in addition to being supportive spouses, helped with xeroxing, word processing, typing, and mailing. Dan Rosenberg, George Esber, Steve Butler, and Steve Nussbaum provided moral support and a critical editorial eye when needed. Cheri Gaddis and Velma DeBruler assisted with typing the manuscript. Finally, we are grateful to our editor at University of California Press, Stanley Holwitz, for his support and help.

Introduction

ONE

The Culture of Conflict: Field Reality and Theory

Carolyn Nordstrom and JoAnn Martin

In the history of relations between the world's leading states certain features stand out prominently since the end of the eighteenth century. One is that infrequent wars have alternated with long periods of peace . . . since 1945, another forty years of peace already. (HINSLEY 1987:63)

The history of humanity is one long succession of wars and conflicts. . . . Approximately 150 wars or conflicts have been fought since the end of World War II claiming some 20 million lives. Polemological institutes have counted a mere 26 days of total peace since the end of World War II. (BEDJAOUI 1986:24)

PORTRAYING VIOLENCE ETHICALLY

The widespread sociopolitical violence in the world, especially in the Third World, has altered the terrain of ethnographic research, raising new questions and requiring different types of ethnographic presentations. Anthropologists and other social scientists are confronting the challenge of portraying violence without encouraging or rationalizing it. We are, as Michael Taussig (1987) suggested, searching for a position from which we can speak and write against repression.

Questions concerning repression, resistance, and warfare take on a critical tone for those who, like the authors represented in this volume, conduct in-depth field research on, and in, violent conditions. Given the extent of sociopolitical conflict, and the dearth of dynamic theoretical frameworks geared toward understanding the phenomenon of modern—and what might even be called postmodern—violence, what ethnographic voice do responsible researchers give to the perpetrators and to the victims of sociopolitical violence? What theoretical perspectives best portray the destabilizing effect of violence on cultures? How is conflict "lived" by the people caught in its throes?

The study of sociopolitical violence is marked by a distinct set of difficulties above and beyond those associated with any field research. Notwithstanding the currently popular notion that domination in the modern world depends more on regimes of truth than on violence, the latter remains central to competing claims for power both among and within states.

In modern struggles for power, social scientists frequently find themselves placed in the fictional position of a "powerful subject" who is trying to decipher the strategies and moves of a crafty opponent. Analysis becomes centered around specifying "the 'shots' that a power is capable of making in relation to given facts" (de Certeau 1988:6). For example, whenever a conflict impinges on matters of "national security," the news media looks for leading "experts" to predict the moves the various actors will take. Social scientists are in effect asked to devise a strategy to serve the interests of their own country as though they were directing foreign policy. The process legitimates a way of thinking about violence and conflict that emanates from a position of power. Often, it is a way of thinking that is enmeshed in structural and institutional frameworks, and thereby misses the dynamics associated with the actual experience of violence.

In contrast, the ethnographer's "imagination" (Mills 1959), which is central to this volume, is nurtured through a different subject, one whose perspective may be formed more in tactics of survival rather than strategies of power. For the ethnographer's subject violence may not be a means to an end, but a powerful component of sociocultural reality.

Field Reality

The field reality made explicit in the essays in this book stands in contrast to the picture of conflict conveyed to outside observers by textual analyses and media sources. The "images" of conflict that are carried to outsiders by the visual and print media focus on dramatic vignettes that are intended to convey sociopolitical "truths" about the situation in question. In all of these formal portrayals the ideology is clear-cut, the opponents are obvious, and the fight takes place among delineated factions that are politically recognizable. Soldiers fight, ideology teaches, civilians support or suffer the struggles for power.

In fact, notions of witchcraft, bureaucracy, time, and everyday conversations or their repressive silencing are often the arenas in which power struggles are manifest and aggression given a cultural voice; literature and art are mechanisms by which tensions, distresses, and threats are communicated to a larger audience; and claims of just war are often used as ideological whitewashes covering far different practices.

The power of the ethnographer's position is derived from that person's ability to capture experience and to turn that experience into something quite different by drawing on larger theoretical frameworks that contend with problems of power in relation to issues of domination, resistance, and terror. In sharp contrast with traditional studies of sociopolitical violence that focus on political and (para)military institutions, the chapters in this book offer approaches for researching violence as a dynamic sociocultural phenomenon. This research is grounded in people and the way they experience conflict and the enactment of violence. As de Certeau (1980:3) states in dedicating his essay to the ordinary man, "He is the murmur of societies." It is the average person that constitutes the heartbeat of societies—the essential rhythm and lifeblood of social reality.

Field reality as presented here speaks simultaneously as context and theory. Interpersonal social interactions, state formations, and international power relationships are connected in the field context in ways that, although not always transparent to informants, may be captured in an ethnography. The ethnographer writes from a position privileged by an ability to move through different levels: local, national, and international; and by the way theory is drawn into the process of reflecting on "the causes, significance, and implications of . . . experience" (Cocks 1989:95). Thus, the field reality is rich terrain in which the ethnographer can glean the interplay of power relationships across various levels as they are played out in the daily lives of the people involved.

Repression, Resistance, and Local Reality: Culture and Power

The most striking finding of this volume is that repression and resistance generated at the national level are often inserted into the local reality in culturally specific ways. As a result, phenomena that anthropologists have often viewed as results of local processes take on entirely new meaning when viewed in relation to more macro-level political change. Political anxieties and the horrors of political violence are variously expressed in cultural performances, silenced by denial, or disguised in day-to-day representations of self at the local level. When violence reaches grave levels it may overtake the webs of significance informing the entire cultural system. These processes—which are critical to understanding the dynamics of sociopolitical violence—are often overlooked in traditional analyses of conflict that view warfare as a sporadic and exceptional aspect of everyday life, external to family relations, social processes, and cultural realities of the population at large. However, recent theoretical developments have challenged distinctions that might have prevented researchers from capturing the way systems of domination, resistance, and terror may affect every form of social life.

The notion of hegemony as developed by Antonio Gramsci (1971) and elaborated by Raymond Williams (1977, 1980) places culture at the center of analyses of power. Culture as a "lived system of meanings and values" is forged in a context in which not all actors are equally powerful, nor are those in power acting only in response to their own immediate economic interests (Williams 1977:110). Central to the notion of cultural hegemony is the observation that power shapes cultural processes through the deployment of concepts and values in a variety of institutions—many of which are only indirectly linked to a dominant group. Alternative and oppositional practices continually emerge within dominant culture. Furthermore, the meaning of "cultural logics" that are used to oppress a people can become coopted in rebellion as a source of identity (West 1988:23; Williams 1980:40). Thus, the concept of hegemony suggests a more fluid vision of the way power interacts with culture, not a simplistic model in which economic elites plot to control their world.

Gramsci and Williams decenter the concept of power by recognizing that power originates in society, but they both maintain a distinction between "political" and "civil" society. They are always sure that somewhere a dominant group exists whose influence can ultimately be identified (Cocks 1989:4). Foucault, however, is wary of specifying dominant groups: "I do not have in mind a general system of domination exerted by one group over another, a system whose effects, through successive derivations, pervade the entire social body" (Foucault 1976:92). For Foucault, the state is important, not because it exercises institutional power but because it captures and controls power that is rooted in systems of social networks and inscribed on the body (Foucault 1976:224). Taking culture as the central domain of contests for power, ethnographers now emphasize the way culture in all its varied aspects becomes wedded to an expanding capitalist system and/or powerful and repressive states (Comaroff 1985; Fernandez-Kelly 1983; Kapferer 1988; Nash 1977; Ong 1987; Sider 1989; Taussig 1980).

The linkages among various cultural systems mean that culture can no longer be imagined as a cohesive system of beliefs, values, and behavior (Clifford 1988). As the essays in this volume illustrate the inability to demonstrate coherence at the level of culture or at the level of structures of power has encouraged anthropologists to emphasize discourse, performance, and text as indications of the way relations of power are inscribed in images of what is speakable and unspeakable, and to whom and in which contexts. Micro-level attention to discourse as voice, body as script, action as performance, and representation as (ideal) art shatters any conceptions of culture as a consummate whole that determines behavior and channels ways of thinking.

Analytical attention to frameworks of power and domination make little sense without a concomitant conception of struggle and resistance. Practices that anthropologists might once have viewed as a survival of "tradition," when analyzed in relation to structures of domination, emerge as nonessentialist forms of resistance. Tales of the past (Price 1983), jokes (Willis 1977), spirit possession (Ong 1987), and pacts with the devil (Taussig 1980) may be viewed as forms of protest that flourish in contexts that deny history, impose discipline, or profit from wage labor. Resistance may thus be encoded in a wide range of cultural practices that are meaningful by virtue of their opposition to a dominant culture.

When resistance is confined to the level of cultural expressions the task of specifying the nature and form of opposition is often left to the anthropologist—who, inspired with a critical spirit—discerns the hidden meaning behind the informant's statements and practices. In contrast, when informants begin to organize consciously, they specify their own understanding of structures of domination and employ tactics that respond to local circumstances. As the essays in this volume suggest, organized social movements may find enemies and allies in persons and places that the anthropologist, embedded in a tradition of critical theory, would rarely anticipate.

Violence—Manifest and Intangible

Violence itself—as both a phenomenon and a focus of research endeavor—like power, is an "essentially contested" arena (Lukes 1974:9). Many take the approach that "everyone implicated in violence is likely to recognize it as such" (Riches 1986:10). In many ways this is true; violence can come to serve as a metalanguage that is understood—and all too often employed—across social, political, linguistic, and ethnic boundaries when normal channels of communication are ineffective. The notion that violence is incontestable circumvents the problem underscored by Riches that the term *violence,* like *terrorism,* is very much a political designation: both are avoided by perpetrators and the state while being employed by victims who have suffered their consequences.

In fact, not everyone recognizes violence, nor is all violence recognized as such. Scholars such as Thee have forged approaches to violence that include less visible but equally powerful aspects of "structural violence" as well as the more dramatic examples of violence enacted. Research, writes Thee (1980:4), "soon became concerned, apart from the physical and manifest violence, with social and economic violence. Stimulated by the stormy transformation of the international scene in the wake of anticolonial revolution, peace research became conscious of the fact that far more human life on the globe is destroyed by widespread poverty, hunger, avoidable diseases and socioeconomic deprivation than by the overt use of arms." And he concludes, "such conditions reflect a violence embedded in the socioeconomic structure of society—structural violence" (ibid., 5).

Scholars like Bourdieu have expanded the definitions of violence to include symbolic violence, which is maintained in socioeconomic relations cast in less than conscious hegemonic constraints. This is Bourdieu's "unrecognizable, socially recognized violence" (1977:191). Such approaches emphasize that systems of inequality and dominance generate relationships themselves capable of being violent in nature. Expanding the definition of violence, however, makes it a sweeping category that may prove cumbersome. Comaroff (1985) approaches the hegemonic reproduction of violent relationships in a more focused manner. She challenges Bourdieu's focus on the predominantly unconscious replication of these structures by noting that it is in the hazy arena of partial consciousness of social and conceptual action that the conflict of hegemonic force and the voices of resistance are most powerfully articulated.

Expanded definitions of violence have been useful in giving a voice to systems of violence no less powerful by virtue of their intangibility. They clearly demonstrate that violence enacted is but a small part of violence lived. A cautionary note should be raised, however. The expansion of the definitions of violence can also play into the hands of repressive regimes who justify widespread repression by claiming to "see" violence (read "opposition") throughout the population.

A thorny set of questions is raised by the intangibility of violence. There is a tendency in the social sciences to study violence when it is manifested, even while recognizing that its genesis lies in structural violence. In other words, the view supported is that violence ceases when violent actions stop. Yet its ideational manifestation is as crucial as its more concrete expression. Violence, like Simmel's (1950:151) statement on domination, "is not so much the exploitation of the other as much as the mere consciousness of the possibility." Thus, the continual reproduction of violence is in all likelihood linked to the fact that while the legitimacy of its use is contested, its existence as part of the cultural repertoire is not.

EXPLOSIVE SITUATIONS

The essays in this book are organized along a continuum of domination, resistance, and the manifestation of overt violence and terror. They move from situations where domination is embedded in everyday social realities and resistance is unexpressed through the emergence of resistance and overt conflict to situations of extreme sociopolitical violence. We have strived to represent examples of research from around the world indicative of the conflicts and problems people are facing today. All are set within the fundamental assumption that violence is not a natural or genetic characteristic in human populations, and then go on to ask what social and cultural dynamics foment, perpetuate, and resolve conflict.

In grappling with how to approach the study and presentation of sociopolitical violence, the chapters in this volume demonstrate several trends. First, they place studies of violence in the field of violence. Second, authors in this volume work with issues of sociopolitical violence within a larger framework that contends with problems of power struggles. Finally, the authors seek to wed context with analysis as a comprehensive presentation. In this way, the field reality can speak simultaneously as data, as ethnographic product, and as theoretical construction combined.

The types of violence and the ways in which they are manifested vary over time and space; so, too, do the theories intended to explain them, as the first two chapters demonstrate. Jeff Sluka's chapter, "The Anthropology of Conflict" (chap. 2), introduces the major theoretical arenas that have defined contemporary anthropological investigation into cross-cultural conflict. Sluka's view is an optimistic one: anthropologists, taking critical perspectives seriously, continually hone and refine viable approaches to representing conflict as a manifest phenomenon that raises pressing moral issues.

In a parallel to Sluka's contribution, John Bodley (chap. 3) challenges pat constructions of contemporary political conflict and genocide. His chapter gives voice to two essentially muted arenas of research into sociopolitical violence: the wholesale genocide of tribal peoples and the responsibility of the theoretician, the anthropologist, and—one might add—the apologist, in directly affecting the policies and the justifications for tribal genocide or protectionism. This essay takes on added significance given Bodley's estimates that around fifty million tribal people have been killed in the last century—figures, interestingly, that are seldom included in statistics of war-related casualties. His chapter is a reminder that power is not relegated to monolithic politicomilitary institutions alone, but extends into the halls of academia itself.

Domination

Part I deals with situations of domination and resistance that are embedded in the everyday context of the social order and in which resistance is more discursive than enacted, more latent than overt. Conflict and oppression are culturally diffused, and resistance is socially subordinated to the interests of controlling powers.

James Scott's essay (chap. 4) focuses on representations of self embodied in discursive formations established around unequal power relations (landlord vs. tenant; slave vs. master, etc.). Power viewed in terms of distributions of authority is the basis of Scott's discussion, with a primary focus on the dialogic expression of power. In an illuminating series of case studies, Scott portrays the careful negotiations of hidden and public transcripts that give voice to the frustrations and grievances of inequality. The reproduction of power relations in daily society is a cogent process but one, he notes, that is at least partially influenced by all the actors involved, dominant and powerless alike. Individual interactions and ongoing social dynamics at the micro level lay the foundation for larger sociopolitical dramas when tensions finally erupt and the separation between the hidden and public transcript breaks down.

Longina Jakubowska (chap. 5) investigates the connection between domination and the construction of social identity among Israeli Bedouins. She demonstrates the way the Israeli state constructs ethnic identity as a technology of power. In the Israeli-Palestinian conflict ethnic affiliation becomes a way of controlling groups by marginalization. Jakubowska finds that while the traditional cultural vitality of the Bedouin has suffered from these policies, they have attempted to renegotiate the marginalization process to resist Israeli-imposed ethnic identity, and have turned to religion as a way of preserving their social and political distinctiveness. Her essay suggests the ways in which ethnicity, which has so often been analyzed as a source of group pride, may in the context of a repressive state become an undesirable social construct.

Edgar Winans's (chap. 6) focus on the occurrences of "man-beast" killings in Tanzania is an excellent example of how anthropologists are beginning to reconceptualize local-level events in relationship to more macro-level political changes. Winans argues that the "man-beast" killings of livestock that increased sharply around the time of independence reflected the tensions that emerged when radical political change was taking place and questions of power were in doubt. He demonstrates that violence cannot be understood if defined as directed solely against the physical person, and argues that conflict and tensions are often expressed within the framework of the cultural template of a people. By recasting these killings in light of the pressures brought about by independence, Winans's analysis stands as a cogent rebuttal to earlier functional explanations of such killings and to studies that cast politics solely in terms of institutional factors.

Resistance

The chapters in Part II deal with consciously enacted resistance and struggle. Tensions and conflicts are expressed in discursive formations, social interactions, and cultural texts, as well as in practices. Chapters 7 to 10 demonstrate ways in which domination and resistance are carried throughout the social and conceptual universe of a population as conflict takes shape. Conflict is culturally articulated: movies, myths, and murals convey rhetoric and ideology; spirits become arenas of contention; and time, irony, and historical narrative become modes of resistance and rebellion.

Jean-Paul Dumont's essay (chap. 7) begins Part II by addressing the question of violence. His essay moves in an appropriately abrupt fashion from the local context in the Philippines to the Hollywood movie, *The Killing Fields*. The dramatic shift in context provides a telling juxtaposition: Marcos's use of the movie to convey political threat to the population at large—a move neatly satirized by the average citizen—stands alongside the way in which people actually grapple with the daily specter of violence in their lives. His chapter demonstrates the way international politicocultural relationships, the powerful celluloid representations of the media, and the political intrigues that take place on the national level coalesce to influence popular culture and the individual's struggle with political and personal realities. Dumont's essay (chap. 7) employs an ironic technique to capture the irony of undertaking research on violence at the local level in the context of the repressive Marcos regime in which violence, by politicopublic decree, does not exist.

The multiple dimensions of conflict becomes apparent in a second chapter on the Philippines (chap. 8), in which Philip Parnell analyzes tactics of resistance that are employed by organizations of squatter communities in Manila. In addition to distilling the basic strategies of resistance and power articulated by the actors themselves, he gleans the more intangible strategies that have come to define the field of struggle: time, irony, and concepts of home are used by squatters as tools to influence sociopolitical change. Parnell's research suggests that both conflict and time look very different to people depending on the place they occupy in the social, economic, and political ladder. The struggles represented in this chapter are not all external: Parnell points to the difficulties that an ethnographer—born and raised in a culture where thwarted time and compounded conflicts are to be avoided—has in understanding this type of social movement.

Martin's chapter illuminates the processes by which ideals of resistance become actualized. Her study of storytelling in Mexico captures a process whereby constructs of identity and conceptualizations of resistance merge in a public voice to initiate sociopolitical action. The chapter suggests the extent to which patterns of domination and resistance are engraved in historical memory and reproduced through narratives. By following the unfolding story of revolutionary identity taking on a social force and cohesiveness, she illustrates that the truth about the past is created by storytellers who weave their tales of revolution around the possibilities and necessities of present-day configurations of power relationships. The power of narrative to promote historical consciousness lies in the way form, creativity, and individual and community biographies are brought together in the story. The chapter highlights the ways in which forms of resistance may be encoded in practices that nourish a consciousness of history even in the face of structures of domination.

Wars are fought on many fronts, and Jeff Sluka's essay (chap. 10) describes the multiple levels on which conflict is manifested. More than 400 years of conflict in Northern Ireland have given rise to a war waged simultaneously in the chambers of politicians, the battlefields (read "streets") of Belfast, and the communities of the average citizen. How is the struggle elucidated and kept alive in the everyday lives of the Irish? One important way is through murals. For political activists, concrete becomes canvas, and art becomes strategy and weapon. Painting serves as political process and revolutionary voice. From the first appearance of a crude and hasty style of graffiti to the emergence of a group of professional muralists, the stages in the development of the conflict in Northern Ireland are reflected in the buildings and walls of the city. Political art is an inherent part of conflict and war, as is (para)military confrontation and lethal communal violence.

Terror

The chapters in Part III address circumstances of entrenched, and often dirty, warfare. Violence is not dialogically suggested, socially muted, nor conceptually subtle: it is a stark fact of life and a major cause of death in the countries discussed here. The mechanisms that underlay the development of overt aggression discussed above, have, in Part III, emerged as prominent features of a social landscape molded by the harsh demands of people embroiled in oppression, resistance, and warfare.

Marcelo Suárez-Orozco's study (chap. 11) of the Argentine dirty war uses a psychocultural approach to make sense of both the denial of disappearances during the height of the dirty war and the present-day compulsion to speak and write of the terror generated at that time. His chapter emphasizes that the terror of the years of the dirty war cannot, and did not, end with the democratic election of Raul Alfonsin because the practice of disappearances interrupts the mourning process. The political and psychological come together in the form of movements such as the Mothers of the Plaza and other groups who continue to hope for the return of their loved ones alive. In the process of analyzing Argentina's dirty war, Suárez-Orozco suggests that the terror of colonialism may not help us to understand present-day cultures of terror in Latin America, and that decentered notions of power may in fact disguise the high levels of coordination that are needed to carry out terror.

Drawing on her fieldwork among civilian victims of dirty war strategies in Mozambique and Sri Lanka, Carolyn Nordstrom illustrates that distance from the enactment of violence has a good deal to do with the way we theorize about it. The space between violence and theory has enabled researchers to ascribe a reasonableness to warfare that belies the civilian experience. The differences are qualitative: while researchers have long acknowledged that unarmed civilians become trapped between competing (para)militaries, Nordstrom (chap. 12) argues that the attack against civilians *is* the defining strategy of modern dirty war. These technologies of warfare, she suggests, serve to inculcate an epistemology of the absurd. The repercussions of this extend beyond maimed bodies and burned-out towns. By attacks that devastate the social and cultural foundations of a society, and by remarkably senseless and brutal assaults against civilians, cultural and epistemological viability are themselves challenged for all those whose life-worlds are increasingly defined as life on the frontlines.

CONCLUSION

Violence is not a socioculturally fragmented phenomenon that occurs "outside" the arena of everyday life for those affected. It is part and parcel of life for the millions of people who live under oppressive, repressive, or explosive politicomilitary conditions. If we are to understand peace and conflict, it is to people themselves, to the social dynamics and cultural phenomena that inform them, that we must turn.

This stands at odds with traditional studies of sociopolitical violence that have long focused on the formal institutions credited with defining, waging, and resolving aggression: political, (para)military, security, and legal. Within these formal institutions warfare is viewed as a contest between opponents who consciously, if not rationally, compete for control of resources, employ strategies and develop weapon systems. Many social scientists have unwittingly adopted these concerns into their theories and analysis. While these arenas of analysis are important, focusing solely on them may prove a mistake in trying to understand the patterns of conventional and nonconventional war, domination and repression, and terror and resistance that characterize sociopolitical violence in the world today.

It is not only naive to assume that conflict takes place within an arena demarcated by the formal institutions designated as responsible for waging and controlling aggression. It is dangerous. On average, 90 percent of all war-related deaths now occur among civilian populations. What ethnographic voice conveys the social reality of these unarmed victims of aggression—the families who essentially live their lives on the frontlines of today's conflicts—if researchers focus on the politicomilitary systems whose members may declare war, but certainly do not bear the brunt of it? Worse, who gives resonance to those repressed, tortured, and disappeared in undeclared wars? Violence starts and stops with the people that constitute a society; it takes place in society and as a social reality; it is a product and a manifestation of culture. Violence is not inherent to power, to politics, or to human nature. The only biological reality of violence is that wounds bleed and people die.

This volume suggests that the field reality is an appropriate court for understanding the various levels of power and struggle as they are played out in the daily lives of people. Contemporary social and philosophical theory allows that there are multiple and contradictory field realities. People live in small-scale communities informed by negotiated popular knowledge and the authority of traditions, and by more formalized educational institutions responsive to the demands of the state. Individual and collective identities are indelibly marked by the effects of global economy and political processes within and among nation-states. All of these various influences on the field reality are reflected in our theories about domination, resistance, and violence.

Theoretical representation is one of the many voices of the field reality—as are the voices of power imposed, of power negotiated, and of violence suffered. Viewed in isolation, each voice tells a different story, yet all are essential components of the full story. Thus the concept of the field reality helps us to negotiate the pitfalls of the determinism of grand theory and the indeterminacy of the field itself—of power, struggle, and violence as enacted and experienced.

With one-third of the world's countries presently engaged in war, and two-thirds regularly practicing human rights abuses in order to control their populations—not to mention the frequent sporadic and often very destructive instances of explosive communal violence around the world—two things become evident. First, social scientists, no matter what their field of study, will in all likelihood confront some instance of sociopolitical violence in the field. Understanding these processes are invaluable for surviving them. Second, researchers who choose to focus on sociopolitical violence in any of its guises need viable field methodologies and theoretical frameworks. Anthropology can become more responsive to these issues by developing texts—both cultural and educational—to address fundamental questions surrounding violence and its resolution. The topics raised in this volume should encourage a basic rethinking of the conceptual foundations that surround sociopolitical violence and the way it is played out in the world today. The essays represent an initial step in designating theoretical frameworks for studying violence that elucidate field realities that enhance knowledge of conflict processes and human(e) dynamics with a more critical and global perspective.

REFERENCES

Bedjaoui, Mohammed, ed.
    1986   *Modern Wars.* London: Zed Books.
Bourdieu, Pierre
    1977   *Outline of a Theory of Practice.* New York: Cambridge University Press.
Clifford, James
    1988   *The Predicament of Culture: Twentieth-Century Ethnography, Literature, and Art.* Cambridge, Mass.: Harvard University Press.
Cocks, Joan
    1989   *The Oppositional Imagination: Feminism, Critique and Political Theory.* New York: Routledge.
Comaroff, Jean
    1985   *Body of Power, Spirit of Resistance: The Culture and History of a South African People.* Chicago: University of Chicago Press.

de Certeau, Michel
1980   "On the Oppositional Practices of Everyday Life." *Social Text,* Fall
       1980:3–43.
1988   *The Writing of History.* Trans. Tom Conley. New York: Columbia
       University Press.
Fernandez-Kelly, Maria Patricia
1983   *For We Are Sold, I and My People: Women and Industry in Mexico's Fron-
       tier.* Albany: State University of New York Press.
Foucault, Michel
1976   *The History of Sexuality.* Vol. 1: *An Introduction.* Trans. Robert Hurley.
       New York: Vintage Books.
Gramsci, Antonio
1971   *Selections from the Prison Notebooks.* Ed., trans. Quintin Hoare and
       Geoffrey Nowell Smith. New York: International Publishers.
Hinsley, F. H.
1987   "Peace and War in Modern Times." In *The Quest for Peace,* pp. 63–
       79, R. Vayrynen, ed. London: Sage Publications.
Kapferer, Bruce
1988   *Legends of People, Myths of State.* Washington, D.C.: Smithsonian In-
       stitution Press.
Lukes, Steven
1974   *Power: A Radical View.* London: Macmillan.
Mills, C. Wright
1959   *The Sociological Imagination.* Oxford: Oxford University Press.
Nash, June
1977   *We Eat the Mines and the Mines Eat Us: The Dependency and Exploitation
       in Bolivian Tin Mines.* New York: Columbia University Press.
Ong, Aihwa
1987   *Spirits of Resistance and Capitalist Discipline: Factory Work in Malaysia.*
       Albany: State University of New York Press.
Price, Richard
1983   *First Time: The Historical Vision of an Afro-American People.* Baltimore:
       Johns Hopkins University Press.
Riches, David, ed.
1986   *The Anthropology of Violence.* New York: Basil Blackwell.
Sider, Gerald M.
1989   *Culture and Class in Anthropology and History: A Newfoundland Illustra-
       tion.* Cambridge: Cambridge University Press.
Simmel, Georg
1950   *The Sociology of Georg Simmel,* trans., ed. K. H. Wolff. New York: The
       Free Press.
Sivard, Ruth Leger
Annual *World Military and Social Expenditures.* Leesburg, Va.: World Priorities.

Taussig, Michael
    1980   *The Devil and Commodity Fetishism in South America.* Chapel Hill: University of North Carolina Press.
    1987   *Shamanism, Colonialism, and the Wild Man.* Chicago: University of Chicago Press.
Thee, Marak
    1980   "The Scope and Priorities in Peace Research." Paper prepared for the Consultations on Peace Research, United Nations University, Toyko. December 8–13, 1980.
West, Cornel
    1988   "Marxist Theory and the Specificity of Afro-American Oppression." In *Marxism and the Interpretation of Culture,* pp. 17–29, C. Nelson and L. Grossberg, eds. Urbana: University of Illinois Press.
Williams, Raymond
    1977   *Marxism and Literature.* Oxford: Oxford University Press.
    1980   *Problems in Materialism and Culture.* London: Verso.
Willis, Paul
    1977   *Learning to Labor: How Working Class Kids Get Working Class Jobs.* New York: Columbia University Press.

TWO

The Anthropology of Conflict

Jeffrey A. Sluka

In the beginning was violence, and all history can be seen as an unending effort to control it. (BALANDIER 1986:499)

The manipulation of violence is one of the functions of power, which has its origin in violence and is maintained by managing it. (BALANDIER 1986:501)

Conflict cannot be excluded from social life . . . "peace" is nothing more than a change in the form of the conflict or in the antagonists or in the objects of the conflict, or finally in the chances of selection.
(WEBER, *cited in* COSER 1968:232)

The money required to provide adequate food, water, education, health and housing for everyone in the world has been estimated at 17 billion a year. It is a huge sum of money . . . about as much as the world spends on arms every two weeks. (NEW INTERNATIONALIST *poster*)

This world . . . is not spending money alone [on arms]. It is spending the sweat of its labours, the genius of its scientists, the hopes of its children. This is not a way of life at all in any true sense. Under the cloud of war it is humanity hanging on a cross of iron. (Former U.S. President DWIGHT D. EISENHOWER, *cited in* WISEMAN 1986:12)

It appears to me that relations among caste/race groups, ethnic groups and classes are becoming starkly simplified—that the lines are being clearly drawn between those who have and those who have not; between the rich and poor; between high caste and low; between "developed" nations and "developing" ones. The subtleties and complexities seem to be diminishing, and with them the niceties are being dropped. Naked power is being resorted to more unabashedly as the conflict becomes more evident, the contenders more clearly identified, the means less camouflaged, the rules less constraining, noblesse oblige less practiced, the use of force more blatant, the stakes greater, the rewards and injuries more stark. Therefore, I think, the incidence, the likelihood and the impact of overt conflict between unequals is increasing both within and between societies and nations.
(BERREMAN 1977:235)

INTRODUCTION

It has been estimated that since 3600 B.C. there have been something on the order of 3,500 major wars and 10,500 minor wars worldwide, producing approximately one billion direct battle deaths (Beer 1974: 30). The ICIHI (1986:24) notes that "the history of mankind is one long succession of wars and conflicts. . . . In over 3,400 years of documented human history, only 250 have been years of peace. War is thus the normal state of relations between men." The Commission also notes that there have been at least 150 wars since the end of World War II, resulting in the deaths of approximately twenty million people, and only twenty-six days of world peace (ICIHI 1986:24). Even that must be viewed as a very conservative reckoning because it depends on what one means by a day "without war," and because the Commission counted only wars between states. They did not count "internal wars," of which there have been far more, and which have been responsible for more deaths. Tiranti (1977:6) calculated that in the decade between 1958 and 1966 there were at least 164 "significant conflicts," including 15 official wars between states; 76 guerrilla insurgencies; and 73 revolts, coups, and uprisings. Clearly, if we count both the internal and external wars since the end of World War II, there have been at least several hundred wars, producing perhaps as many as 100 to 150 million deaths, and not a single day of world peace. In fact, it is fair to say that in a number of places war has become a permanent feature or "way of life."[1] In 1985 the world spent over $660 billion (U.S.) on arms, at a time when over 600 million people were malnourished (*New Internationalist* 1986:16). According to UNESCO, one day's global military spending could save the lives of all of the fifteen million children who die each year from starvation and disease (Wiseman 1986:12). In 1986, the UN-declared "Year of Peace," there were fifteen ongoing wars (defined as conflicts producing over 1,000 annual deaths) (Brazier 1986:6). The point is that "for a decade or two, conflicts have clearly been more frequent, more serious, and more radicalized" (ICIHI 1986:25), and the fact that today the study of social conflict has become a dominant anthropological interest is a reflection of this world historical trend.

Anthropologists have long noted that because social life inevitably entails frustrations and incompatibilities between individuals and groups, conflict is a basic form of human interaction that occurs in all social systems. Another way of saying this is that anthropologists view social conflict as a cultural universal. As Bohannan (1967:xii) has put it, "conflict is just as basic an element as sex in the mammalian and cultural nature of man." However, while it is true that all societies exhibit patterns of conflict, just as they all exhibit patterns of conformity and cooperation, it is no less important an anthropological observation that there is a wide range in the degree and forms of conflict exhibited across human societies (Nader 1968:238).

While there is a long history in anthropology of interest in social conflict, in 1961 Robert LeVine (1961:3, 14) noted that "theoretical attention to social conflict is relatively new in anthropology," and there was "no unified theoretical or methodological orientation" in anthropological approaches to the study of social conflict. That is still the case today. Contemporary anthropological approaches to the study of conflict vary considerably according to the perspectives and interests of particular researchers and are characterized by a high degree of theoretical eclecticism. This is a characteristic of sociocultural anthropology in general, and should be recognized as a strength rather than a weakness. The other strengths anthropologists bring to the study of conflict are also reflections of the strengths of sociocultural anthropology in general. These include a cross-cultural and comparative perspective, a holistic approach, reliance on participant observation, concentration on local-level or microanalysis, and a commitment to getting as close as possible to the participant's (or "emic") point of view. Perhaps the major weakness, or even fallacy, in conflict studies by social scientists outside anthropology has been the often glaring omission of any substantive consideration of the subjective, experiential, meaningful, or "cultural" dimension.

Within anthropology, "conflict" is a broadly defined concept and widely interpreted phenomenon. Conflict between individuals, groups, and classes has been an abiding interest, and anthropologists have produced both ethnography and theory with respect to the study of social conflict in all of its various manifestations. Anthropological interest in conflict is wide-ranging; from personal motivation in conflict, through the social structures and dynamics of specific conflict situations, to interest in the global nature of contemporary militarism. A good deal has been written on the anthropology of war,[2] and a number of anthropologists have written about issues of particular contemporary relevance—such as state terror (Walter 1969) and the "culture of terror" (Suárez-Orozco 1987; Taussig 1984), terrorism (Leach 1977), alternatives to war (Mead 1968), and the "cold war" (Turner and Pitt 1988). But while it is true that anthropologists have always been interested in social conflict, they are more interested in this subject today than they were in the past.

Early theoretical work by anthropologists on the subject of social conflict was at first shaped by the great sociological thinkers—Durkheim, Weber, Simmel, and Marx—and then influenced primarily by structural-functionalism and indirectly by the frustration-aggression (or relative deprivation) hypothesis (LeVine 1961:3). The earliest anthropologists were interested in the cultural manifestations of conflict and war within and between so-called primitive or tribal peoples. Up to the end of World War II, anthropologists were primarily interested in social order, and the first half of this century saw them producing detailed ethnographic discriptions and analyses of specific practices regarding conflict and warfare in relatively small societies. However, even when the dominant interest was the problem of social order, anthropologists were also interested in conflict. But they were interested in it primarily as an aspect of "stable" societies, particularly in terms of how various forms of institutionalized conflict operated or "functioned" to help maintain the existing sociopolitical order (e.g., Coser 1956; Gluckman 1955, 1963). This interest in both order and conflict in stable societies was expressed in the common anthropological opposition between "custom," or order, and conflict.

In the post-World War II era, particularly the late 1950s and 1960s, anthropological interest in social conflict was greatly stimulated by the national liberation struggles and other conflicts associated with the process of decolonization in the Third World (where the majority of anthropologists worked), by the cold war threat of thermonuclear holocaust, and, particularly in the United States, by the Vietnam War (Bramson and Goethals 1964; Fried et al. 1968). These world historical conditions were responsible for a shift in the focus of primary interest from social order in relatively stable societies to social conflict in societies undergoing rapid change (e.g., Beals and Siegel 1966). By the late 1960s this shift in interest from conflict in stable societies to conflict in rapidly changing ones was complete. This was recognized by Elizabeth Colson, who noted that "in a period of contending interests, most [anthropological] studies deal with competition, with conflict, and with rapid change" (Colson 1968:192).

This shift in interest also produced new theoretical formulations that challenged the dominant structural-functional perspective. Along with changing world historical conditions, the development of the conflict perspective was a result of criticisms of certain weaknesses in the structural-functional tradition of studying social control and order. One criticism was that this approach failed "to take into account fundamental conflicts of interest between different groups or sectors in society, conflicts not accounted for by a model of functional equilibrium and systems maintenance" (Seymour-Smith 1986:51). Other major criticisms of the structural-functional approach were that it neglected processes of change and failed to consider conflict as an ongoing process (Seaton and Claessen 1979:12). The emerging perspective on social conflict therefore emphasized conflict and process, rather than order and structure. By the end of the 1950s, Dahrendorf (1958) had developed a hybrid structure-conflict approach. While this was for many years vigorously contested by structural-functionalists, today this dual approach, combining interest in structures and processes, has become accepted mainstream theory.

SOCIAL CONFLICT DEFINED

It is interesting to note that "conflict" is rarely explicitly defined in anthropological writings on the subject. When it has been explicitly defined, the definitions have varied, depending on the particular perspectives and interests involved. The definition most widely cited by anthropologists is that presented by Lewis Coser in 1956. Coser (1968:232) defined social conflict as "a struggle over values and claims to status, power, and scarce resources, in which the aims of the conflicting parties are not only to gain the desired values but also to neutralize, injure, or eliminate their rivals." Social conflict involves a test of power between antagonistic parties, and while such conflict may include violence, other more subtle but equally significant forms of conflict exist as well. Symbolic, economic, and legal conflict come readily to mind as examples of nonviolent forms of social conflict. Among social scientists, anthropologists have been particularly, although certainly not exclusively, interested in these more subtle, symbolic forms and dimensions of conflict.

BASIC AXIOMS IN THE ANTHROPOLOGY OF SOCIAL CONFLICT

The theoretical eclecticism and diversity of approaches and interests in the anthropology of social conflict make it impossible to produce a coherent theoretical paradigm of the subfield. However, in broad terms, contemporary anthropological interest in this area does seem to be marked by a number of identifiable paradigmatic elements. There are at least four major interrelated approaches, five key, analytic concepts, and four basic theoretical axioms. The four interrelated approaches are (1) a cultural perspective that focuses on the relationship between conflict and learned, shared, and transmitted systems of symbolic meanings; (2) a perspective that combines interest in conflict from both individual-subjective and group-social perspectives; (3) a perspective that combines interest in both the processes of conflict and the structures that underlie them; and (4) a perspective that incorporates elements of both structure or system and power-conflict theory. The key analytic concepts are culture, symbolism, structure, process, and power, and the basic axioms are the rejection of the biological hypothesis; that conflict is a cultural universal, but is also culturally relative, varying in form, intensity, and even meaning from one society to another; the relationship between forms of social structure and forms and intensity of conflict; and recognition of the dual or ambiguous nature of conflict.

Rejection of the Biological Hypothesis

While some anthropologists have been interested in human aggression and the relationship between human biology and social conflict, aggression has not been a major interest in anthropology. Anthropologists (e.g., Holloway 1968; Montagu 1973) have mainly had to confront this issue because of the immense and enduring popularity of the "killer instinct" hypothesis, popularized by people like Lorenz (1966) and Ardrey (1966). As Ferguson (1984:8) points out, "Our supposedly aggressive 'nature' has been invoked repeatedly as the root cause of war," and of conflict and violence in general.

Along the lines of the old nature-nurture debate, there are two views of the primary cause of social conflict: (1) the view that conflict is a form of learned behavior that is culturally determined and (2) the view that conflict is biologically determined, the product of "natural" human aggressiveness. (There is also a third view, popular with some sections of the public but rejected for serious consideration by anthropologists, that the ultimate cause of social conflict is "evil" or human depravity.) In general, anthropologists have rejected the instinctive theory of aggression, and have argued against the biological hypothesis of the causes of social conflict (e.g., Mead 1940). This anthropological rejection of the biological hypothesis is a long-standing one. For example, in 1941 Malinowski (cited in Bramson and Goethals 1964:260) argued that "war cannot be regarded as a fiat of human destiny in that it could be related to biological needs or immutable psychological drives. All types of fighting are complex cultural responses due not to any direct dictates of an impulse, but to collective forms of sentiment and value."

Thus, few anthropologists believe that conflict, violence, and aggression are human biological necessities, and they have generally viewed them as forms of learned behavior that are culturally, rather than biologically or psychologically, constructed and defined. In the introduction to an edited volume of articles on the anthropology of violence,

Riches (1986:23) notes that "among the anthropologists in the orthodox traditions there is one agreement . . . that social and cultural factors, together with ecological setting, are the chief factors influencing the type and frequency of violence in any social situation."

One of the most important points anthropologists have made about conflict refers to its sources, particularly the sources of violence. Anthropologists hold that conflict and violence are products not of our genes but of particular forms of social relations. There is simply no credible evidence that either the forms or degree of conflict and violence exhibited within any society are instinctive, inevitable, or the result of perverse human nature. One major contribution that anthropologists have made to our understanding of social conflict and violence is that these forms of human behavior cannot be dismissed as exceptional, irrational, immoral, meaningless, a sign of social pathology, or the result of either the actions of "evil men" or the putative presence of "violent instincts." Theories of "innate depravity," such as those propounded by Ardrey (1966) and Lorenz (1966), are scientifically unsound and socially and politically dangerous. The genetic theory of social conflict is a political argument, and little more than a rationalization legitimizing the status quo. As Robert Nieburg put it over two decades ago, it is "an ideology of complacency, inaction, and defeatism because it justifies the inevitability of violence and the hopelessness of provisional [i.e., social or political] remedies" (1969:37).

The Cultural Perspective

The anthropological literature on conflict demonstrates that conflict is a cultural phenomenon. Anthropologists have argued that conflict is in great part a cultural product, stressed the cultural factors that give rise to or support conflict, and maintained that conflict cannot be viewed apart from the rest of the culture in which it occurs. It is a form of institutionalized social interaction that is culturally defined, and that definition varies from one society to another. It varies not only in form and content but also in the very character and meaning, in subjective terms, that the participants in the conflict themselves attach to it. Conflict relations are objectified, developed, maintained, expressed, or camouflaged by means of symbolic forms and patterns of symbolic action—that is, by symbolism or culture (a complex system of symbolic meanings). For example, Rappaport (cited in Worsley 1986:297) has commented on the varying cultural bases of war, which "has at times been viewed as a pastime or an adventure, as the only proper occupation for a nobleman, as an affair of honor (e.g., in the days of chivalry), [or] as a ceremony (among the Aztecs)." Anthropology therefore provides an intermediate level of analysis between humanity's behavioral potential and its final expression in conflict through the study of the symbolic systems or cultures of human groups.

The anthropological or cultural approach interprets conflict with reference to the norms, values, ideologies, and world-views held by the participants. A basic premise is that members of a given society share culturally patterned characteristics of conflict behavior, and that it is possible to delineate these patterns in the relationship of one member's behavior to another's as well as to the culture as a whole. Based on this premise, anthropologists argue that understanding the cultural context is essential to understanding any specific instance or example of social conflict.

Abner Cohen (1969, 1974, 1979) has been one of the leading contemporary proponents of the cultural or symbolic perspective in anthropology. Cohen (1979:111) argues that "anthropology is essentially the child of Marxism, for it was Marx who initiated the systematic analysis of culture in relation to the power structure." Cohen stresses that anthropology has always been concerned with the interrelationship or "causal interconnections" between two major variables: (1) culture (symbolic forms, styles of life, primary relationships, world-views, and religious, ethnic-racial, and other ideologies) and (2) the struggle between groups for economic and political power. Cohen argues that culture (symbolism) and power are "the two major variables that pervade all social life," and that anthropology is best suited to the analysis of the relations between the two domains. From this cultural or symbolic perspective, the anthropology of social conflict focuses on the analysis of the dynamic relationship between conflict, cultural symbols, and power relations (politics and economics).

Cohen takes a two-dimensional approach, arguing that "political man is also symbolist man." He argues (1979:99) that "all normative culture is two-dimensional"—that is, both instrumental and expressive, political and symbolic. On one hand, the political and economic domains are both based on power relations, relations that are "manipulative, technical and instrumental, as men in different situations use one another as means to ends and not as ends in themselves" (Cohen 1969:217). On the other hand, the cultural or symbolic domain is normative, "rooted in the psychic structure of men in society through continual socialisation . . . these symbols are cognitive, in that they direct the attention of men selectively to certain meanings. They are affective, in that they are never emotionally neutral; they always agitate feelings and sentiments. They are conative, in that they impel men to action" (Cohen 1969:217). Cohen (1979: 99) argues that social order and conflict are both effected "in day to day living by moral and ritual obligations that are developed, objectified, and maintained through symbolic forms and symbolic action."

In recent years, Robert Rubinstein and Mary Foster have also emerged as noteworthy proponents of the cultural approach to social conflict. They point out that "a recurrent theme in the anthropological literature is that all social behavior has a symbolic dimension. Although warfare and the construction of peaceful social relationships have much to do with considerations of economics and material force, they also have symbolic aspects that must be taken into account in order to resolve conflicts, avoid war or maintain an established peace" (Rubinstein 1988:28). They have also argued that a "full and effective" understanding of social conflict requires "examining the intricate connections between cultural and symbolic processes and social action" (Rubinstein and Foster 1988:1). They note that factors contributing to both order and conflict must be interpreted in the context of the "symbolic matrix" provided by culture, and that failure to do so "yields a lifeless and misleading picture" of the dynamics of social life (Rubinstein and Foster 1988:4, 5).

Another important recent example of a cultural approach to the analysis of conflict is James Scott's (1985) book on peasant resistance, which focuses on the "meaning centred"—that is, symbolic or cultural—analysis of class relations and conflicts. Scott refers to everyday acts of small-scale resistance as "small arms fire in the class war" and deals with both cautious resistance and calculated conformity as everyday responses to situations of exploitation and repression. He maintains that "The struggle between rich and poor . . . is not merely a struggle over work, property rights, grain, and cash. It is also a struggle over the appropriation of symbols, a struggle over how the past and present shall be understood and labeled, a struggle to identify causes and assess blame, a contentious effort to give partisan meaning to local history" (1985:xv). Scott points out that the forms that class conflict takes are based on shared world-views or culture: "Neither gossip nor character assassination, for example, makes much sense unless there are shared standards of what is deviant, unworthy, impolite" (1985:xvii).

Another recent anthropological study of conflict that relies on cultural analysis is a volume of articles on the "war system" edited by Falk and Kim (1980:160), who argue that anthropologists

can make an important contribution to the enhancement of cross-cultural (and cross-national and cross-ideological) communications in warmaking

and peacemaking by clearly defining such culturally transmitted definitions of social variables as: strength and weakness; conflict and cooperation; hero and villain; victory and defeat; ascribed and achieved statuses;
justice and injustice; equality and hierarchy; submission and dominance;
dependence and independence; and legitimate and illegitimate authority.
These variables all relate to both behavioral and structural attributes of
any organized human society.

They, too, maintain that the major contribution anthropologists make
to the study of conflict is the analysis of the symbolism associated with
each of these behavioral and structural attributes.[3]

Conflict and Social Structure

In anthropology, it is axiomatic that all social or cultural systems have
organizational characteristics that predispose them toward particular
kinds and degrees of social conflict. The structural approach to the study
of conflict views conflict as an inherent and ineradicable component of
social structures, emphasizes the social structural sources of conflict, and
holds that social structure shapes the specific form that conflict takes.
The association of forms of social structure with frequency and type or
form of conflict has received substantial cross-cultural verification, and
it is fair to say that the interrelation of forms of social structure with the
frequency and form of conflict remains a cornerstone of current anthropological research on conflict.[4]

Conflict as Process

In anthropology, most contemporary approaches to the study of conflict focus on the social dynamics or processes of conflict. The process
approach was developed by political anthropologists in the late 1950s
and 1960s, such as Swartz, Turner, and Tuden, who argued that "all
politics . . . will at some time in their course involve processes of conflict
over the distribution, allocation, and use of public power" (Swartz et al.
1966:27). This approach developed out of the shift in emphasis from
static and synchronic analysis of stable or relatively unchanging societies
to diachronic studies of societies or contexts undergoing rapid change,
and from recognition that structural-functional analysis alone is not
sufficient. In the process approach, the emphasis is on dynamic political
phenomena—on processes of conflict and cooperation, such as competition, factionalism, struggle, conflict resolution, conflicts of interest and
values, the pursuit of public goals, and the struggle for power—rather
than on structure and function.

However, it should be noted that this interest in conflict as a social process represents a change of emphasis and interest rather than an outright rejection of structural-functionalism or system theory. Conflict involves both structures and processes, relationships and actions, and one must consider both. This shift in emphasis results from recognition that structural-functional analysis alone is not sufficient. Thus, the process perspective represents a dual or hybrid structure-process approach.

The Dual Nature of Conflict

Because conflict immediately impresses us with its socially destructive force, it is easy to neglect its positive or socially constructive aspects. However, Simmel (1955:14) was perhaps the first to promulgate what has now become an axiom in the anthropology of conflict—namely, that conflict has a dual nature. "Actual society," he argued, "does not result only from . . . social forces which are positive [integrating], and only to the extent that the negative factors do not hinder them. This common conception is quite superficial: Society . . . is the result of both categories of interaction [positive and negative or integrating and disintegrating], which thus both manifest themselves as wholly positive" (1955:16). Conflict and order are inextricably interwoven—opposed and yet complementary. Conflict has both functional and dysfunctional aspects, it can produce social order and stability or disorder and change, be unifying or divisive, result in social fission or social fusion, and be progressive or reactionary. Human social life is a precipitate not only of processes of cooperation but also, simultaneously, of a dialectic between processes of conflict and accommodation.

Coser also recognized the dual nature of conflict, and argued that it is incorrect to make a sharp distinction between system and power-conflict models of society:

> Peace and feuding, conflict and order, are correlative. Both the cementing and the breaking of the cake of custom constitute part of the dialectic of social life. One is hence ill-advised to distinguish sharply a sociology of order from a sociology of conflict, or a harmony model of society from a conflict model. Such attempts can only result in artificial distinctions. The analysis of social conflicts brings to awareness aspects of social reality that may be obscured if analytical attention focuses too exclusively on phenomena of social order; but an exclusive attention to conflict phenomena may obscure the central importance of social order and needs to be corrected by a correlative concern with the ordered aspects of social life. We deal here not with distinct realities but only with differing aspects of the same reality, so that exclusive emphasis on one or the other is likely to lead the analyst astray. Perhaps we need return now to Charles Horton

Cooley's statement: "The more one thinks of it the more he will see that conflict and co-operation are not separable things, but phases of one process which always involves something of both." (Coser 1968:235–236).

Thus, the dual nature of conflict reinforces the argument that a dual or hybrid system-conflict theoretical perspective is best suited to the study of conflict.

That anthropologists have long recognized the dual nature of conflict is reflected in the long-standing tradition of using binary oppositions such as "custom and conflict" (Gluckman 1955), "order and rebellion" (Gluckman 1963), "cooperation and conflict" (Mead 1961), "conflict and accommodation" (DeVos 1982), and "conformity and conflict" (Spradley and McCurdy 1972), to refer to the basic dynamics of human social and cultural life. That the dual nature of conflict is well recognized in anthropology is further indicated by the fact that studies of the problem of social order are often presented as contributions to the anthropology of conflict. For example, in the introduction to his classic study of social order in the New Guinea highlands, Ronald Berndt points out that "any problem of social order must inevitably take up the problem of conflict" (1962:vi).

Another axiom in the anthropology of conflict that is related to and reinforces the view of the dual nature of conflict is the observation that conflict and violence can contribute not only to social stability, order, and the maintenance of the status quo but also to social disequilibrium and change. System (structural-functional) theorists have been interested primarily in the contribution that conflict can make to social order, while power-conflict theorists have been interested primarily in the contribution that conflict can make to social change. Marx's perspective was that one particular form of conflict—class conflict—is the central mechanism of social change and progress. The relationship between conflict, stability, and change has been aptly summarized by Seymour-Smith, who observes that "Conflict is a primary source or stimulus for social change, for, when it cannot be handled by institutionalized mechanisms of dispute settlement, the opposing parties will be forced to create new strategies either to resolve the conflict or avoid the situation which produces it" (1986:51).

The dual nature of conflict leads to an important observation with regard to its "evaluation." The question is whether conflict is viewed as something that is positive, negative, both, or neither. Many would argue, of course, that the only objective perspective is neutrality. Here, I merely want to suggest that some anthropologists may have either an explicit or implicit value position with regard to various forms of social conflict and violence. This position is to some degree inherent in their theoretical perspectives, and sometimes influences their interpretations. None of the dominant theoretical perspectives in anthropology today interpret conflict as being inherently or wholly either positive or negative, but in each of these perspectives there is a tendency to interpret some forms of conflict positively and others negatively. For example, in Marxist perspectives conflict is evaluated positively as long as it leads to progressive change. But conflict that reinforces the status quo is viewed negatively. In structural-functional perspectives the opposite interpretation applies. Conflict is viewed positively if it ultimately contributes to social order, and negatively if it leads to a breakdown of social order. Durkheim, Parsons, and Warner considered conflict to be dysfunctional or negative, but others have taken a diametrically opposed position, such as Fanon (1963) and Sartre (Preface in Fanon [1963]), who argued that conflict in general, and violence in particular, is a positive—indeed, necessary— part of the process of decolonization. Ultimately, the evaluation of conflict appears to depend on whether one places more value on social stability or on social change. It is important to know, I think, where any particular anthropologist stands on the evaluation issue.

CONCLUSION: CONFLICT IN THE
CONTEMPORARY WORLD

Conflict and group violence in all their forms (e.g., material and symbolic) can be effective, rational, and even moral strategies of political action or means of achieving political ends. What Nieburg (1969:9) said over two decades ago about violence still applies to conflict in general:

> It is self-defeating to study violence as if it were obscene, nor does recognition of its relevance condone or encourage it. Quite the contrary is true. Like many things, violence is deeply ambiguous in all its aspects, containing both functional and dysfunctional tendencies, capable of both positive and negative outcomes.

Nieburg went on to observe that the tactics of confrontation politics have proved to be effective strategies for improving the bargaining position of disadvantaged groups and achieving progressive social change, while the preferred tactics of political participation, petition, and peaceful demonstration, "working through the establishment," have generally proved to be less effective, often achieving only abstract and token effects (1969:9). I suggest that this is because of one of the basic axioms of power-conflict theory, the proposition that no powerful, dominant, or relatively advantaged group willingly or easily relinquishes their position of advantage. Tragically, the rich and powerful are almost never persuaded to change through reasoned argument or moral persuasion. The mobilization of power is the major, if not only, means of achieving progressive change in stratified societies.

The social causes of conflict and political violence in nation-states can be traced directly to the correlates of social stratification—major institutionalized inequalities in access to wealth, status, and power (or, in Weber's terms, "life chances"). Social stratification leads to such conflict-inducing factors as ethnic, religious, and ideological discrimination; socioeconomic deprivation; political inequality and its correlates such as infringement of rights, injustice, and oppression; the absence of effective channels of peaceful or systemic resolution of grievances and conflicts; and, of course, exploitation and alienation.

As Berreman has noted, wherever there is significant disparities between social groups in access to life chances, "there is suffering and conflict because these are systems which assure privilege to some at the expense of others, and people do not acquiesce easily to that situation. When they do, it is not because they agree to its legitimacy or inevitability, but because they know the uses of power" (1977:229). Berreman argues that systems of social stratification are "everywhere characterized by conformity rather than consensus, by conflict rather than tranquility, by enforcement rather than by endorsement, by resentment rather than contentment" (1977:229).

If the causes of social conflict and political violence are inherent in the stratified social structures of our modern nation-states, we cannot hope to remove or alleviate those causes without altering those structures. As such, perhaps we are, for the most part, doomed to treating these things symptomatically. The only effective long-term means of reducing the incidence of social conflict and political violence is to work to resolve or reduce the professed grievances of groups whose only effective political recourse is to employ these means. And if it is true that we cannot eliminate social inequality, oppression, exploitation, and injustice (i.e., stratification and its correlates), we can certainly reduce their scope and intensity. Every incremental reduction in the scope and intensity of these causes can be expected to produce a corresponding incremental reduction in the scope and intensity of world conflict.

Berreman has observed that

Present trends suggest a worldwide polarization in access to power, privilege and resources—the gap between the "haves" and the "have nots" increases with a diminishing willingness among the poor to continue to suffer deprivation, and among the wealthy to ameliorate it. The disparities must be ended, and inevitably will be, by conflict if not by accommodation. It would be to the advantage of everyone that it be done graciously, quickly and well, lest it occur brutally, perhaps by holocaust. (1977:236)

A degree of conflict and violence may be inevitable in social life, but no social condition is inevitable. Social conditions are created by people, and what people create, they can change. Social conditions can, at the very least, be changed so that conflict and violence will no longer appear as the only effective political recourse many oppressed and powerless groups have at their disposal. As psychologists Kardiner and Ovessey pointed out forty years ago in *The Mark of Oppression*, "there is only one way that the products of oppression can be dissolved, and that is to stop the oppression" (1951:387).

NOTES

1. For example, the Karen people of Burma have been fighting a "low-intensity" war for over four decades, there has been continuous war in Eritrea and Tigray for nearly three decades, and in 1989 the war in Northern Ireland passed the two-decade mark. A number of other such examples could be cited as well.

2. See, for instance, four edited volumes on the anthropology of war (Bohannon 1967; Ferguson 1984; Fried et al. 1968; Nettleship et al. 1975). Anthropologists have been particularly interested in "primitive war" (Malinowski 1941; Schneider 1950; Turney-High 1949; Vayda 1968), war and the state or the evolution of war (Cohen 1974; Lesser 1968; Otterbein and Otterbein 1970; Webster 1975), and peasant war and/or revolt (Alavi 1973; Friedrich 1970; Wolf 1969).

3. Other important examples of contemporary cultural approaches to the study of social conflict include David Parkin's (1978) work on the cultural definition of political action, a volume of articles on the anthropology of violence edited by Riches (1986), and a cultural analysis of the Cold War recently published by Turner and Pitt (1988).

4. In bands, "tribes," and chiefdoms the structural lines of conflict tend to follow the organizational lines established by kinship—conflicting groups are generally households, lineage segments, lineages, and clans. In state-level (or stratified) societies conflict arises between various organizations of common interest—class, status (particularly ethnicity), and party.

REFERENCES

Alavi, Hamza
   1973   "Peasants and Revolution." In *Imperialism and Revolution in South Asia*, K. Gough and H. Sharma, eds. New York: Monthly Review Press.

Ardrey, Robert
1966   *The Territorial Imperative*. New York: Atheneum Publishers.
Balandier, Georges
1986   "An Anthropology of Violence and War." *International Social Science Journal* 110:499–511.
Beals, Alan R., and Bernard J. Siegel
1966   *Divisiveness and Social Conflict*. Stanford: Stanford University Press.
Beer, Francis A.
1974   *How Much War in History: Definitions, Estimates, Extrapolations and Trends*. Beverly Hills: Sage Publications.
Berndt, Ronald M.
1962   *Excess and Restraint*. Chicago: University of Chicago Press.
Berreman, Gerald D.
1977   "Social Barriers: Caste, Class and Race in Cross-Cultural Perspective." *Papers in Anthropology* 18(2):217–242.
Bohannan, Paul, ed.
1967   *Law and Warfare: Studies in the Anthropology of Conflict*. Garden City: Natural History Press.
Bramson, L., and G. Goethals, eds.
1964   *War: Studies From Psychology, Sociology, Anthropology*. New York: Basic Books.
Brazier, Chris
1986   "Pacific Force." *New Internationalist* 163:4–6.
Cohen, Abner
1969   "Political Anthropology: The Analysis of the Symbolism of Power Relations." *Man* 4(2):215–235.
1974   *Two-Dimensional Man: An Essay on the Anthropology of Power and Symbolism in Complex Society*. Berkeley, Los Angeles, London: University of California Press.
1979   "Political Symbolism." *Annual Review of Anthropology* 8:87–113.
Colson, Elizabeth
1968   "Political Anthropology: The Field." In *The Encyclopedia of the Social Sciences*, pp. 189–193, D. Sills, ed. New York: Crowell, Collier & Macmillan.
Coser, Lewis
1956   *The Functions of Social Conflict*. New York: Free Press.
1968   "Conflict: Social Aspects." In *The Encyclopedia of the Social Sciences*, pp. 232–236, D. Sills, ed. New York: Crowell, Collier & Macmillan.
Dahrendorf, Ralf
1958   "Toward a Theory of Social Conflict." *Journal of Conflict Resolution* 2(2):170–183.
DeVos, George
1982   "Ethnic Pluralism: Conflict and Accommodation." In *Ethnic Identity: Cultural Continuities and Change*, pp. 5–41, G. DeVos and L. Romanucci-Ross, eds. Chicago: University of Chicago Press.

Falk, Richard, A., and Samuel S. Kim, eds.
1980   *The War System: An Interdisciplinary Approach.* Boulder, Colo.: Westview Press.

Fanon, Frantz
1963   *The Wretched of the Earth.* Preface by Jean Paul Sartre. Harmondsworth: Penguin Books.

Ferguson, R. Brian, ed.
1984   *Warfare, Culture, and Environment.* New York: Academic Press.

Fried, Morton, Marvin Harris, and Robert Murphy, eds.
1968   *War: The Anthropology of Armed Conflict and Aggression.* Garden City: Natural History Press.

Friedrich, Paul
1970   *Agrarian Revolt in a Mexican Village.* Chicago: University of Chicago Press.

Gluckman, Max
1955   *Custom and Conflict in Africa.* Glencoe: Free Press.
1963   *Order and Rebellion in Tribal Africa.* London: Cohen & West.

Holloway, Ralph L.
1968   "Human Aggression: The Need for a Species-Specific Framework." In *War: The Anthropology of Armed Conflict and Aggression,* pp. 29–48, Morton Fried, Marvin Harris, and Robert Murphy, eds. Garden City: Natural History Press.

ICIHI
1986   "Modern Wars: The Humanitarian Challenge." In *Proceedings of a Report of the Independent Commission on International Humanitarian Issues* (presented by M. Bedjaoui). London: Zed Books.

Kardiner, Abram, and Lionel Ovessey
1951   *The Mark of Oppression.* Cleveland: World Publishing Company.

Leach, Edmund
1977   *Custom, Law and Terrorist Violence.* Edinburgh: Edinburgh University Press.

Lesser, Alexander
1968   "War and the State." In *War: The Anthropology of Armed Conflict and Aggression,* pp. 92–96, Morton Fried, Marvin Harris, and Robert Murphy, eds. Garden City: Natural History Press.

LeVine, Robert A.
1961   "Anthropology and the Study of Conflict." *Journal of Conflict Resolution* 5(1):3–15.

Lorenz, Konrad
1966   *On Aggression.* New York: Harcourt, Brace & World.

Malinowski, Branislaw
1941   "An Anthropological Analysis of War." *American Journal of Sociology* 46:521–550.

Mead, Margaret
1940   "Warfare is Only an Invention—Not a Biological Necessity." *Asia* 40:402–405.

1961   *Cooperation and Conflict among Primitive Peoples.* Boston: Beacon Press.

1968   "Alternatives to War." In *War: The Anthropology of Armed Conflict and Aggression,* pp. 215–228, Morton Fried, Marvin Harris, and Robert Murphy, eds. Garden City: Natural History Press.

Montagu, Ashely

1973   *Man and Aggression.* London: Oxford University Press.

Nader, Laura

1968   "Conflict: Anthropological Aspects." In *The Encyclopedia of the Social Sciences,* pp. 236–242, D. Sills, ed. New York: Crowell, Collier & Macmillan.

Nettleship, Martin A., Dale R. Givens, and Anderson Nettleship, eds.

1975   *War: Its Causes and Correlates.* The Hague: Mouton.

New Internationalist

1986   "Building Peace and Justice." *New Internationalist* 163.

Nieburg, H. L.

1969   *Political Violence.* New York: St. Martin's Press.

Otterbein, Keith, and Charlotte Swanson Otterbein

1970   *The Evolution of War: A Cross-Cultural Study.* New Haven, Conn.: HRAF Press.

Parkin, David

1978   *The Cultural Definition of Political Response.* New York: Academic Press.

Riches, David, ed.

1986   *The Anthropology of Violence.* London: Basil Blackwell.

Riches, David, and Mary LeCron Foster, eds.

1988   *The Social Dynamics of Peace and Conflict: Culture in International Security.* Boulder, Colo.: Westview Press.

Rubinstein, Robert A.

1988   "Anthropology and International Security." In *The Social Dynamics of Peace and Conflict,* pp. 17–34, R. Rubinstein and M. Foster, eds. Boulder, Colo.: Westview Press.

Schneider, Joseph

1950   "Primitive Warfare: A Methodological Note." *American Sociological Review* 15:727–777.

Scott, James C.

1985   *Weapons of the Weak: Everyday Forms of Peasant Resistance.* New Haven, Conn.: Yale University Press.

Seaton, S. L., and H. J. M. Claessen, eds.

1979   *Political Anthropology: The State of the Art.* New York: Mouton.

Seymour-Smith, Charlotte

1986   *Dictionary of Anthropology.* Boston: G. K. Hall.

Simmel, George

1955   *Conflict and the Web of Group Affiliations.* Glencoe: Free Press.

Spradley, David, and David McCurdy, eds.

1972   *Conformity and Conflict: Readings in Cultural Anthropology.* Boston: Little, Brown.

Suárez-Orozco, Marcelo M.
  1987   "The Treatment of Children in the 'Dirty War': Ideology, State Ter-
          rorism and the Abuse of Children in Argentina." In *Child Survival:
          Anthropological Perspectives on the Treatment and Maltreatment of Chil-
          dren,* pp. 227–246, N. Scheper-Hughes, ed. Dordrecht, The Nether-
          lands: D. Reidel Publishing Co.
Swartz, Marc J., Victor Turner, and Arthur Tuden, eds.
  1966   *Political Anthropology.* Chicago: Aldine Publishing Co.
Taussig, Michael
  1984   "Culture of Terror: Roger Casement's Putumayo Report and the
          Explanation of Torture." *Comparative Study of Society and History*
          26:467–497.
Tiranti, Dexter
  1977   "The Barrel of a Gun." *New Internationalist* 51:5–7.
Turner, P., and D. Pitt, eds.
  1988   *Cold War and Nuclear Madness: An Anthropological Analysis.* Columbia,
          S.C.: Bergin & Garvey.
Turney-High, H. H.
  1949   *Primitive War: Its Practices and Concepts.* Columbia: University of
          South Carolina Press.
Vayda, Andrew P.
  1968   "War: Primitive Warfare." In *The Encyclopedia of the Social Sciences,*
          pp. 468–472, D. Sills, ed. New York: Crowell, Collier & Macmillan.
Walter, E. V.
  1969   *Terror and Resistance.* New York: Oxford University Press.
Webster, David
  1975   "Warfare and the Evolution of the State." *American Antiquity* 40:464–
          470.
Wiseman, John
  1986   "Beyond the Cross of Iron." *New Internationalist* 163:12–13.
Wolf, Eric R.
  1969   *Peasant Wars of the Twentieth Century.* New York: Harper & Row.
Worsley, Peter
  1986   "The Superpowers and the Tribes." In *Peace and War: Cross-Cultural
          Perspectives,* pp. 293–306, M. Foster and R. Rubinstein, eds. New
          Brunswick: Transaction Books.

THREE

Anthropology and the Politics of Genocide

John H. Bodley

The modern global assault by nation-states on small-scale, self-sufficient tribal peoples was an immense human tragedy that impoverished the planet. Autonomous tribal peoples provided a glimpse of a world without writing, cities, taxes, or ruling elites, before they were transformed by conquering states. Tribals merit special attention not only because they maximized the advantages of low-density population, low per capita consumption, and long-term stability but also—and perhaps even more importantly—because some 200 million contemporary "indigenous peoples" seek to maintain the relative political autonomy, economic self-reliance, and social equality that made small-scale cultures so successful.

Millions of tribals died in the hundred years before 1920, when they were forced to surrender nearly half of the globe. There can be no precise figures, but I have estimated that tribal populations may have been reduced by as much as 50 million during this period (Bodley 1990). This was genocide and ethnocide on a vast scale. Furthermore, such genocide continues today. For example, in 1968 the Brazilian government's Indian Protection Service was disbanded after it was implicated in the deaths of thousands of forest Indians who were exterminated to clear the way for land development. In Bangladesh, it has been estimated that 185,000 tribals were killed by government troops between 1977 and 1984 after the Chittagong Hill tribal area was opened to large-scale settlement by outsiders (*IWGIA Newsletter 1984* [International Work Group for Indigenous Affairs] 37:15–17). As many as 150,000 Papuans may have died between 1963 and 1983 as the Indonesians expanded their control over tribal areas in former Dutch New Guinea (Korwa 1983;

Nietschmann 1985). Contrary to the orthodox view that violence against tribals is both "natural" and inevitable, I argue that independent tribal societies were forced to a premature end. Tribals continue to be threatened by inhumane political choices that can be changed.

Genocidal violence directed against tribals by national governments is often overlooked by political scientists concerned with conflict because tribals have been politically invisible and tribal genocide may not be recognized as war because tribals are not considered to be sovereign nations by the states claiming control over their territories. Nevertheless, the destruction of tribals must be considered a deliberate and violent political act carried out as national policy in order to gain access to the natural resources controlled by tribal peoples.

The majority of nineteenth-century anthropologists were intensely aware of the impending tragic end of tribal cultures, but rather than working to prevent it, the majority espoused "scientific" evolutionary theories that explained the destruction and suggested that it was inevitable. In my view, such "theories" were actually self-serving political opinions, not well-founded scientific judgments.

A significant minority of idealistic anthropologists and other well-informed individuals did argue for the independence of tribal peoples. Unfortunately, their viewpoint was largely ignored during the critical early decades of this century because the debate mistakenly focused on tribal "preservation" rather than self-determination. The real political issue of the basic human right of tribal peoples to self-determination was not widely recognized by anthropologists until the liberal political movements of the late 1960s. In the meantime, many concerned anthropologists, who prided themselves on their "realism," successfully promoted "just and humane" conquest policies for threatened tribal peoples. Their compromise sought to reduce the human cost of ethnocide, but it delayed acceptance of the self-determination approach and ultimately proved unable to prevent massive depopulation of tribal areas.

VANISHING DATA AND THE REALITY OF GENOCIDE

Regardless of the inherent vitality of tribal peoples, the overwhelming historical reality, which was well established early in the nineteenth century, was that tribal peoples died and their cultures disintegrated when Europeans invaded tribal territory. The British Parliamentary Select Committee on Aborigines acknowledged this basic fact in their official reports of 1836–37. Even Charles Darwin included a discussion of the "extinction of savage tribes" in his 1871 *The Descent of Man,* and very matter-of-factly attributed it to "competition" with civilized races. (Darwin 1871:228–231).

The history of "Victorian anthropology" has recently been examined in detail by George Stocking (1987), who shows clearly the relationship between the colonial enterprise and the class structure of Britain and the development of what we now view as outrageously racist anthropological thinking in which tribals were simply objectified as "savage others."

From the 1870s on, the extinction of tribals was a frequent theme in the Anthropology Section of the British Association for the Advancement of Science and at the meetings of the Royal Anthropological Institute (RAI). Throughout this period there was a clear sense of the historical significance of tribal genocide. For example, in 1881 the physical anthropologist W. H. Flower declared before the British Association: "than any previous one, the destruction of races, both by annihilation and absorption, is going on" (Flower 1882:688).

Perhaps the most striking demonstration that anthropologists fully appreciated the scope of the destruction of tribal peoples was the frantic urgency to save the vanishing data, which became a major theme at professional meetings beginning in the 1870s. Colonel A. H. Lane Fox (Pitt-Rivers) was one of the first to sound the alarm, declaring in his address to the Anthropology Section of the British Association in 1872 that vital data is "rapidly disappearing from the face of the earth" (Pitt-Rivers [Lane Fox] 1872:171). Colonel Lane Fox joined E. B. Tylor, John Lubbock, and others to prepare the original version of "Notes and Queries" as a guide to salvage anthropology.

By the end of the nineteenth century, the triumph of evolutionary theory was such that in 1897 Royal Navy Lieutenant B. T. Somerville presented a paper to the RAI that would today be seen as a totally outrageous apology for the extermination of a people, but it was published in the Institute's journal without critical comment. At the end of his "ethnographical notes" on the natives of New Georgian the Solomon Islands, Somerville noted that the population was in rapid decline and would probably be exterminated. Whatever the cause, Somerville was not bothered by the prospect of extinction, and commented that the "elimination" of these "lazy natives" would be "no great loss to the world" because they would be replaced by a more energetic people (Somerville 1897).

By the early decades of this century, prominent anthropologists, sensing that it was already too late to save tribals, bemoaned the great loss for anthropology caused by the mass exterminations. For example, in

1929, Henry Balfour, in his presidential address to the British Association for the Advancement of Science meeting in South Africa, declared that it was a "tragedy" that "so much of the invaluable and once accessible material should have been allowed to die away unstudied" (1930: 154). Radcliffe-Brown, in his presidential address to anthropologists at the British Association in 1931, called it "almost tragic" that just as anthropology had developed the appropriate theoretical approaches to study tribal cultures, they were being "destroyed with appalling rapidity" (1932:160).

REALISTS VERSUS IDEALISTS

Everyone agreed that civilization was destroying tribals, yet when policy implications were considered, a major philosophical split emerged between the realists and the idealists. The realists accepted the "reality" of national expansion. They assumed that tribals would ultimately be unable to survive as independent peoples and would either physically disappear or become integrated into the dominant society. Thus, the realists appeared to accept genocide on a staggering scale as a regrettable by-product of national expansion. Idealists were both more critical of the frontier process and more optimistic about the possibility of tribals maintaining their political and cultural integrity.

Realists

The realists had their roots in the social Darwinist imperialism of the nineteenth century. Several realist subgroups can be distinguished. The imperialist humanitarians wanted "justice" for dispossessed tribals and hoped to minimize the damage. Often their motivation was more religious than scientific, and many were not anthropologists. This approach originated with the Aborigines Protection Society (APS) (1839) and eventually led to alliances between anthropologists, missionaries, and governments, such as Brazil's Indian Protectorate Service (1910) and the Summer Institute of Linguistics (SIL) missionary-linguists (1947). The Aborigines Protection Society (APS) fought hard to defend tribals on the British colonial frontier, but never questioned the justice of colonial expansion itself. The APS simply felt that conquest could be carried out both more humanely and more economically and lobbied for policies that would curb the worst abuses associated with tribal dispossession.

Scientific imperialists date from the founding of anthropology as a scientific discipline, and were exemplified by the unsuccessful nineteenth-century RAI effort to establish an Imperial Bureau of Ethnology, as a support for the colonial enterprise and to serve as a repository for vanishing data. The scientific imperialists included the scientific interventionists and applied anthropologists, who sought to combine scientific respect for tribal culture with economic development and integration into the national society; and the salvage anthropologists, whose primary concern was with saving vanishing data.

The term *applied anthropology* was coined by RAI president Lane Fox Pitt-Rivers in 1881 to classify a paper entitled "On the Laws Affecting the Relations between Civilized and Savage Life . . . ," which was read before the RAI by colonial administrator Sir Bartle Frere (1881). Sir Frere felt that natural law required savages to surrender their political autonomy and transform their culture in order to survive.

Realist anthropologists often masked the politics of genocide by emphasizing that tribals simply died when they came into contact with civilization. They stressed the irreconcilable differences between tribal and civilized societies. While unwilling to condemn colonial expansion itself, they felt that the damage could be minimized. This view was expressed by physical anthropologist W. H. Flower in his presidential address to the RAI in 1883, where he declared that "the mere contact of races generally ends in the extermination of one of them. If such disastrous consequences cannot be altogether averted, we have it still in our power to do much to mitigate their evils" (Flower 1884:493).

It should have been obvious that "contact" was a euphemism for "conquest" and that this was a political process, not "natural law"—yet early applied anthropologists were confident that they were engaged in science and not politics. Reverend Edwin W. Smith, missionary president of the RAI, argued in 1934 that anthropology should be a "coldly neutral," value-free science when in the service of "practical undertakings." It was not to be yoked to "politics, to religion, to nationalism, (or) to philosophy," value-based policy opinions were not to be passed off as science. However, for Smith, anthropology was "not an enemy of progress," and did not advocate preserving tribal people. Smith even cited the preeminent British Scientist, Sir Julian Huxley, to the effect that African tribals could not be preserved in human zoos. However, Huxley (1931:137) in fact stated that preservation would not work because it was not British policy, implying that a policy change could make preservation work under appropriate conditions. Huxley was actually in favor of preservation of Congo pygmies.

The Idealist Preservationists

In contrast to the proexpansionist conservatism of the established humanitarian and anthropological organizations, a small minority of well-informed individuals consistently argued that tribal cultures were still viable and could be saved—if the appropriate authorities had the will to do so. This position proved both unpopular and unprofitable, and unfortunately focused on "preservation," thereby giving critics an easy target to attack. Realists conveniently interpreted "preservation" to mean "imposed" and therefore inhumane "preservation." However, fundamentally the idealist argument was really political. The common theme was that tribals should be left alone, free of outside intrusion.

At least three main groups shared this general perspective: scientific preservationists, humanitarian preservationists, and environmental conservationists. These distinctions are drawn somewhat arbitrarily according to the apparent motivation for the "leave them alone" argument. Scientific preservationists wanted tribals saved for scientific purposes, usually in order to save the vanishing data. Humanitarian preservationists wanted tribals left alone because they felt this was the only way to prevent their ultimate destruction. Later this humanitarian approach evolved into the human rights position of the indigenous-peoples organizations, which stressed the political rights of people to maintain control over their territories and cultures. The environmental conservationists worked to preserve both tribal cultures and their natural environments. The struggle of conservationists to include tribals in environmental sanctuaries has a long history beginning with George Catlin in 1832 and has achieved significant results since 1960 (Bodley 1988, 1990).

Human Zoos: The Scientific Preservationists

From 1872 to 1938 arguments for tribal preservation because of their scientific value were surprisingly frequent. This was a variation on the vanishing-data theme, but it was sometimes mixed with humanitarian and even liberal political sentiments. For example, in 1872, Joseph Kaines, a member of the Royal Anthropological Institute, told the British Association that anthropologists should work to preserve disappearing tribals as a "duty" because the development of their science depended on tribal survival. This approach is here treated as "idealist" because it acknowledges that the existence of independent tribals is possible if governments chose to permit it, while a "realist" would simply argue that tribal survival could never be policy. Scientific preservationists could also be seen as "imperialists" because they treat tribals as objects and would, in effect, deny their right to self-determination.

A tribal preservation resolution was approved by the Australian Association for the Advancement of Science (ANZAAS) in 1923. The resolution called for the segregation of certain select, but unspecified, areas in the Pacific containing "uncontaminated" tribal peoples in order to preserve them for study. A special committee was set up in order to monitor demographic conditions within the tribal areas to be designated. Included on the committee were Australian ethnologist-zoologist Baldwin Spencer and British social anthropologist George Henry Pitt-Rivers. Partly at the urging of the RAI, vast reserves were in fact created for aborigines in central Australia at this time, but whatever the intent of the Committee, it soon became clear that these areas were not sanctuaries where aborigines would be free to live independently. Mission stations and government welfare posts were spread throughout the reserves. The land was not even legally owned by the aborigines, and they were not allowed to prevent development such as mining if the government approved. Official Australian policy remained firmly assimilationist until the mid-1970s.

In 1932 the International Congress of Americanists (ICA) passed a resolution calling for "conservation" of Indian peoples in South America for scientific purposes (ICA 1934, 25:xlv). A similar preservation theme emerged at the 1938 International Congress of Anthropological and Ethnological Sciences (ICAES), where a special research committee was established "For the Study of Governmental Measures for the Conservation of Aboriginal Peoples Whose Ways of Life Are of Scientific Interest." This committee included such prominent anthropologists as Radcliffe-Brown, Alfred Kroeber, Paul Rivet, Diamond Jenness, and Donald Thomson, but its efforts were interrupted by the war. Radcliffe-Brown was in most respects a realist and generally worked in support of colonial expansion, but he was also interested in saving the data. His involvement with the 1938 committee was apparently his closest approach to an idealist position, but he clearly felt that tribals could not maintain their independence in the long run.

Leave Them Alone: Humanitarian Preservationists

While avoiding a self-interested concern with the preservation of scientific data, the humanitarian preservationists focused on the rights of tribals to be left alone and the critical importance of tribal control of resources. Unfortunately, they often still used the rhetoric of cultural preservation and thus had difficulty gaining support.

Charles Wellington Furlong, who visited Tierra del Fuego in 1907/08, recommended before the ICA in 1915 that the governments of Chile and Argentina should permanently reserve the Ona's territory for their "sole use." He urged that the reserve be restocked with wild guanaco in order to maintain the Ona's primary subsistence resource. Through such a policy, he argued, the Ona "would be saved and the tribe preserved" (1915:444).

Australian physical anthropologist Frederic Wood Jones took an emphatic antimissionary, pro-humanitarian preservationist stance toward tribal aborigines in his 1926 presidential address before the Anthropology Section of ANZAAS. As a supporter, he cited the distinguished British explorer A. F. R. Wollaston, who in 1920 had recommended before the Royal Geographical Society that the New Guinea interior be left "as a native reserve where these people can live their own life" with no outside interference. Wood Jones quoted the full-page text of Wollaston's remarks together with the RAI's 1920 petition to the Australian government calling for reserves "on which the natives might be protected from contact with the deleterious elements in White and Asiatic Civilization" (*Man* [1920], 20[12]:89–96, 191).

Wood Jones accepted as a scientifically respectable verdict that such reserves would be the only way to guarantee "the racial survival for such people as the Australian aborigine" (1928:509). He argued that it was land appropriation and prolonged contact with civilization that doomed aborigines to a "lingering but certain death." In a clear departure from the reservation system earlier proposed by Baldwin Spencer (1913), which provided for missionaries, schooling, and the interests of settlers, Wood Jones instead advocated "real reserves" that would allow continuation of tribal culture and traditions.

A similar policy approach was advocated by anthropologist Donald Thomson, who was commissioned by the Australian Federal Government in 1934 to make policy recommendations for the Arnhem Land Aboriginal reserve. He concluded that the 1,500 fully independent aborigines who remained in Arnhem Land were "on the road to extinction" because the government permitted outside interference. Thomson clearly felt that it was still possible for the aborigines to maintain themselves as self-sufficient tribals if given a chance, and that the government would be directly responsible if they were allowed to die. He recommended that aborigines be left in occupation of their own territory and steps be taken to "preserve their culture intact" by keeping settlers and missionaries out. Thomson's recommendations were contained in three separate reports to the government and in papers presented to scientific meetings before the Australia and New Zealand Association for the Advancement of Science in 1937, the British Association, the RAI, and the ICAES in 1938.

Colombian anthropologist Juan Friede, in a paper to the thirtieth International Congress of Americanists (ICA) in 1952, referred specifically to the "rights" of Amazonian Indians to maintain their language and customs, while keeping all outsiders out of their territory. There was no suggestion in Friede's argument that Indians be preserved so that they could be studied. He saw it as simply a matter of their basic human rights. At the following ICA two years later (1954), the human rights approach was strongly endorsed in a resolution on Brazilian Indians. Paulo Duarte and Herbert Baldus, senior Brazilian ethnologist and secretary general of the ICA executive commission, respectively, addressed their resolution to the president of Brazil (ICA 1955, 31[1]:lxix–lxx). They noted that the future survival of many Indian groups in Brazil was threatened because their lands were being invaded in complete disregard for their constitutional rights. They specifically endorsed proposals placed before the Brazilian Parliament by the Indian Protectorate Service designed to increase the legal protection of Indian lands, requesting funds to demarcate tribal lands and for the creation of the Xingu Indian Park. The emphasis in this resolution was on "survival of Indian tribes," and there was no mention of their acculturation or integration into the national society as an objective. Likewise, the resolution was not linked to any concern for the scientific value of vanishing data. It was strictly a matter of human rights. The Xingu project was specifically endorsed because it would permit the maintenance of the intertribal system, which, if broken, "would condemn the tribes to extermination."

You Can't Leave Them Alone: The Realists Prevail

The conflict between the realists and the idealists was continuous. The realists lumped all the idealists with the scientific preservationists and accused them of seeking to establish human zoos as a form of enforced primitivism to preserve their data. The "human zoo" charge, and the related accusations of romanticism and antiprogress, effectively halted the scientific preservationist movement by 1938, and effectively retarded any attempts to gain political support for independent tribals. After stinging attacks by Firth (1944) and Elkin (1946) it became almost impossible for anthropologists to argue for "preservation," and when the ICAES Committee on the Conservation of Aboriginal Peoples reconvened in 1956, attention was shifted to the dual realist program of data salvage and applied anthropology.

Perhaps the central figure in the rejection of idealist approaches, after Reverend Smith, was A. P. Elkin, Australian anthropologist and Christian minister, who followed the realist anthropology of Radcliffe-Brown and Malinowski. Elkin was an influential and outspoken advocate of "justice" for aborigines. He was certainly a liberal for the Australia of the 1930s, but his main concern was to gain humane treatment for aborigines as individuals; he was not interested in safeguarding aboriginal lands and maintaining their independence. In direct opposition to Thomson, Elkin stressed the need for "raising of the Aborigines in the scale of culture," and declared, "To leave them alone is impossible" (Elkin 1935:207).

In view of Elkin's obvious sympathies for the aborigines as human beings, it may seem strange that he was unwilling to support their right to full self-determination by arguing along with Thomson and Wood Jones that whites must be excluded from tribal reserves. Elkin would not have wanted missionaries excluded. In addition to his position as chair of the University of Sydney Anthropology Department, editor of *Oceania*, and member of the powerful Australian National Research Council, Elkin was ultimately dependent on funds provided by the Australian government and the Rockefeller Foundation, who clearly supported realist policies. Furthermore, Elkin's immediate predecessor, Radcliffe-Brown, had ominously endorsed the realist position when he declared that "the Australian Aborigines, even if not doomed to extinction as a race, seem at any rate doomed to have their cultures destroyed" (1930:3). Within this context, Elkin's position made good political sense. In his 1934 summary of the "future of Aborigines" written for *Oceania*, Elkin wanted there to be no doubt when he declared: "It should be stated quite clearly and definitely that anthropologists connected with the [Anthropology] Department in the University of Sydney have no desire to preserve any of the aboriginal tribes of Australia or of the islands in their pristine condition as 'museum specimens' for the purpose of investigation; this charge is too often made against anthropologists" (1934:2).

Raymond Firth, speaking before the RAI in 1943, was equally emphatic in rejecting tribal preservation, stating: "We do not want to keep the people primitive; we know (perhaps better than most) that it cannot be done" (Firth 1944; *Man* 44 [8]:19–22). For both Elkin and Firth, this political opinion was clearly posed as a statement of scientific fact.

The clearest indication of the political strength of realist anthropologists can be seen in International Labor Organization (ILO) Convention 107 (1957), which clearly endorsed integration and development over tribal autonomy. In 1954 the ILO convened a Committee of Experts to debate policy prior to the drafting of Convention 107. According to Horace Miner (1955), the Committee was divided between the "protectionists" led by Brazilian anthropologist Darcy Ribeiro, who favored respect for tribal culture and a very slow rate of change, and Asian representatives who argued for rapid change. In the end the realist position won out. As Miner explained, "The realist recognizes the inevitability of increasing encroachment of civilization on the remaining outposts of preliterate culture" (1955:441). The realists battled among themselves over the rate of change, with the scientific interventionists generally favoring greater caution and respect for the culture and the religious humanitarians pushing for more rapid integration. Neither saw any possibility of leaving tribals alone.

CONCLUSION

Modern nation-states have carried out expansionist policies that have devastated tribal peoples in order to facilitate the extraction of resources from tribal territories. These policies have resulted in genocidal wars of conquest that differ little in substance from the numerous wars fought between states, although the outcome for tribals has consistently been more brutal. The significant difference between the violence perpetrated between states and tribals versus that between states and states is that the latter has been thoroughly analyzed and formal mechanisms for conflict resolution have been sought. Violence against tribals has been virtually invisible. The object of this chapter was to draw attention to the essentially political nature of tribal genocide and to demonstrate that anthropologists and anthropological theory have been part of this genocidal process.

Anthropological involvement in the violence against tribals has been indirect, but significant. Anthropologists were obviously aware of the fate of specific tribal groups. For a century they watched as group after group was exterminated by government policies, yet they made no attempt to halt the violence because prevailing evolutionary theory declared that the disappearance of tribals was natural and inevitable. When evolutionary theory declined, anthropologists found that functionalist theory facilitated "scientific intervention" in the conquest process and helped reduce but did not eliminate the violence of political conquest. Postcolonial development anthropologists tended to accept the conquest of internal tribal areas within independent states as inevitable nation-building progress.

In the preceding sections anthropologists whose theoretical assumptions about evolution, development, and progress masked the political dimension of violence against tribals were grouped together as "realists," while those who questioned these assumptions and explicitly recognized the political dimension while advocating the independence of tribals were called "idealists." By the end of the colonial era, the scientific preservationists were the only idealists to generate any significant interest within the anthropological establishment. But they were easily discredited in the postcolonial era. Tribal preservation came to be seen as inhumane, antiprogress, imperialist, and antinational integration. The humanitarian preservationists and environmental conservationist approaches had great difficulty gaining any widespread support because they were so contrary to the mainstream of anthropological theory, and because their proposals were easily confused with the negative connotations of scientific preservationism.

Realist perspectives dominated policymaking until 1968, when idealist organizations such as the International Work Group for Indigenous Affairs (IWGIA) began to redefine the tribal survival problem as a community human rights issue and came to the support of the emerging indigenous political organizations. This shift coincided with global concerns over war, the arms race, political oppression, poverty, and environmental deterioration. By the late 1960s it had become painfully obvious that national expansion along the world's last great resource frontiers, such as in Brazil, really did kill Indians and destroy the tropical rain forest. It was also becoming clear that tribals would not be the only victims, because uncontrolled development could degrade ecosystems throughout the world and disrupt the global biosphere.

Today many anthropologists are willing to openly condemn government development policies that threaten the survival of tribal peoples, and they argue that tribals, or "indigenous peoples," should be given the political independence to control their own resources and internal affairs, and to work out their own relationship with their neighbors. International Labor Organization Convention 107 is now being rewritten to more closely reflect the directly expressed aspirations of indigenous peoples to control their own futures. Unfortunately, the present success of the idealist perspective came too late for countless tribal groups who were swallowed up by frontier genocide. An anthropology more aware of its own political ideology might have pioneered more humane cultural policies decades earlier.

REFERENCES

ANZAAS (Australian and New Zealand Association for the Advancement of Science)
    1924   Summary of Resolutions, Section F. Committee on Vital Statistics of Primitive Races. *Report of the 16th Meeting* (1923) 16:xlv–xlvi.

Balfour, Henry
    1930   "South Africa's Contribution to Prehistoric Archaeology." British
            Association for the Advancement of Science, *Report of the 97th Meet-
            ing* (1929) 97:153–163.
Bodley, John H.
    1988   "Umweltschutzer unterstutzen Stammesvolker." In *Die neuen "Wil-
            den,"* pp. 54–65, Peter E. Stuben, ed. Okozid 4. Giessen, Germany:
            Vocus-Verl.
    1990   *Victims of Progress,* 3d ed. Mountain View, Calif.: Mayfield Publishing
            Co.
Darwin, Charles
    1871   *The Descent of Man.*
Elkin, A. P.
    1934   "Anthropology and the Future of the Australian Aborigines." *Oce-
            ania* 5(1):1–18.
    1935   "Presidential Address: Anthropology in Australia, Past and Pres-
            ent." *Report of the 22nd Meeting of ANZAAS* 22:196–207.
    1946   "Conservation of Aboriginal Peoples Whose Modes of Life Are of
            Scientific Interest." *Man* 46(81):94–96.
Firth, Raymond
    1944   "The Future of Social Anthropology." *Man* 44(8):19–22.
Flower, W. H.
    1882   "Chairman's Address for Anthropology." British Association for the
            Advancement of Science, *Report of the 51st Meeting* (1881) 51:688.
    1884   "President's Address on the Aims and Prospects of the Study of An-
            thropology." *Journal of the Royal Anthropological Institute* 13:488–507.
Frere, Sir H. Bartle
    1881   "On the Laws Affecting the Relations between Civilized and Savage
            Life, as Bearing on the Dealings of Colonists with Aborigines." *Jour-
            nal of the Royal Anthropological Institute* 11:313–354.
Friede, Juan
    1952   "Los Cofan: Una Tribu de la Alta Amazonia Colombiana." *Proceed-
            ings of the International Congress of Americanists* 30:202–219.
Furlong, Charles Wellington
    1915   "The Haush and Ona, Primitive Tribes of Tierra del Fuego." *Pro-
            ceedings of the International Congress of Americanists* 19:432–444.
Great Britain, House of Commons
    1837   "Report of the Select Committee on Aborigines (British Settle-
            ments)." House of Commons, *Imperial Blue Book,* no. VII, p. 425.
Huxley, Julian
    1931   *Africa View.* New York: Harper & Row.
ICA (International Congress of Americanists)
    1934   "Resolutions." *Proceedings of the International Congress* 25:xlv.

ICAES (International Congress of Anthropological and Ethnological Sciences)
    1938   *Proceedings, Second Congress,* Copenhagen.
Kaines, Joseph
    1873   "Western Anthropologists and extra-Western Communities." British
            Association for the Advancement of Science, *Report of the 42nd Meet-
            ing* (1872) 42:189–190.
Korwa, Fred
    1983   "West Papua: The Colonisation of West Papua." *IWGIA Newsletter*
            (35/36):192–197.
Miner, Horace M.
    1955   "Planning for the Acculturation of Isolated Tribes." *Proceedings of
            the International Congress of Americanists* 31(1):441–446.
Nietschmann, Bernard
    1985   "Indonesia, Bangladesh: Disguised Invasion of Indigenous Na-
            tions." *Fourth World Journal* 1(2):89–126.
Pitt-Rivers, Major General A. (Lane Fox)
    1873   "Anthropology: Address to the Department of Anthropology." Brit-
            ish Association for the Advancement of Science, *Report of the 42nd
            Meeting* (1872) 42:157–175.
    1874   Report of the Committee Consisting of Colonel Lane Fox, Dr. Bed-
            doe, Mr. Franks, Mr. Francis Galton, Mr. E. W. Brabrook, Sir J. Lub-
            bock, *Bart.,* Sir Walter Elliot, Mr. Clements R. Markham, and Mr.
            E. B. Tylor, Appointed for the Purpose of Preparing and Publishing
            Brief Forms of Instructions for Travellers, Ethnologists, and other
            Anthropological Observers." British Association for the Advance-
            ment of Science, *Report of the 43rd Meeting* (1873) 43:482–488.
    1882   "Anniversary Address to the Anthropological Institute of Great Brit-
            ain and Ireland." *Journal of the Royal Anthropological Institute* 11(4):
            488–509.
Radcliffe-Brown, A. R.
    1930   Editorial. *Oceania* 1(1):1–4.
    1932   "The Present Position of Anthropological Studies." British Associa-
            tion for the Advancement of Science, *Report of the 99th Meeting*
            (1931) 99:159–171.
Smith, Edwin W.
    1934   "Anthropology and the Practical Man." *Journal of the Royal Anthro-
            pological Institute* 64:xiii–xxxvii.
Somerville, Boyle T.
    1897   "Ethnographical Notes in New Georgia, Solomon Islands." *Journal
            of the Royal Anthropological Institute* 26:357–412.
Spencer, Baldwin
    1913   "Preliminary Report on the Aboriginals of the Northern Territory."
            The Parliament of the Commonwealth of Australia, Northern Ter-
            ritory of Australia, *Report of the Administrator for the Year 1912,* pp.
            36–52.

Stocking, George W., Jr.
1987   *Victorian Anthropology*. New York: The Free Press, Macmillan.
Thomson, Donald F.
1938a   "Recommendations of Policy in Native Affairs in the Northern Territory of Australia." The Parliament of the Commonwealth of Australia, no. 56, f.2945.
1938b   "Problems of Administration among the Australian Aborigines: A Correction." *Man* 38 (185).
1938c   "The Australian Aborigine and the Problems of Administration." British Association for the Advance of Science, *Report of the 108th Meeting*, 108:463–464.
Wollaston, A. F. R.
1920   "Remarks on 'The Opening of New Territories in Papua.'" *The Geographical Journal* (June):457–458.
Wood Jones, Frederic
1928   "The Claims of the Australian Aborigine." Eighteenth Australia New Zealand Association for the Advancement of Science, Perth, 1926, *Report* 18:497–519.

PART ONE

Domination

Pl. 1. "Native Police Dispersing the Blacks" from *Among Cannibals*
by Carl Lumholtz.

FOUR

Domination, Acting, and Fantasy

James C. Scott

I tremble to speak the words of freedom before the tyrant.
(*Coryphaeus, in Euripides,* The Bacchae)

If the expression "speak truth to power" still has a utopian ring to it, even in modern democracies this is surely because it is so rarely practiced. The dissembling of the weak in the face of power is hardly an occasion for surprise. It is ubiquitous—so ubiquitous, in fact, that it makes an appearance in many situations in which the sort of power being exercised stretches the ordinary meaning of "power" almost beyond recognition. Much of what passes as normal social intercourse requires that we routinely exchange pleasantries and smile at others about whom we may harbor an estimate not in keeping with our public performance. Here we may perhaps say that the power of social forms embodying etiquette and politeness require us often to sacrifice candor for smoother relations with our acquaintances. Our circumspect behavior may also have a strategic dimension; this person to whom we misrepresent ourselves may be able to harm or help us in some way. George Eliot may not have exaggerated in claiming that "there is no action possible without a little acting."

The "acting" that comes of civility will be of less interest to us in what follows than the acting that has been imposed throughout history on the vast majority of people. I mean the public performance required of those subject to elaborate and systematic forms of social subordination: the worker to the boss, the tenant or sharecropper to the landlord, the serf to the lord, the slave to the master, the untouchable to the Brahmin, or a member of a subject race to one of the dominant race. With rare, but significant, exceptions the public performance of the subordinate will—out of prudence, fear, and the desire to curry favor—be shaped to appeal to the expectations of the powerful. I shall use the term *public transcript* as a shorthand way of describing the open interaction between subordinates and those who dominate.[1] The public transcript, where it is not positively misleading, is unlikely to tell the whole story about power relations. It is frequently in the interest of both parties to tacitly conspire in misrepresentation. The oral history of a French tenant farmer, "Old Tiennon" covering much of the nineteenth century is filled with accounts of a prudent and misleading deference: "When he [the landlord who had dismissed his father] crossed from Le Craux, going to Meillers, he would stop and speak to me and I forced myself to appear amiable, in spite of the contempt I felt for him."[2]

Old Tiennon prides himself on having learned, unlike his tactless and unlucky father, "the art of dissimulation so necessary in life."[3] The slave narratives that have come to us from the U.S. South also refer again and again to the need to deceive:

> I had endeavored so to conduct myself as not to become obnoxious to the white inhabitants, knowing as I did their power, and their hostility to the colored people. . . . First, I had made no display of the little property or money I possessed, but in every way I wore as much as possible the aspect of slavery. Second, I had never appeared to be even so intelligent as I really was. This all colored at the south, free and slaves, find it particularly necessary for their own comfort and safety to observe.[4]

As one of the key survival skills of subordinate groups has been impression management in power-laden situations, the "performance" aspect of their conduct has not escaped the more observant members of the dominant group. Noting that her slaves fell uncharacteristically silent whenever the latest news from the front in the Civil War became a topic of white conversation, Mary Chesnut took their silence as one that hid something: "They go about in their black masks, not a ripple of emotion showing; and yet on all other subjects except the war they are the most excitable of all races. Now Dick might be a very respectable Egyptian Sphynx, so inscrutably silent he is."[5]

Here I will venture a crude and global generalization that I will later want to qualify severely: the greater the disparity in power between dominant and subordinate and the more arbitrarily it is exercised, the more the public transcript of subordinates will take on a stereotyped, ritualistic cast. In other words, the more menacing the power, the thicker the mask. We might imagine, in this context, situations ranging all the way from a dialogue among friends of equal status and power on one hand to the concentration camp on the other hand, in which the public transcript of the victim bears the mark of mortal fear. Between these extremes are the vast majority of the historical cases of systematic subordination that will concern us.

Cursory though this opening discussion of the public transcript has been, it alerts us to several issues in power relations—each of which hinges on the fact that the public transcript is not the whole story. First, the public transcript is an indifferent guide to the opinion of subordinates. Old Tiennon's tactical smile and greeting mask an attitude of anger and revenge. At the very least, an assessment of power relations read directly off the public transcript between the powerful and the weak may portray a deference and consent that is possibly only a tactic. Second, to the degree that the dominant suspect that the public transcript may be "only" a performance, they will discount its authenticity. It is but a short step from such skepticism to the view, common among many dominant groups, that those beneath them are deceitful, shamming, and lying by nature. Finally, the questionable meaning of the public transcript suggests the key roles played in power relations of disguise and surveillance. Subordinates offer a performance of deference and consent while attempting to discern, to read, the real intentions and mood of the potentially threatening powerholder. As the favorite proverb of Jamaican slaves captures it: "Play fool, to catch wise."[6] The power figure, in turn, produces a performance of mastery and command while attempting to peer behind the mask of subordinates to read their real intentions. The dialectic of disguise and surveillance that pervades relations between the weak and the strong will help us, I think, to understand the cultural patterns of domination and subordination.

The theatrical imperatives that normally prevail in situations of domination produce a public transcript in close conformity with how the dominant group would wish to have things appear. The dominant never control the stage absolutely, but their wishes normally prevail. In the short run, it is in the interest of the subordinates to produce a more or less credible performance, speaking the lines and making the gestures that they know are expected of them. The result is that the public transcript is—barring a crisis—systematically skewed in the direction of the libretto, the discourse, represented by the dominant. In ideological terms the public transcript will typically, by its accommodationist tone, provide convincing evidence for the hegemony of dominant values, for the hegemony of dominant discourse. It is in precisely this public domain where the effects of power relations are most manifest, and any analysis based exclusively on the public transcript is likely to conclude that subordinate groups endorse the terms of their subordination and are willing, even enthusiastic, partners in that subordination.

A skeptic might well ask at this point how we can presume to know, on the basis of the public transcript alone, whether this performance is genuine. What warrant have we to call it a "performance" at all, thereby impugning its authenticity? The answer is, surely, that we cannot know how contrived or imposed the performance is unless we can speak, as it were, to the performer offstage, out of this particular power-laden context, or unless the performer suddenly declares openly, on stage, that the performances we have previously observed were just a pose.[7] Without a privileged peek backstage or a rupture in the performance we have no way of even calling into question the status of what might be a convincing but feigned performance.

If subordinate discourse in the presence of the dominant is the public transcript, we shall use the term *hidden transcript* to characterize discourse that takes place "offstage," beyond direct observation by power-holders. The hidden transcript is thus derivative in the sense that it consists of those offstage speech, gestures, and practices that confirm, contradict, or inflect what appears in the public transcript.[8] We do not wish to prejudge, by definition, the relation between what is said in the face of power and what is said behind its back. Power relations are not, alas, so straightforward that we can call what is said in power-laden contexts as "false" and what is said offstage as "true." Nor can we simplistically describe the former as a realm of necessity and the latter as a realm of freedom. What is certainly the case, however, is that the hidden transcript is produced for a different audience and under different constraints of power than is the public transcript. By assessing the discrepancy *between* the hidden transcript and the public transcript we may begin to judge the impact of domination on public discourse.

The abstract and general tone of the discussion thus far is best relieved by a concrete illustration of the possibly dramatic disparity between the public and hidden transcript. It is drawn from slavery in the antebellum U.S. South. Mary Livermore, a white governess from New England, recounted the reaction of Aggy, a normally taciturn and deferential black cook, to the beating the master had given her daughter. The daughter had been accused, apparently unjustly, of some minor theft and then beaten while Aggy looked on, powerless to intervene. *After* the master had finally left the kitchen, Aggy turned to Mary, whom she considered her friend, and said:

Thar'a day a-comin'! Thar's a day a-comin'! . . . I hear the rumblin ob de chariots! I see de flashin ob de guns! White folks blood is a runnin on the ground like a ribber, an de dead's heaped up dat high! . . . Or Lor! Hasten de day when de blows, an de bruises, and de aches an de pains, shall come to de white folks, an de buzzards shall eat dem as dey's dead in de streets. Or Lor! roll on de chariots, an gib the black people rest and peace. O Lor! Gib me de pleasure ob livin' till dat day, when I shall see white folks shot down like de wolves when dey come hungry out o'de woods.[9]

One can imagine what might have happened to Aggy if she had delivered this speech directly to the master. Apparently her trust in Mary Livermore's friendship and sympathy was such that a statement of her rage could be ventured with comparative safety. Alternatively, perhaps she could no longer choke back her anger. Aggy's hidden transcript is at complete odds with her public transcript of quiet obedience. What is particularly striking is that this is anything but an inchoate scream of rage; it is a finely drawn and highly visual image of an apocalypse, a day of revenge and triumph, a world turned upside down using the cultural raw materials of the white man's religion. Can we even conceive of such an elaborate vision rising spontaneously to her lips unless the beliefs and practice of slave Christianity had prepared the way carefully? In this respect our glimpse of Aggy's hidden transcript, if pursued further, would lead us directly to the offstage culture of the slave quarters and slave religion. Whatever such an investigation would tell us, this glimpse itself is sufficient to make any naive interpretation of Aggy's previous and subsequent public acts of deference impossible both for us and most decidedly for Aggy's master, should he have been eavesdropping behind the kitchen door.

The problem we face in examining a public transcript of deference amounts to this: how can we estimate the impact of power relations on action when the exercise of power is nearly constant? We can only begin to measure the influence of a teacher's presence on a classroom of students once he or she leaves the room—or when *they* leave the room at recess. Aside from what they say, the typical explosion of chatter and physical exuberance released when school is out, compared with their previous behavior in the classroom, does tell us something retrospectively about the effect of the school and the teacher on behavior. The motives behind acts of deference will remain opaque to us until and unless the power that prompts it weakens or else we can speak confidentially, backstage to those whose motives we wish to understand.

It is particularly in this latter realm of relative discursive freedom, outside the earshot of powerholders, where the hidden transcript is to be sought. The disparity between what we find here and what is said in the presence of power is a rough measure of what has been suppressed from open political communication. The hidden transcript is, for this reason, the privileged site for nonhegemonic, contrapuntal, dissident, subversive discourse. To this point I have used the terms hidden and public *transcript* in the singular when, in fact, the plural would be more accurate and would convey the great variety of sites where such transcripts are generated. The illustration which follows—the crudity and linearity of which would have to be modified—provides an initial sense of this plurality of transcripts in the case of slavery.[10]

As a hypothetical slave is found among audiences progressively toward the more secluded (right) side of the continuum shown in figure 4.1, the slave's discourse is *relatively* freer of intimation from *above*. Stated in slightly different terms, power over discourse is typically, but not always, less lopsided the more the slave is cloistered within that individual's most intimate circle. This is decidedly *not*, however, to assert that the slave's actions before a harsh master are necessarily sham and pretense while that individual's conduct with immediate family and close friends is necessarily genuine and true. The reason we may not leap to this simplifying conclusion is that power relations are ubiquitous. They are surely different at opposite ends of the continuum, but they are never absent.[11]

The difference in power relations toward the hidden-transcript segment of the continuum is that they are generated among those who are mutually subject, often as peers, to a larger system of domination. Although the slave may be freer vis-à-vis the master in this setting, it does not follow that relations of domination do not prevail among the slaves. Power relations among subordinates are not necessarily conducted along democratic lines at all. Among the inmates of prisons who are all subject to a common domination from the institution and its officers, there frequently develops a tyranny as brutal and exploitive as anything the guards can devise. In this domination within domination, subordinate prisoners must measure their words and conduct perhaps more carefully before dominant prisoners than they do before prison officials. Even if relations among subordinates may be characterized by symmetry and mutuality, the hidden transcript that develops in this case may be experienced as no less tyrannical despite the fact that all have had a hand in shaping it. Consider, for example, the ethos that often prevails among workers that penalizes any laborer who would deliberately try to curry the favor of the bosses. The words used from below to describe such

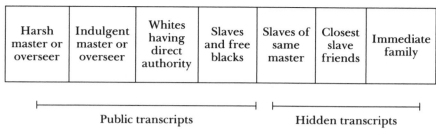

Harsh master or overseer	Indulgent master or overseer	Whites having direct authority	Slaves and free blacks	Slaves of same master	Closest slave friends	Immediate family

Public transcripts   Hidden transcripts

Figure 4.1 Hypothetical discursive sites, arranged by audience, under slavery.

behavior (toady, ass-kisser, rate-buster, boot-licker) are designed to prevent it. They may be supplemented by glares, shunning, and perhaps even beatings.

The power relations generated among subordinate groups are often the only countervailing power to the determination of behavior from above. Tenant farmers in the Malaysian village I studied had developed a strong norm among themselves, condemning anyone who might try to secure or enlarge one's acreage by offering the landlord a higher seasonal rent than the current local tenant now paid. Fifteen years ago someone apparently defied the norm; since then the family is poorly regarded and has not been spoken to or invited to feasts by any kin or friends of the offended family. In a comparable case no Andalusian farmworkers were said to dare work for less than the minimum wage. If they did, they would be given the cold shoulder, ostracized, or branded "low" or a "creeper." [12] The strength of the sanctions deployed to enforce conformity depends essentially on the cohesiveness of the subordinate group and how threatening they view the defection. In nineteenth-century rural Ireland when a tenant broke a rent boycott by paying the land agent, he was likely to find his cow "houghed" in the morning: its Achilles tendon severed so that the tenant would have to destroy it himself. All such cases are instances of the more or less coercive pressure that can be generated to monitor and control deviance among a subordinate group. [13] This pressure serves not only to suppress dissent among subordinates but may also place limits on the temptation to compete headlong with one another—at the expense of all—for the favor of the dominant.

Returning to figure 4.1, the dialectical relationship between the public and hidden transcripts is obvious. By definition, the hidden transcript represents discourse—gesture, speech, practices—that is ordinarily excluded from the public transcript of subordinates by the exercise of power. The practice of domination, then, *creates* the hidden transcript.

If the domination is particularly severe, it is likely to produce a hidden transcript of corresponding richness. The hidden transcript of subordinate groups, in turn, reacts back on the public transcript by embodying a subculture and by opposing its own variant form of social domination against that of the dominant elite. Both are realms of power and interests.

Given the dialectical link between the public and hidden transcripts, there is much to be gained in comparing forms of domination that share some distinctive features. Elsewhere I have attempted to show that slavery, serfdom, untouchability, and racial domination share certain characteristics that tend to produce a wide divergence between the public and the hidden transcript of subordinate groups.[14]

These forms of domination are institutionalized means of extracting labor, goods, and services from a subject population. They embody formal assumptions about superiority and inferiority, often in elaborate ideological form, and a fair degree of ritual and "etiquette" regulates public conduct within them. In principle, at least, status in these systems of domination is ascribed by birth, mobility is virtually nil, and subordinate groups are granted few, if any, political or civil rights. Although they are highly institutionalized, these forms of domination typically contain a strong element of personal rule. Here I have in mind the great latitude for arbitrary and capricious conduct by master toward slave, by lord to serf, or by Brahmin to untouchable. Thus these forms of domination are infused by an element of personal terror that may take the form of arbitrary beatings, sexual violations, and other insults and humiliations. Whether they occur in relation to any particular subordinate, the ever-present knowledge that they might seems to color the relationship as a whole. Finally, like most large-scale structures of domination, the subordinate group has a fairly extensive offstage social existence that, in principle, affords it the opportunity to develop a shared critique of power.

This structural family resemblance is an important analytical underpinning to my argument. I do not intend, in other words, to make "essentialist" assertions about the immutable characteristics of slaves, serfs, untouchables, the colonized, or subjugated races. What I do want to claim, however, is that similar structures of domination, other things equal, tend to provoke responses and forms of resistance that also bear a family resemblance to one another. My analysis, therefore, is one that runs roughshod over differences and specific conditions that others would consider essential, in order to sketch the outlines of broad approach. This broad approach, I hope, can help us to understand better the quiet "prehistory" of what may become violent conflicts. If, in addition, it also sheds some small light on other forms of domination such as class, gender, status, and on total institutions such as prisons, so much the better, but I can't sustain any such claims here.

CONTROL AND FANTASY—
THE BASIS OF THE HIDDEN TRANSCRIPT

When vengeance is tabled, it turns into an illusion, a personal religion, a myth which recedes day by day from its cast of characters, who remain the same in the myth of vengeance. (Milan Kundera, "The Joke")

It is plain enough thus far that prudent subordinates will ordinarily conform by speech and gesture to what they know is expected of them— even if that conformity masks a quite different offstage opinion. What is not perhaps plain enough is that, in any established system of domination, it is not just a question of masking one's feelings and producing the correct speech acts and gestures in their place. Rather, it is often a question of controlling what would be a natural impulse to rage, insult, anger, and the violence that such feelings prompt. There is no system of domination that does not produce its own routine harvest of insults and injury to human dignity—the appropriation of labor, public humiliations, whippings, rapes, slaps, leers, contempt, ritual denigration, and so on. Perhaps the worst of these, many slave narratives agree, was not personal suffering but rather the abuse of one's child or spouse while one had little choice but to look on helplessly. This inability to defend oneself or members of one's family (i.e., to act as mother, father, husband, or wife) against the abuses of domination is simultaneously an assault on one's physical body and one's personhood or dignity. The cruelest result of human bondage is that it transforms the assertion of personal dignity into a mortal risk. Conformity in the face of domination is thus occasionally—and unforgettably—a question of suppressing a violent rage in the interest of oneself and loved ones.

The existential dilemma at work here is captured by contrasting it briefly with Hegel's analysis of the duelist. A person challenges another to a duel because he judges that his honor and standing (including often that of his family) have been mortally insulted. He demands an apology or retraction, failing which his honor can be satisfied only by a duel to the death. What the challenge to a duel says, symbolically, is that to accept this insult is to lose standing, without which life is not worth living [the ideal code, seldom rigorously followed, of the warrior aristocrat].

Who wins the duel is symbolically irrelevant; it is the challenge that restores honor. If the challenger loses, he paradoxically wins his point by demonstrating that he was willing to wager his physical life in order to preserve his honor, or "name." The very logic of the duel makes its status as an ideal apparent; any code that preaches the assertion of standing and honor at the expense of life itself is likely to have many lukewarm adherents in a pinch.

For most bondsmen through history, whether untouchables, slaves, serfs, captives, minorities held in contempt, the trick to survival, not always mastered by any means, has been to swallow one's bile, choke back one's rage, and conquer the impulse to physical violence. It is this systematic *frustration of reciprocal action* in relations of domination that, I believe, helps us understand much of the content of the hidden transcript. At its most elementary level the hidden transcript represents an acting out in fantasy—and occasionally in secretive practice—of the anger and reciprocal aggression that is denied by the presence of domination.[15] Without the sanctions imposed by power relations, subordinates would be tempted to return a blow with a blow, an insult with an insult, a whipping with a whipping, a humiliation with a humiliation. It is as if the "voice," to use Albert Hirschman's term, which they are refused in the public transcript finds its full-throated expression backstage. The frustration, tension, and control necessary in public give way to unbridled retaliation in a safer setting, where the accounts of reciprocity are, symbolically at least, finally balanced.[16]

Later in our analysis we will want to move beyond this elementary, individual, and psychologistic view of the hidden transcript to its cultural determinants, its elaboration, and the forms in which it is expressed. For the moment, however, it is important to recognize that there is an important wish-fulfillment component to the hidden transcript.[17]

The greater part of Richard Wright's account, in *Black Boy*, of his youth in Mississippi is infused with the attempt to control anger among whites and, in turn, to give vent to that anger in the safety of black company.[18] His efforts at stifling his anger is a daily, conscious effort—one that does not always succeed.

> Each day in the store I watched the brutality with growing hate, yet trying to keep my feelings from registering in my face. When the boss looked at me I would avoid his eyes.[19]

> I feared that if I clashed with whites I would lose control of my emotions and spill out the words that would be my sentence of death.[20]

Among his friends during work breaks, the talk frequently turned to fantasies of retaliation and revenge. The fantasies are explicit and often take the form of rumors about what has happened elsewhere. For example,

> Yeah, if they hava race riot around here, I'm gonna kill all the white folks with poison.

> My momma says, that old white woman where she works talked about slapping her and ma said, 'Miz Green, if you slaps me, I'll kill you and go to hell to pay for it.'

> They say a white man hit a colored man up north and that colored man hit that white man, knocked him cold, and nobody did a damned thing.[21]

Wright explains that a "latent sense of violence" surrounded all the offstage talk about whites and that such talk was the "touchstone of fraternity" among the black boys who gathered at the crossroads.

Further evidence for the link between the practical need to control anger and its reflection in fantasy may be illustrated by the findings of a remarkable, if basically flawed, study of the psychological consequences of racial domination on blacks written in the 1940s: Abram Kardiner and Lionel Ovesey's *The Mark of Oppression*.[22] As they understand it, any response to an all-powerful other will be some combination of idealization and hatred. The behavioral expression—whether with manipulative intent or not—of idealization would be ingratiation. Idealization might also take the form of emulation—the use of skin-lightening creams, hair straighteners, and other attempts to distance oneself from the oppressors' stereotype of blacks. This last strategy, for all but a very few, is bound to be futile. What is relevant for our purposes, however, is that both ingratiation and emulation (up to a point) readily find an outlet in the public transcript, precisely because they reaffirm the superiority of the dominant group. The equivalent manifestations of hatred—we may call them *insolence* and *rejection*—cannot, by definition, however, be expressed openly in the public transcript. They must either be insinuated cleverly into the public transcript to avoid retaliation or else expressed offstage. The hidden transcript comes, in this way, to be the repository of the assertions, whose open expression would be dangerous.

In their summaries of individual profiles, Kardiner and Ovesey emphasize that the major psychological problem for blacks was the control of aggression and its consequences. The aggression they find is not unconsciously repressed so much as consciously suppressed. One of their subjects, "G. R." is described as being aware of his anger and capable of expressing it, but only when it is safe to do so. "This means that he is engaged in a constant process of control. He must be ever vigilant and he dare not act or speak on impulse."[23] Putting the issue in terms appropriate to virtually any subordinate group, they conclude:

> The conspicuous feature of rage lies in the fact that it is an emotion that primes the organism for motor expression. Hate is an attenuated form of rage, and is the emotion toward those who inspire fear and rage. The difficult problem for those who are constantly subject to frustration is how to contain this emotion and prevent its motor expression. The chief motive for the latter is to avoid setting into motion retaliatory aggression.[24]

The effort to control open aggression, knowing that it leads almost inevitably to harsh retaliation, was not always successful. Those who did assert themselves defiantly won themselves a place in black folklore— that of the "baaaad Nigger"—that is one of both admiration and fearful awe. Admiration, for having acted out the hidden transcript and fearful awe, for having often paid for it with their lives. As we shall see later, the more common folk hero of subordinate groups—blacks included— has historically been the trickster figure who manages to outwit his adversary and escape unscathed.

Some indirect evidence for the effort required to control anger comes from studies of slavery that indicate the circumstances under which the control might momentarily lapse. Mullin, in his study of slavery in eighteenth-century Virginia, finds repeated evidence that on those occasions when the masters declared a holiday and provided liquor, intoxicated slaves were said to become "aggressive and hostile, insolent, impudent, bold, stubborn."[25] It was as if alcohol loosened slightly the normal inhibitions against aggressive talk, thereby allowing a portion of the hidden transcript to find its way onto the stage.

Whenever a rare event legitimately allowed the black community to vicariously and publicly savor the physical victory of a black man over a white man, that event became an epoch-making one in folk memory. The fight between Jack Johnson and Jim Jeffries (the "White Hope") in 1910 and Joe Louis's subsequent career, which was aided by instant radio transmission of the fights, were indelible moments of reversal and revenge for the black community. "When Johnson battered a white man (Jeffries) to his knees, he was the symbolic black man taking out his revenge on all whites for a lifetime of indignities."[26] Lest such moments be seen purely as a safety valve reconciling blacks to their quotidian world of white domination, there were racial fights in every state in the South and in much of the North immediately after the 1910 fight. The proximate causes varied but it is clear that in the flush of their jubilation, blacks became momentarily bolder in gesture, speech, and carriage, and this was seen as a provocation, a breech of the public transcript by much of the white community. Intoxication comes in many forms.

Fantasy life among dominated groups is also likely to take the form of *schadenfreude*: joy at the misfortunes of others. This represents a wish for negative reciprocity, a settling of scores when the high shall be brought low and the last shall be first. As such, it is a vital element in any millennial religion. Natural events that seem to conform to this wish—as with the Johnson-Jeffries fight—will typically become the focus of symbolic attention. In the case of the black community in the twentieth century, the sinking of the *Titanic* was such an event. The drowning of large numbers of wealthy and powerful whites (the larger losses in steerage were ignored) in their finery aboard a ship that was said to be unsinkable seemed like a stroke of poetic justice to many blacks. It can be said to have "captured the imagination" of blacks in the nearly literal sense of being a prophetic enactment of their hidden transcript. "Official" songs about the loss of the *Titanic* were sung ironically ("It was *saaad* when the great ship went down"). Other songs were composed and sung within the black community. A fragment of one serves to indicate the jubilation at the reversals:

> All the millionaires looked around at Shine [a black stoker] say,
> "Now Shine, oh, Shine, save poor me."
> Say, "We'll make you wealthier than one Shine can be."
> Shine say, "you hate my color and you hate my race."
> Say, "Jump overboard and give those sharks a chase."
> And everybody on board realized they had to die.
> But Shine could swim and Shine could float,
> And Shine could throw his ass like a motorboat.
>
> Say Shine hit the water with a hell of a splash,
> And everybody wondered if that Black sonovabitch could last
> Say the Devil looked up from hell and grinned
> Say, "He's a black, *swimming motherfucker*.
> I think he's gon come on in."[27]

At a more cosmic level we have the effort by subordinate groups to call down a curse on the heads of their aggressors. The elaborate curse, such as that which Aggy invoked against her white master before emancipation and cited earlier, embodies a far more complex symbolic message than the individual dream of a specific revenge against a specific oppressor or the glee at the victory of a black prize-fighter. The curse is an open prayer—even if confined to the backstage audience—embodying an intricate and lovingly ornate vision of revenge. From the perspective of magic, the curse, if properly prepared and recited, will bring about the wish it expresses. Long after emancipation, in the 1920s, Zora Neale Hurston, black novelist and anthropologist, collected such an elaborate curse from the Deep South. Its length precludes full quotation, but an excerpt will convey its controlled rage:

> O Man God, I beg that this I ask for my
>   enemies shall come to pass
> That the South wind shall scorch their bodies
>   and make them wither and shall not be
>   tempered to them
> That the North wind shall freeze their blood
>   and numb their muscles.
>
> I pray that death and disease shall be
>   forever with them and that their crops
>   shall not multiply and their cows, their
>   sheep, their hogs and all their living
>   possessions shall die of starvation and
>   thirst.
>
> I pray that their friends shall betray them
>   and cause them loss of power, of gold and
>   of silver, and that their enemies shall
>   smite them until they beg for mercy,
>   which shall not be given them.
>
> O Man God, I ask you for all these things
>   because they have dragged me in the dust
>   and destroyed my good name; broken my
>   heart and caused me to curse the day that
>   I was born. So be it.[28]

Considering the curse in its entirety, it would be difficult to imagine a more comprehensive damnation with all the details visualized. The revenge is explicit in the curse itself, which begins and ends with the invocation of the oppressions for which the curse is just retribution.

To understand the more luxuriant fantasies of the hidden transcript, they must be seen not alone but instead as the reaction to domination in the public transcript. The inventiveness and originality of these fantasies lies in the artfulness with which they reverse and negate a particular domination.[29] No one recognized this more fully than W. E. B. Du Bois, who wrote of the double-consciousness of the American black arising from racial domination: "Such a double life with double thoughts, double duties, and double social classes, must give rise to double words and double ideals, and *tempt the mind to pretense or revolt, to hypocrisy or radicalism.*"[30]

Occasionally, Du Bois thought of individual blacks as representing one or the other consciousness. Those given to "revolt" or "radicalism" were those who "stood ready to curse God and die" while those given to "pretense" and "hypocrisy" had forgotten that "life is more than meat and the body more than raiment." We can, I think, more usefully think of the former as the hidden transcript and the latter as the public transcript embodied in the same individual, the former being the site of the rage and anger generated by the necessity of preserving a deferential or obsequious public demeanor despite humiliations. If Du Bois associated the "radicalism" more with the North and the "hypocrisy" with the South, this was probably because blacks were somewhat freer to speak their mind in the North.

The hidden transcript that Aggy revealed in the comparative safety of friendship is occasionally openly declared in the face of power. When, suddenly, subservience evaporates and is replaced by open defiance, we encounter one of those rare and dangerous moments in power relations. Mrs. Poyser, a character from George Eliot's *Adam Bede* who finally spoke her mind, provides an illustration of the hidden transcript storming the stage. As tenants of the elderly Squire Donnithorne, Mrs. Poyser and her husband had always resented his rare visits when he would impose some new and onerous obligation on them and treat them with disdain. He had

> a mode of looking at her which, Mrs. Poyser observed, "allays aggravated her; It was as If you was an insect, and he was going to dab his fingernail on you." However, she said, "your servant, sir" and curtsied with an air of perfect deference as she advanced towards him: she was not the woman to misbehave toward her betters, and fly in the face of the catechism, without severe provocation.[31]

This time the Squire came to propose an exchange of pasture and grain land between Mr. Poyser and a new tenant that would almost certainly be to the Poyser's disadvantage. When assent was slow in coming, the Squire held out the prospect of a longer-term farm lease and ended with the observation—a thinly veiled threat of eviction—that the other tenant was well-off and would be happy to lease the Poyser's farm in addition to his own. Mrs. Poyser—"exasperated" at the Squire's determination to ignore her earlier objections "as if she had left the room," and at the final threat—exploded. She "burst in with the desperate determination to have her say out this once, though it were to rain notices to quit, and the only shelter were the workhouse."[32] Beginning with a comparison between the condition of the house—frogs on the steps of the flooded basement, rats and mice coming in through the rotten floorboards to eat the cheeses and menace the children—and the struggle to pay the high rent, Mrs. Poyser let fly her personal accusations as she realized that the Squire was fleeing out the door toward his pony and safety:

> You may run away from my words, sir, and you may go spinning underhand ways o' doing us a mischief, for you've got old Harry to your friend, though nobody else is, but I tell you for once as we're not dumb creatures to be abused and made money on by them as ha' got the lash i' their hands, for want o' knowing how t' undo the tackle. An if I'm th' only one as speaks my mind, there's plenty o' the same way o' thinking i' this parish and the next to 't, for your name's no better than a brimstone match in everybody's nose.[33]

Such were Eliot's powers of observation and insight into her rural society that many of the key issues of domination and resistance can be teased from her story of Mrs. Poyser's encounter with the Squire. At the height of her peroration, for example, Mrs. Poyser insists that they will not be treated as animals despite his power over them. This, together with her remark about the Squire looking on her as an insect, and her declaration that he has no friends and is hated by the whole parish, focus on the issue of self-esteem. While the confrontation may originate in the exploitation of an onerous tenancy, the discourse is one of dignity and reputation. The practices of domination and exploitation typically generate the insults and slights to human dignity, which, in turn, foster a hidden transcript of indignation. Perhaps one vital distinction to draw between forms of domination lies in the kinds of indignities that the exercise of power routinely produces.

Notice also how Mrs. Poyser presumes to speak not just for herself but for the whole parish. She represents what she says as the first public declaration of what everyone has been saying behind the Squire's back. Judging from how rapidly the story traveled and the unalloyed joy with which it was received and retold, the rest of the community also felt that Mrs. Poyser had spoken for them as well. "It was known throughout the two parishes that the Squire's plan had been frustrated because the Poysers had refused to be 'put upon,' and Mrs. Poyser's outbreak was discussed in all the farmhouses with a zest that was only heightened by frequent repetition."[34] The vicarious pleasure of the neighbors had nothing to do with the actual sentiments expressed by Mrs. Poyser—hadn't everyone been saying the same thing about the Squire among themselves for years? The content, although Mrs. Poyser may have put it with considerable folk elegance, was stale; it was saying it openly (with witnesses) to the Squire's face, which was remarkable and made Mrs. Poyser into something of a local hero. The first open statement of a hidden transcript, a declaration that breaches the etiquette of power relations, which breaks an apparently calm surface of silence and consent, carries the force of a symbolic declaration of war. Mrs. Poyser had spoken (a social) truth to power.

Delivered in a moment of anger, one might say that Mrs. Poyser's speech was spontaneous—but the spontaneity lay in the timing and vehemence of the delivery, not in the content. The content had, in fact, been rehearsed again and again, as we are told: "and though Mrs. Poyser had during the last twelvemonth recited many imaginary speeches, meaning even more than met the ear, which she was quite determined to make to him the next time he appeared within the gates of the Hall Farm, the speeches had always remained imaginary."[35]

Who among us have not had a similar experience? Who, having been insulted or having suffered an indignity—especially in public—at the hand of someone in power or authority over us, have not rehearsed an imaginary speech that they wish they had given or intended to give at the next opportunity?[36] Such speeches may often remain a personal "hidden transcript" that may never find expression, even among close friends and peers. But in *this* case we are dealing with a shared situation of subordination. The tenants of Squire Donnithorne and, in fact, much of the nongentry in two parishes had ample personal reasons to take pleasure in his being publicly humbled and to share vicariously in Mrs. Poyser's courage. Their common class position and their social links thus provided a powerful revolving lens, bringing their collective hidden transcript into focus. One might say, without much exaggeration, that they had together, in the course of their social interchange, *written* Mrs. Poyser's speech for her. Not word for word, of course, but in the sense that Mrs. Poyser's "say" would be her own reworking of the stories, the ridicule, and the complaints that those beneath the Squire all shared. And to "write" that speech for her, the Squire's subjects had to have some secure social space, however sequestered, where they could exchange and elaborate their criticism. Her speech was her personal rendition of the hidden transcript of a subordinate group, and, as in the case of Aggy, that speech directs our attention back to the offstage culture of the class within which it originated.

An individual who is affronted may develop a personal fantasy of revenge and confrontation, but when the insult is merely a variant of affronts suffered systematically by a whole race, class, or stratum, the fantasy can become a collective cultural product. Whatever form it assumes, offstage parody, dreams of violent revenge, millennial visions of a world turned upside down, this collective hidden transcript is essential to any dynamic view of power relations.

Mrs. Poyser's explosion was potentially very costly and it was her daring—some would have said foolhardiness—that won her such notoriety. The word explosion is used deliberately here because that is how Mrs. Poyser experienced it:

> "Theest done it now," said Mr. Poyser a little alarmed and uneasy, but not without some triumphant amusement at his wife's outbreak. "Yis, I know I've done it," said Mrs. Poyser, but I've had my say out, and I shall be the'easier for 't all my life.
>
> There's no pleasure in living, if you're to be corked up for iver, and only dribble your mind out on the sly, like a leaky barrel. I shan't repent saying what I think, if I live to be as old as the Squire.[37]

The hydraulic metaphor George Eliot puts in Mrs. Poyser's mouth is the most common way in which the sense of pressure behind the hidden transcript is expressed. Mrs. Poyser suggests that her habits of prudence and deception can no longer contain the anger that she has rehearsed for the last year. That the anger will find a passage out is not in doubt; the choice is rather between a safer but less psychologically satisfying process of "dribbl(ing) your mind out on the sly" or the dangerous but gratifying full blast that Mrs. Poyser has ventured. George Eliot has, in effect, taken one position here on the consequences for consciousness of domination. Her claim is that the necessity of "acting a mask" in the presence of power produces, almost by the strain engendered by its inauthenticity, a countervailing pressure that cannot be contained indefinitely. As an epistemological matter, we have no warrant for elevating the truth status of Mrs. Poyser's outburst over that of her prior deference. Both are arguably part of Mrs. Poyser's self. Note, however, that as Eliot constructs it, Mrs. Poyser feels she has finally spoken her "mind." Inasmuch as she and others in comparable situations feel that they have finally spoken truthfully to those in power, the concept truth may have a sociological reality in the thought and practice of people whose actions interest us. It may have a phenomenological force in the real world despite its untenable epistemological status. An alternative claim, nearly a logical mirror image of the first, is that those obliged by domination to "act a mask" will eventually find that their faces have grown to fit that mask. The practice of subordination in this case produces, in time, its own legitimacy, rather like Pascal's injunction to those who were without religious faith but who desired it, to get down on their knees five times a day to pray and the acting would eventually engender its own justification in faith. In the analysis that follows I hope to clarify this debate considerably, inasmuch as it bears so heavily on the issues of domination, resistance, ideology, and hegemony that are at the center of my concern.

If the weak have obvious and compelling reasons to seek refuge behind a mask when in the presence of power, the powerful have their own compelling reasons for adopting a mask in the presence of subordinates. Thus, for the powerful as well, there is typically a disparity between the public transcript deployed in the open exercise of power and the hidden transcript expressed safely only offstage. The offstage transcript of elites is, like its counterpart among subordinates, derivative; it consists in those gestures and words that inflect, contradict, or confirm what appears in the public transcript.

Nowhere has the "act of power" been more successfully examined than in George Orwell's essay, "Shooting an Elephant," from his days as a subinspector of police in the 1920s in colonial Burma. Orwell had been summoned to deal with an elephant in heat that had broken its tether and was ravaging the bazaar. When Orwell, elephant gun in hand, finally locates the elephant that has, indeed, killed a man, it is peacefully grazing in the paddy fields, no longer a threat to anyone. The logical thing would be to observe the elephant for a while to ensure that its heat had passed. What frustrates logic for Orwell is that there are now more than 2,000 colonial subjects who have followed and are watching him. He is well worth quoting at length:

> And suddenly I realized that I should have to shoot the elephant after all. The people expected it of me and I had got to do it; I could feel their two thousand wills pressing me forward, irresistibly. And it was at this moment, as I stood there with the rifle in my hands, that I first grasped the hollowness, the futility of the white man's dominion in the East. Here was I, the white man with his gun, standing in front of the unarmed native crowd—seemingly the leading actor of the piece; but in reality I was only an absurd puppet pushed to and fro by the will of those yellow faces behind. I perceived in this moment that when the white man turns tyrant it

is his own freedom that he destroys. He becomes a sort of hollow posing dummy, the conventionalized figure of a sahib. For it is the condition of his rule that he shall spend his life in trying to impress the "natives," and so in every crisis he has to do what the "natives" expect of him. He wears a mask and his face grows to fit it . . . A sahib has got to act like a sahib; he has got to appear resolute, to know his own mind and do definite things. To come all that way, rifle in hand, with two thousand people marching at my heels, and then to trail feebly away, having done nothing—no, that was impossible. The crowd would laugh at me. And my whole life, every white man's life in the East, was one long struggle not to be laughed at.[38]

Orwell's use of the theatrical metaphor is pervasive; he speaks of himself as a "leading actor of the piece," of hollow dummys, puppets, masks, appearances, and an audience poised to jeer if he doesn't follow the established script.

As he experiences it, Orwell is no more free to be himself, to break convention, than a slave would be in the presence of a tyrannical master. If subordination requires a credible performance of humility and deference, so domination seems to require a credible performance of haughtiness and mastery. There are, however, two differences. A slave who transgresses the script risks beating, while Orwell risks only ridicule. Another important distinction is that the necessary posing of the dominant derives not from weakness but rather from the ideas behind their rule, the kinds of claims that they make to legitimacy. A divine king must act like a god, a warrior king like a brave general; an elected head of a republic must appear to respect the citizenry and their opinions; a judge must seem to venerate the law. Actions by elites that *publicly* contradict the basis of a claim to power are threatening. The cynicism of the taped Oval Office conversations in the Nixon White House was a devastating blow to the public transcript claim to legality and highmindedness. Similarly, the existence of special shops and hospitals for the party elites in the socialist bloc profoundly undercut the ruling party's public claim to rule on behalf of the working class.[39]

One might usefully compare forms of domination in terms of the kinds of display and public theater that they seem to require. Another, perhaps even more revealing, way of addressing the same question would be to ask what activities are most sedulously hidden from public view by different forms of domination. Each form of rule will have not only its characteristic stage setting but also its characteristic dirty linen.[40]

Those forms of domination that are based on a premise or claim to inherent superiority by ruling elites would seem to depend heavily on lavish display, sumptuary laws, regalia, and public acts of deference or tribute by subordinates. The desire to inculcate habits of obedience and hierarchy, as in military organizations, can produce similar patterns. In extreme cases display and performance dominate as in the case of the Chinese Emperor Long Qing, whose public appearances were so minutely choreographed that he became virtually a living icon deployed in rituals that risked nothing to improvisation. Offstage, in the Forbidden City, he might carouse as he wished with princes and aristocrats.[41] This may be something of a limiting case, but the attempt by dominant elites to sequester an offstage social site where they are no longer on display and can let their hair down is ubiquitous, as is the attempt to ritualize contact with subordinates so that the masks remain firmly in place and the risk that something untoward might happen is minimized. Milovan Djilas's early critique of Yugoslavia's new party elite contrasted a meaningful but secret backstage with the empty ritual of public bodies:

> At intimate suppers, on hunts, in conversations between two or three men, matters of state of the most vital importance are decided. Meetings of party forums, conferences of the government and assemblies, serve no purpose but to make declarations and put in an appearance.[42]

Strictly speaking, of course, the public ritual that Djilas denigrates does, indeed, serve a purpose inasmuch as the theater of unanimity, loyalty, and resolve are intended to impress an audience. Public ritual of this kind is both real and meaningful; Djilas's complaint is rather that it is also a performance designed to conceal an offstage arena of politics that would contradict it. Dominant groups often have much to conceal and, typically, also have the wherewithal to conceal what they wish. The British colonial officials with whom Orwell served in Moulmein had the inevitable club to repair to in the evenings. There, except for the invisible Burmese staff, they were "among their own," as they might have put it, and no longer strutting before the audience of colonial subjects. Activities, gestures, remarks, and dress that were unseemly to the public role of sahib were safe in this retreat.[43]

Now that the basic idea of public and hidden transcripts has been introduced, I will venture a few concluding observations. For the study of power relations, this perspective alerts us to the fact that virtually all ordinarily observed relations between dominant and subordinate represent the encounter of the *public* transcript of the dominant with the *public* transcript of the subordinate. It is to observe Squire Donnithorne imposing on Mr. and Mrs. Poyser on all those occasions on which, prior to the explosion, she managed to keep up the pretense of being deferential and agreeable. Social science is, in general, then, focused resolutely on the "official" or "formal" relations between the powerful and weak. This is even the case for much of the study of conflict when that conflict has become highly institutionalized. I do not mean to imply that the study of this domain of power relations is necessarily false or trivial—only that it hardly exhausts what we might wish to know about power.

Eventually we would want to know how the *hidden* transcripts of various actors are formed, the conditions under which they do or do not find public expression, and what relation they bear to the public transcript.[44] Three characteristics of the hidden transcript, however, merit clarification beforehand. First, the hidden transcript is specific to a given social site and to a particular set of actors. Aggy's oath was almost certainly rehearsed in various forms among the slaves in their quarters or at the clandestine religious services that we know were common. Orwell's peers, like most dominant groups, would risk less from a public indiscretion, but they would have the safety of the Moulmein Club in which to vent their spleen. Each hidden transcript, then, is actually elaborated among a restricted "public" that excludes—that is, is hidden from—certain specified others. A second and vital aspect of the hidden transcript that has not been sufficiently emphasized is that it contains not only speech acts but also a whole range of practices. Thus, for many peasants, activities such as poaching, pilfering, clandestine tax evasion, and intentionally shabby work for landlords are part and parcel of the hidden transcript. For dominant elites, hidden-transcript practices might include the clandestine use of hired thugs, bribery, and tampering with land titles. These practices, in each case, contravene the public transcript of the party in question and are, if at all possible, kept offstage and unavowed.

Finally, it is clear that the frontier between the public and the hidden transcript is a zone of constant struggle between dominant and subordinate—not a solid wall. The capacity of dominant groups to prevail—although never totally—in defining and constituting what counts as the public transcript and what as offstage is, as we shall see, no small measure of their power. The unremitting struggle over such boundaries is perhaps the most vital arena for ordinary conflict, for everyday forms of class struggle. Orwell noticed how the Burmese managed to insinuate almost routinely a contempt for the British, while being careful never to venture a more dangerous open defiance:

> anti-European feeling was very bitter. No one had the guts to raise a riot, but if a European woman went through the bazaars alone somebody would probably spit betel juice over her dress. . . . When a nimble Burman tripped

me up on the football field and the referee (another Burman) looked the other way, the crowd yelled with hideous laughter. . . . In the end the sneering yellow faces of the young men that met me everywhere, the insults hooted after me when I was at a safe distance, got badly on my nerves. The young Buddhist priests were the worst of all.[45]

Tactical prudence ensures that subordinate groups rarely blurt out their hidden transcript directly. But, taking advantage of the anonymity of a crowd or of an ambiguous accident, they manage in a thousand artful ways to imply that they are grudging conscripts to the performance.

The analysis of the hidden transcripts of the powerful and of the subordinate offer us, I believe, one path to a social science that uncovers contradictions and possibilities, that looks well beneath the placid surface that the *public* accommodation to the existing distribution of power, wealth, and status often presents. Behind the "anti-European" acts that Orwell noted was undoubtedly a far more elaborate hidden transcript, an entire discourse, linked to Burman culture, religion, and the experience of colonial rule. This discourse was not available—except through spies—to the British. It could be recovered only offstage in the native quarter in Moulmein and only by someone intimately familiar with Burman culture. Nor, of course, did the Burmans know—except through the tales that servants might tell—what lay behind the more or less official behavior of the British toward them. That hidden transcript could be recovered only in the clubs, homes, and small gatherings of the colonists. The analyst in any situation like this has a strategic advantage over even the most sensitive participants precisely because the hidden transcripts of dominant and subordinate are, in most circumstances, *never in direct contact.* One participant will be familiar with the public transcript and the hidden transcript of one's own circle, but not with the hidden transcript of the other participant. For this reason, political analysis can be advanced by an analysis that can compare the hidden transcript of subordinate groups with the hidden transcript of the powerful and *both* hidden transcripts with the public transcript that they share. This last facet of the comparison will reveal the effect of domination on political communication.

Just a few years after Orwell's stint in Moulmein a huge anticolonial rebellion took the English by surprise. It was led by a Buddhist monk claiming the throne and promising a utopia that consisted largely of getting rid of the British and taxes. The rebellion was crushed with a good deal of gratuitous brutality and the surviving "conspirators" sent to the gallows. A portion, at least, of the hidden transcript of the Burmans had suddenly, as it were, leapt onto the stage to declare itself openly. Millennial dreams of revenge, visions of just kingship, of Buddhist saviors, of a racial settling of scores of which the British had little inkling were being acted on. In the brutality of the repression that followed one could detect an acting out of the admission that Orwell struggled against and that undoubtedly found open expression in the whites only club that "the greatest joy in the world would be to drive a bayonet into a Buddhist priest's guts." Many—perhaps most—hidden transcripts remain just that: hidden from public view and never "enacted." Nor are we able to tell easily under what precise circumstances the hidden transcript will storm the stage. But if we wish to move beyond apparent consent and to grasp potential acts, intentions as yet blocked, and possible futures that a shift in the balance of power or a crisis might bring to view, we have little choice but to explore the realm of the hidden transcript.

NOTES

1. *Public* here refers to action that is openly avowed to the other party in the power relationship and *transcript* is used in its juridical sense (procès-verbal) of a complete record of what was said. This complete record, however, would also include nonspeech acts such as gestures and expressions.

2. Emile Guillaumin, *The Life of a Simple Man,* ed. Eugen Weber, rev. trans. Margaret Crosland (Hanover, N.H.: University Press of New England, 1983), 83. See also pp. 38, 62, 64, 102, 140, and 153 for other instances.

3. Ibid., 82.

4. Lunsford Lane, "The Narrative of Lunsford Lane, Formerly of Raleigh, North Carolina" (Boston, 1848), quoted in Gilbert Osofsky, ed., *Puttin' on Ole Massa: The Slave Narratives of Henry Bibb, William Wells, and Solomon Northrup* (New York: Harper & Row, 1969), 9.

5. Mary Chesnut, *A Diary from Dixie* (Boston: Houghton Mifflin, 1949), quoted in Orlando Patterson, *Slavery and Social Death: A Comparative Study* (Cambridge, Mass.: Harvard University Press, 1982), 208.

6. Ibid., 338.

7. I bracket, for the moment, the possibility that the offstage retraction or the public rupture may itself be a ruse designed to mislead. It should be clear, however, that there is no satisfactory way to establish definitively some bedrock reality or truth behind any particular set of social acts. I also overlook the possibility that the performer may be able to insinuate an insincerity into the performance itself, thereby undercutting its authenticity for part or all of the audience.

8. This is *not* to assert that subordinates have nothing to talk about among themselves other than their relationship to the dominant. Rather, it is merely to confine the term to that segment of interaction among subordinates that bears on relations with the powerful.

9. Mary A. Livermore, "My Story of the War" (Hartford, Conn., 1889)

quoted in Albert J. Raboteau, *Slave Religion: The "Invisible Institution" of the Antebellum South* (New York: Oxford University Press, 1978), 313.

10. A great deal of important information is purposely omitted from this illustration. As depicted, it is entirely static and does not allow for the development and interaction of transcripts over time. It fails to specify the location and circumstances as well as the audience; a slave speaking with a white shopkeeper while making an ordinary transaction would not be in the same situation as when encountering whites on horseback at night. Finally, it adopts the vantage point of a single individual rather than what might be called the "community of discourse." It does, however, serve to orient a discussion of power and discourse—a discussion that might have any number of illustrative cases—serfdom, caste, wage labor, bureaucracy, school.

11. No real social site can be regarded as a realm of entirely "true" and "free" discourse unless, perhaps, it is the private imagination to which, by definition, we can have no access. Disclosure to anyone else immediately brings power relations into play, and psychoanalysis—which aims at the disclosure of repressed truth in a tolerant, encouraging atmosphere—is, at the same time, a highly asymmetrical power relationship.

12. See Juan Martinez-Alier, *Labourers and Landowners in Southern Spain*, St. Anthony's College Oxford Publications no. 4 (London: Allen and Unwin, 1971), 126.

13. Where such domination *within* domination is pronounced, it becomes possible to speak of a hidden transcript within the hidden transcript. Subordinates may be too intimidated by the exercise of domination within the group to say or do anything at odds with what is required. Notice also that when such a situation develops, powerholders among subordinates may well come to have something of vested interest in the overall pattern of domination, which is a precondition of their own power.

14. See James C. Scott, *Political Arts of the Powerless: Interpreting the Hidden Transcript of Subordinate Groups* (Yale University Press: in press).

15. One might, speculatively, parallel analysis of the cultural products of hatred and anger that cannot find direct expression on one hand and the cultural products of love that cannot find direct expression on the other hand. At one extreme are apocalyptic visions of a world upside down and, at the other, a poetry of complete mystical union with the beloved. If we were to proceed in terms of Habermas's analysis of the "ideal speech situation," the hidden transcript would represent the whole reciprocal conversational reply of the subordinate, which, for reasons of domination, cannot be spoken openly. Habermas excludes, by definition, all "strategic" action and dominated discourse from the ideal speech situation and, hence, from the search for rational consensus. What domination achieves, in this context, is the fragmentation of discourse so that much of what would be a cohesive, integrated discourse is sequestered into the hidden transcript of the subordinate and the hidden transcript of the dominant. See, for example, Thomas McCarthy, *The Critical Theory of Jürgen Habermas* (London: Hutchinson, 1978), chap. 4, 273–352.

16. Something very like this equilibrium view of the hidden transcript is invoked by Hochschild in the relatively benign world of flight attendants:

> But in the public world of work, it is often part of an individual's job to accept uneven exchanges, to be treated with disrespect or anger by a client, all the *while closeting into fantasy the anger one would like to respond with.* Where the customer is king, unequal exchanges are normal, and from the beginning customer and client assume different rights to feeling and display. The ledger is supposedly evened by a wage.

The fantasy in this case involves mostly imagined acts of retaliation to insults of the "what I would like to do if I didn't have to be prudent" kind. Flight attendants thus "pictured" themselves trading insults with abusive passengers, spilling drinks on their laps, putting large doses of a laxative in their coffee, and so forth. Wish fulfillment this most definitely is. See Arlie Russell Hochschild, *The Managed Heart: The Commercialization of Human Feeling* (Berkeley, Los Angeles, London: University of California Press, 1983), 85–86.

17. Understanding the hidden transcript in this fashion might seem the equivalent of calling it the site of "ressentiment," as Nietzsche used the term. "Ressentiment" arises from the repeated repression of feelings of hatred, envy, and revenge that cannot be acted out. In this respect, at least, the term fits. But for Nietzsche, the psychological dynamics of "ressentiment" depend on these emotions having *literally* no possible outlet—no externalization—so that they come eventually to lie below the level of conscious thought. In our case, it is the social site of the hidden transcript that provides the opportunity for these emotions to take a collective, cultural form and be acted out. As Scheler notes, once an "ill-treated servant can vent his spleen in the ante-chamber, he will remain free from the inner venom of ressentiment"; see Max Scheler, *Ressentiment,* trans. William W. Holdheim, ed. Lewis A. Coser (Glencoe, Ill.: Free Press, 1961). See Friedrich Nietzsche, *On The Geneology of Morals,* trans. Walter Kaufman and F. J. Hollingsdale, particularly "First Essay," secs. 8, 10, 11, 13; "Second Essay," secs. 14–16 (New York: Vintage, 1969). I was made aware of the relevance of Nietzsche's concept by the fine sociological study of contemporary domestic servants by Judith Rollins, *Between Women: Domestics and Their Employers* (Philadelphia: Temple University Press, 1985).

18. Richard Wright, *Black, Boy: A Record of Childhood and Youth* (New York: Harper and Bros., 1937).

19. Ibid., 159.

20. Ibid., 175.

21. Ibid., 67–69.

22. Abraham Kardiner and Lionel Ovesey, *The Mark of Oppression,* subtitled *Explorations in the Personality of the American Negro* (Cleveland: Meridian Books, 1962). First published in 1951. This book is in the tradition of the "modal personality" school of cultural studies that Kardiner pioneered.

23. Ibid., 104.

24. Ibid., 304. Kardiner and Ovesey went to some lengths to secure an unbiased picture of the fantasy life of their subjects. Results of Rorschach Tests and Thematic Apperception Tests (TATS), both standard projective tests, were

submitted to a panel for blind evaluation. Here, in an imaginative realm with few constraints, the assessment was that "the bulk of their emotional strivings are organized along the lines of aggression. Their inner existences are turbulent with the urge to hit out, hurt, and destroy." The protocols were frequently the mirror image of the control and measured words required in the public transcript of domination. Here one found much of the released violence and revenge that was otherwise suppressed. Ibid., 322.

25. Gerald W. Mullin, *Flight and Rebellion: Slave Resistance in 18th Century Virginia* (New York: Oxford University Press, 1972), 100. Wright, *Black, Boy,* 162, quotes a drunken black man saying the following couplet: "All these white folks dressed so fine / Their ass-holes smell Just like mine." For drink and self-assertion among women, see, for example, Mary Field Belenky et al., *Women's Ways of Knowing: The Development of Self, Voice, and Mind* (New York: Basic Books, 1986), esp. 25.

26. Al-Tony Gilmore, *Bad Nigger!: The National Impact of Jack Johnson* (Port Washington, N.J.: Kennikat Press, 1975), 5. Knowing the likely impact of showing the film, the local and state authorities passed ordinances to ban its showing in local theaters. Ibid., 76–82.

27. D. C. Dance, ed., *Shuckin' and Jivin': Folklore from Contemporary Black Americans* (Bloomington: University of Indiana Press, 1978), 215–216, (emphasis in original). The reversals here and elsewhere in the song are multiple. Shine, the black stoker from the hot engine room below decks, swims home to new sexual triumphs while the white passengers on the upper decks plunge with the ship to the cold bottom of the sea.

28. Quoted by Alice Walker, "Nuclear Exorcism," *Mother Jones* (September–October, 1982), 20. Alice Walker began a speech at a nuclear disarmament rally with this curse in an effort to explain why many blacks were not much interested in signing nuclear-freeze petitions. Their "hope for revenge" made them look on nuclear destruction brought about by a white-ruled world with equanimity if not malevolent pleasure. One has, she implies, no right expecting civic-spiritedness from those whose experience of community has mostly been that of victims.

29. A standard and much commented on traditional woman's fantasy involves an inversion of dependence in which the dominant male, in this case the object of affection, would be imagined as becoming blind or crippled and thus helpless. The woman entertaining such a fantasy imagines both the harm and the devoted care that would demonstrate both power and affection.

30. W. E. B. Du Bois, "On the Faith of the Fathers," in *The Souls of Black Folk* pp. 210–225, W. E. B. Du Bois, ed. (New York: New American Library [Signet Classic, 1969]), 221–222.

31. George Eliot, *Adam Bede* (Hammondsworth: Penguin Books, 1981), 388–389.

32. Ibid., 393.

33. Ibid., 394.

34. Ibid., 398.

35. Ibid., 388.

36. We are, I think, apt to have the same fantasy when we are bested in argument among equals or insulted by a peer. The difference is simply that asymmetrical power relations do not interfere with the declaration of the hidden transcript in this case.

37. Ibid., 395. For readers unfamiliar with *Adam Bede* who would like to know how things turned out, the Squire died providentially some months later, lifting the threat.

38. George Orwell, *Inside the Whale and Other Essays* (Hammondsworth: Penguin, 1962), 95–96.

39. Similar inequalities are not nearly so symbolically charged in Western capitalist democracies that are publicly committed to defend property rights and make no claims to be run for the particular benefit of the working class.

40. We all recognize homely versions of this truth. It is, parents sense, unseemly to argue publicly in front of their children, especially over their discipline and conduct. To do so is to undercut the implicit claim that parents know best and are agreed about what is proper. It is also to offer their children a political opportunity to exploit the revealed difference of opinion. Generally, parents prefer to keep the bickering offstage and to present a more or less united front before the children.

41. Ray Huang, *1571: A Year of No Significance* (New Haven: Yale University Press, 1981).

42. Milovan Djilas, *The New Class* (New York: Praeger, 1957), 82.

43. I suspect that it is for essentially the same reason that the subordinate staff in virtually any hierarchical organization tend to work in open view while the elite work behind closed doors, often with anterooms containing *private* secretaries.

44. I overlook, deliberately for the moment, the fact that there are, for any actor, several public and hidden transcripts depending on the audience being addressed.

45. Orwell, *Inside the Whale*, 91. A shouted insult seems hardly a hidden transcript. What is crucial here is the "safe distance" that renders the insulter anonymous: the message is public but the messenger is hidden.

REFERENCES

Belenky, Mary Field, et al.
    1986   *Women's Ways of Knowing: The Development of Self, Voice, and Mind.* New York: Basic Books.
Chesnut, Mary
    1982   *A Diary from Dixie.* Boston: Houghton Mifflin, 1949. Quoted in Orlando Patterson, *Slavery and Social Death: A Comparative Study.* Cambridge, Mass.: Harvard University Press.

Dance, D. C., ed.
1978   *Shuckin' and Jivin': Folklore from Contemporary Black Americans.* Bloomington: University of Indiana Press.
Djilas, Milovan
1957   *The New Class.* New York: Praeger.
Du Bois, William Edward Burghardt
1969   "On the Faith of the Fathers." In *The Souls of Black Folks.* New York: New American Library Signet Classics.
Eliot, George
1981   *Adam Bede.* Hammondsworth: Penguin Books.
Gilmore, Al-Tony
1975   *Bad Nigger!: The National Impact of Jack Johnson.* Port Washington, N.J.: Kennikat Press.
Guillaumin, Emile
1983   *The Life of a Simple Man,* Eugen Weber, ed., rev. trans. Margaret Crosland. Hanover, N.H.: University Press of New England.
Hochschild, Arlie Russell
1983   *The Managed Heart: The Commercialization of Human Feeling.* Berkeley, Los Angeles, London: University of California Press.
Huang, Ray
1981   *1571: A Year of No Significance.* New Haven: Yale University Press.
Kardiner, Abram, and Lionel Ovesey
1962   *The Mark of Oppression: Explorations in the Personality of the American Negro.* Cleveland: Meridian Books.
Lane, Lunsford
1969   "The Narrative of Lunsford Lane, Formerly of Raleigh, North Carolina." In *Puttin' on Ole Massa: The Slave Narratives of Henry Bibb, William Wells, and Solomon Northrup,* Gilbert Osofsky, ed. New York: Harper & Row.
Livermore, Mary A.
1978   "My Story of the War" (Hartford, Conn., 1889). Quoted in Albert J. Raboteau, *Slave Religion: The "Invisible Institution" of the Antebellum South.* New York: Oxford University Press.
Martinez-Alier, Juan
1971   *Labourers and Landowners in Southern Spain.* St. Anthony's College Oxford Publications no. 4. London: Allen and Unwin.
McCarthy, Thomas
1978   *The Critical Theory of Jürgen Habermas.* London: Hutchinson.
Mullin, Gerald W.
1972   *Flight and Rebellion: Slave Resistance in 18th Century Virginia.* New York: Oxford University Press.
Nietzsche, Friedrich
1969   *On the Geneology of Morals.* Trans. Walter Kaufman and F. J. Hollingsdale. New York: Vintage Books.

Orwell, George
   1962   *Inside the Whale and Other Essays.* Hammondsworth: Penguin Books.
Rollins, Judith
   1985   *Between Women: Domestics and Their Employers.* Philadelphia: Temple
         University Press.
Scott, James C.
   In press *Political Arts of the Powerless: Interpreting the Hidden Transcript of Sub-
         ordinate Groups.* New Haven: Yale University Press.
Sheler, Max
   1961   *Ressentiment.* Trans. William W. Holdheim, ed. Lewis A. Coser. Glen-
         coe, Ill.: Free Press.
Walker, Alice
   1982   "Nuclear Exorcism." *Mother Jones* (September–October):20–21.
Wright, Richard
   1937   *Black Boy: A Record of Childhood and Youth.* New York: Harper & Row.

FIVE

Resisting "Ethnicity":
The Israeli State and Bedouin Identity

Longina Jakubowska

In the summer of 1985 the principal of a local Bedouin school, himself a Bedouin in his late twenties, announced to a group of his friends in a voice trembling with anger: "if it was not enough what they are doing to us, now they tell us we are an ethnic group." "They" referred to the Israeli state.

This statement became the departure point for my inquiry into the politics of ethnicity. Through examining the case of the Negev Bedouin,[1] I argue that the Israeli state has assumed hegemony over ethnic designations, imposing its own definitions on the identity of the constituent groups in order to manipulate intergroup relations. The outrage of the Bedouin school principal was shared by the audience, and this led me to reconsider the question of Bedouin identity. What seemed to me during my fieldwork as an "identity vacuum" among the Bedouin actually formed the core of resistance against the hegemonic power of the state to define their culture and assign their identity. Bedouin politics of marginalism and their refusal to be labeled an ethnic group constitutes an opposition to the Israeli politics of separatism and "de-Arabization" of the chosen Arab groups. The strategy of marginalism is a continuation of the pastoral nomadic ethos and is employed to reject the prevailing political discourse of Israel phrased in the idiom of conflicting nationalities, the Israeli and the Palestinian.

I argue that the concepts of ethnicity and identity are cognitively distinct for the Bedouin. Identity is understood by them as inherent to the people: it is an internalized cultural construction embedded in the social system and manifested in practices of everyday life. Bedouin regard ethnicity as a political construct imposed by outside powers as means of control and domination. In this chapter I will argue that although settlement of the Bedouin by the Israeli state is presented as modernization, it is intended by the state, and perceived by the Bedouin as a means of political domination and cultural destruction. The presentation of the Bedouin as an ethnic group is a political construct created to accomplish the same end. Bedouin maintenance of marginality and isolationism is a refusal to participate in the discourse of nationalism and an effective means of resistance against state hegemony over identity.

THE BEDOUIN OF THE NEGEV

Geographically the Negev is a triangle with its base in the north at the foothills of the Judean mountains and its apex in the south at Eilat. The arid climate and scanty vegetation of the desert could in the past support only a small pastoral nomadic population. In fact, through the successive conquests of the Egyptian Mameluks, the Ottoman Turks, and even the British Mandate, the nomadic Bedouin maintained sole occupancy of the Negev. The earliest population census carried out in the Negev[2] by the British administration in 1922 estimated the Bedouin at 55,000, with the heaviest concentration in the Beer Sheva region,[3] the area ecologically best suited for animal raising and extensive agriculture.

While pastoral nomadism shows historical continuity and cultural distinctiveness as a mode of livelihood, its populations experience shifts across its boundaries over time (Barth 1961). Pastoral nomadism expanded or contracted according to demands and constraints of both the physical and the political environments (Rosen n.d.; Salzman 1980). Historically, the Negev Bedouin incorporated peasants who, because of drought or loss of land, migrated inland from Egypt and coastal Palestine and adopted the nomadic ethos (Jakubowska 1985; Marx 1967).

The Bedouin were organized in territorial units, *ashai'r* (sing. *ashirah*), headed by *shiukh* (sing. *sheikh*), along the lines of a segmentary lineage system augmented by the absorption of the occasional influx of individual peasant families and the Negro slaves. Slavery, as practiced by the Bedouin, had a character of personal patron-client relationships. The slaves were regarded as cultural "minors." Slavery was prohibited by the Ottoman authorities at the turn of the century. The slaves, collectively called *'abid,* remained a distinct social category. Similarly, the peasants, *fellahin,* constituted a separate group. Although the *'abid* are not slaves, nor do the *fellahin* practice agriculture, this classification is part of the

Bedouin social perception today. Neither group was incorporated into the lineage structure and, consequently, as the territory was controlled by core lineages, became the latter's political and economic clients.[4] Although internally stratified, the Bedouin are homogeneous in culture and language, and identify themselves collectively as "Bedouin." However, this division into social strata, lineages, and religious and occupational groups in Israel,[5] provided the Israeli state with an instrumental tool in conducting local politics, similar to the colonial tactic of divide and conquer.[6]

THE BEDOUIN AND STATE POWER

Living in ecologically and politically marginal areas, the Bedouin largely avoided direct involvement with the state. They confronted it only when their territories were threatened, and were thus able to maintain a degree of independence. Both the mistrust of any state and the belief in their own persistence and continuity irrespective of political circumstances are deeply embedded in the Bedouin ethos. These sentiments are aptly illustrated by a popular saying: "governments come and go but the Bedouin stay." The statement is usually followed by the enumeration of states—it applied to the Ottoman Empire, to the British Mandate, and so it will to Israel. In the imagery of the Bedouin the state assumes only a temporary dimension and an ephemeral nature.

The consecutive states, however, did yield greater than superficial influence on the Bedouin affairs. For example, the Ottoman Land Code of 1858, which met with little compliance at the time, is at present severely affecting the land rights of the Bedouin. The tacit resistance it encountered illustrates well the Bedouin attitude toward state policies.

The law required land registration. Its purpose was to fix rights to landownership through obligatory title deeds. Fearing taxation or potential conscription, the Negev Bedouin avoided inscribing their property in the Land Register.[7] The subsequent British Mandate ordinance of 1921 forbade unauthorized land use and squatting. Although the Negev was de facto occupied by the Bedouin, from the point of view of the state they held the territory illegitimately. Granot (1952:106), a historian, notes: "since very little of the land in this sub-district [Beer Sheva] is inscribed in the Land Registers of the Government, a landowner here is not a landowner in the full sense, as his right has not been confirmed to him officially."

Laws and ordinances passed by state powers, although significant for the future of the Negev Bedouin, seemed of little relevance to their daily life. Indeed, the Ottoman Turks and the British alike rarely intervened in Bedouin affairs (Marx 1967).

The Bedouin continued their strategy of avoidance and marginalism in their initial relationship with the next state, Israel. The proclamation of the state of Israel in 1948, the consequent protest by the Arab states, and the war that followed, minimally involved the Negev Bedouin. Although technically Palestinians, they were hardly aware of it. The Bedouin did not offer resistance, form military units, or take active part in the fighting. Many fled, while some collaborated with the Israeli forces. Their skills in desert tracking proved very useful in warfare in detecting movements across the largely unguarded southern borders. Hence they were allowed to enlist in the Israeli army desert tracking units. This fact, perceived by the Palestinians as joining the enemy, acquired symbolic significance in Palestinian politics and contributed to the rift that developed between the different sections of the Arab population.

The initial policy of Israel toward the Bedouin was marked by ambivalence. Although the Bedouin did not present a direct threat, as Arabs they were considered a potential security risk. After the 1948 war the Israeli army continued occupation of the Negev. In 1950 a military government was instituted for all Arab-inhabited areas. The Negev was placed under the military administration, which retained its jurisdiction until 1966. The Bedouin who had remained in the Negev were forcibly moved and confined to a restricted zone that constituted approximately 10 percent of the territory previously utilized by them. The area was declared closed, enabling the military governor to impose strict controls on movements across its borders. The Bedouin were allowed to leave the zone only with special permits issued in limited numbers. An indication of the severity of restrictions on Bedouin movements is that until 1957 they could not even travel to Beer Sheva on market day without prior permission by the military authorities. Instability in the area continued as Bedouin were uncertain whether to stay in Israel or leave for the neighboring Arab countries. Some, as late as 1959, were expelled to Jordan and Egypt, an action that was reversed only after the intervention of the United Nations (Jiryis 1976). By 1960, the number of Bedouin in the Negev had dwindled to 16,000 (Marx 1967).

The most damaging development to pastoral nomadism was the confiscation of land. This the state accomplished through "a doctrine of expulsion at first, which later turned into a doctrine of land expropriation, using legal means (Marx and Sela' n.d.:4).[8] The state expropriated 93 percent of the Negev under the Land Acquisition Law, which, following the Ottoman Land Code of 1858, did not recognize Bedouin landholding rights. Consequently, the Israeli state did not provide for any form of compensation for the confiscated lands. The Bedouin were barred from returning to and using the territories previously occupied by them. Individuals could be granted annually renewable leases on small parcels of land if the land was not utilized by the Jewish agricultural cooperatives (*moshavim* or *kibbutzim*) that sprouted in the Negev. The severely diminished area available to the Bedouin for pasture and farming led to elimination of pastoral nomadism as a primary source of livelihood. The Bedouin were prompted to enter the unskilled labor force servicing Jewish towns and settlements.

The policies of Israel were directed at eradicating the Bedouin as a viable political entity and nullifying them as a potential threat to the security of the Jewish state. First, the state restricted Bedouin to a reservation. Later the Bedouin economic base was further undermined by the expropriation of land and the people brought under the control of the state. The land-leasing system created dependence on the administration and struck to the very heart of the Bedouin ethos of autonomy.[9] The repressive measures taken by the state made nomadism as a way of life the symbol of freedom. Its loss became the loss of communal honor and the symbol of domination.

Israel's labor policy toward the Bedouin was exploitative in character. Although citizens since 1952, the Bedouin, and Arabs in general, could find employment only if there was a need for additional labor. This depended on the condition of the state economy and its ability to absorb the surge of Jewish immigration, which was given priority on the labor market as well as in other services extended by the state. The Bedouin were able to obtain labor permits and jobs only erratically, and those were not sufficient to provide a stable income.

The military administration and the subsequent authorities continued the strategies of indirect governance instituted by their colonial predecessors, the foremost of which was control through exploiting the divisive elements of the local structures. The 1948 war and its aftermath scattered the Bedouin and disrupted their organizational framework. Sections and even individual members of particular tribes emigrated in uneven numbers. This changed the established balance of power among the Bedouin groups, which consequently needed to be created anew. Israeli authorities took an active part in reassigning tribal membership and affiliations, monitoring them through the issuing of obligatory identity cards. The absence of many former leaders facilitated the appointment of new sheikhs, who, although not holding legitimate authority in the eyes of the Bedouin, became instruments of state control through their position as intermediaries between the government and the people.[10] Occasional relocation of groups in the Negev in the period following the military administration was intended to break the Bedouin attachment to the land. The same was true of the system of individual land leases prohibiting renewal of the same parcel for more than two consecutive years. The sporadic relocation of Bedouin groups further destabilized the society. It also prevented the formation of unified opposition. Inhabitants of one particular settlement were resettled at least three times despite being assured each time that their relocation was permanent.

Treated as passive political objects, Bedouin in some instances tried to influence their fate by coopting the ideology of the rulers. In order to obtain a position equitable to Jewish citizens, one tribe claimed to be the descendants of the lost Hebrew tribe.

SETTLEMENT AS POLITICAL AND CULTURAL DOMINATION

With their land claimed by the state, the majority of Bedouin were blocked from pursuing pastoral nomadism. Having few other alternatives, they began to settle on the lands that they considered their own, thus reaffirming their rights to them. No longer pastoral nomads, they entered the unskilled labor force, working for Israeli industries and agriculture in ever-increasing numbers. Once the military administration was abolished in the Negev, small hamlets built of wooden planks and sheets of tin began to appear. These spontaneous settlements, many of which were not larger than a few huts, were declared illegal by the state. But permanent habitation was also discouraged—applications for building permits were rejected, and encampments were sporadically destroyed, their inhabitants harassed. Helicopters flying low and hovering over a complex unavoidably left the hamlets covered with a cloud of sand. None of the encampments were provided with clinics, schools, roads, or piped water. Bedouin who retained their nomadic life-style—a population that was rapidly decreasing—were periodically raided by the officers of the Land Administration, an agency of the government that was responsible for the enforcement of land utilization laws. The Land Administration justified its actions by the violation of the prohibition against using land without the permission of the state, but in essence they were directed against the continuation of nomadism. The Ministry of Agriculture, claiming that the black goats commonly kept by the nomads eroded the desert environment, employed its paramilitary unit, the "Green Patrol," to confiscate them and to punish the Bedouin for grazing. Although this assertion of environmental damage was invalidated by Israeli conservationists, it did not stop the overzealous actions of the "Green Patrol."[11] Tents were pulled down, herds were confiscated, and people moved to another area. Stories of occasional violence, of infants dying from exposure to cold, and of women shot after inadvertently wandering into a military zone where maneuvers were held echoed through the desert. Bedouin protests in Israeli legal courts against the seizure of herds proved expensive and ineffectual. Even when the case was won, many animals died while they were held under quarantine in livestock detention centers.

The steps taken by the state led toward the total sedentarization of Bedouin in a manner consistent with the political and economic needs of the country. The population of Israel steadily grew; there was an increased demand to accommodate Jewish towns and settlements and a rising need for natural resources. Furthermore, Israeli evacuation from the Sinai under the Camp David Accords (1976) necessitated moving military bases to the Negev. This implied removal of the Bedouin from the area designated for the military to large, densely populated urban settlements. The plan assured minimal use of land resources and maximal dependence of the Bedouin on the Israeli market economy.

Sedentarization of the Bedouin was publicly presented as modernization and expressed in the language of paternalism. My interviews with government officials who were carrying out the settlement project yielded contemptuous phrases: "the Bedouin have progressed 1,000 years during the 35 years of the Israeli rule," "they are not capable of organizing themselves, they constantly fight with each other [various Bedouin groups] so the Jews must head the local council," statements reminiscent of the "white man's burden." Although considered "experts on Bedouin," these officials often were ignorant of consequences of their own policies. The first settlement established for the Bedouin was standing nearly empty for a number of years. The design copied from Arab villages in northern Israel did not take into account the unique aspects of the Bedouin social structure.[12]

In the late 1980s about 90 percent of the Negev Bedouin (of a total population of 60,000, according to the 1982 census) live in one of five urban settlements, the largest of which exceeds 20,000. The first was built in 1968, the last is still under construction. In the vast emptiness of the desert one can distinguish from miles away the numerous gray cement houses that make up the Bedouin settlements.

The Bedouin do not really "live" in those houses. Most activities of the daily life and all the ritual celebrations are conducted outdoors, in the open spaces between the buildings. Most households have outdoor kitchens where one cooks on the open fire, where people gather to eat and to talk, retiring only for the night to the unfurnished abode. Visitors are entertained on a veranda sheltered from the street by vines or rugs, or in a tent, which many people still maintain, although in a minuscule version of the traditional one. Only non-Bedouin strangers are received inside the house.

Ironically, the Bedouin have to buy the allotted one-*dunam*[13] plot on which to build a house. Although the government made an exception to the rule that land cannot be owned but only leased, the Bedouin as yet have not received land deeds. Furthermore, only those Bedouin who vacated the area needed for the construction of the military airport, a consequence of the removal of Israeli bases from the Sinai, received compensation for the land lost. In spite of its policy of denying the Bedouin rights to landownership, the government entered negotiations with them for the sake of expediency in the light of the gravity of providing for the security of Israel's border with Egypt. The talks were angrily stopped for a while when the Bedouin realized the disadvantageous disparity between the compensation offered to them and the Jewish evacuees from the Sinai.

Only a small fraction of the Bedouin have ever received compensation. Some refused to accept a monetary award, or move to settlements designed for them, in the belief that doing so would mean forfeiting their lands forever. Of those who did settle in the government-sponsored urban complexes most were from the lower strata of the Bedouin society, the aforementioned *fellahin* (peasants) and *'abid* (descendants of slaves). For these strata, who already depended on wage labor, settlement offered the opportunity for political emancipation from dominant Bedouin lineages as well as the promise of access to health clinics, schools, electricity, and water, which were withheld from the unauthorized hamlets. Yet, living in urban complexes did not diminish the Bedouin's sentimental attachment to the land they once occupied. On many occasions I was led on a special trip by a Bedouin who would bring his children along to show the piece of land that his family once tilled and grazed its herds on and which he still considers rightfully his. Children memorize the names of the valleys and *wadis* bordering their family land, names that then acquired a different meaning as they became symbols of the Bedouin noble past.

In 1981, at the beginning of my fieldwork, when I was seeking contacts and a family to take me in, I sensed an ambivalence among the urban Bedouin about whether the name *Bedouin* applied to them. If I came to study the Bedouin, I should go further south, to the Sinai, where the real Bedouin still live, I was told. At first I believed that the Bedouin were experiencing an identity crisis or identity vacuum, but the question of the Bedouin identity was more complicated.

The Bedouin are certainly no longer pastoral nomads. The minuscule herds of five or so goats that they keep, the few olive trees and tomato and pepper plants that grow in the kitchen garden contribute little to the family's income. The settlements have a severely limited infrastructure beyond that of road network, electricity, and water access. There is no industry and no business larger than small shops. Most needs, including employment, must be met outside the settlement. Men are employed in construction, trucking, or various other jobs for daily wages[14] for Jewish businesses in neighboring towns. At the time of my research some families took advantage of the booming construction industry by forming small family-owned businesses that contract their services to large Israeli companies. Although most Bedouin are unwilling to be employed directly by the state, they are linked to and dependent on the Israeli economy through the processes of production and consumption.

Invariably the skills necessary for survival in an urban environment are different from those required in the desert. Literacy in Hebrew and knowledge of the workings of the Israeli bureaucracy become indispensable. Because only the younger people are privy to obtaining at least a basic education, generational authority relations have been affected by the need for different types of knowledge. The younger generation is more comfortable, entrepreneurial, and successful in managing the intricacies of the state and local administration in pursuit of building and business permits, identity cards, health insurance, and the numerous other papers created by the bureaucratic apparatus. The sight of a teenage boy leading his father through the corridors of various administrative offices in Beer Sheva and translating for him is not uncommon.

There is a noticeable generational difference with regard to the meaning and the manner of expressing "Bedouinness." I was visiting a sick acquaintance of mine in the Beer Sheva hospital, and an elderly man decided to accompany me. To my surprise, my companion was dressed in the full traditional Bedouin garment, including a short knife tucked behind his belt that had to be surrendered at the hospital entrance. Such clothing is rarely worn nowadays, except on important ceremonial occasions, which a hospital visit was not, but as he explained, he wore it so "they [the Jews] know who I am." His statement expressed pride and

defiance toward the Jewish hospital staff, known for their offhanded
and condescending treatment of the Bedouin. In contrast, young men
who worked in the city were careful about hiding their Bedouin origins.
They usually kept two sets of clothing, one worn in the settlement and
the other wherever they expected to come in contact with the Jews. The
"Bedouin" clothes, they say, are saturated with smells of smoke from the
open kitchen fires and are not neat enough for dealing with Jews. Being
a Bedouin, and appearing as one, carried a stigma of primitivism among
the Israelis with whom they needed to interact. If one is a Bedouin it is
better to look like a "civilized" one, the young men remark. The fact
that some pride themselves on being able to pass for Jews of Oriental
descent reflects the extent to which Bedouin have internalized their assigned lower social status.

Physically the Bedouin settlements are no more isolated than Jewish
towns are from one another. Located twenty to forty kilometers from
Beer Sheva, they are connected through the bus network to other towns.
In social terms, these settlements belong to another sphere. Bedouin settlements are designated for the Bedouin; nobody else is allowed to live
there. Only those who have business there go there. In order to get to
a Bedouin town one must board the Israeli bus which stops at the edge
of the settlement, where the visitor must descend and change to a Bed-
ouin-operated, or "Bedouin," bus. This bus runs a circular route within
the town at unspecified times and stops wherever passengers need to get
off. Women sit in the front, men in the back; people greet each other
and the driver, request that he change the radio station to their liking;
children take rides for one stop without pay, and some get lost and need
to be taken home. The ease with which the passengers behave stands in
stark contrast to their discomfort on "Jewish" buses. It exemplifies a classification the Bedouin employ in their everyday life. This consists of the
juxtaposition of diametrically opposing concepts: objects and behaviors
are polarized into "Bedouin" and "Jewish." "Bedouin" stands for warm,
familiar, and inherently good. "Jewish" means formal, cold, standoffish,
sometimes deceitful, and inevitably worse in quality. "Bedouin" meat,
eggs, and coffee taste better, are sought after and hence generate higher
prices at the market than do their "Jewish" counterparts. Ignorant, offensive, or out-of-bounds behavior is by the same logic labeled "Jewish."

When the Bedouin look at the political hierarchy they cannot help
but notice that everyone in a position of authority above the level of
neighborhood is Jewish. Bedouin settlements are not self-governed.
Local councils are represented by Jewish officials of those government
ministries that by the nature of their task must deal with the Bedouin

(such as the respective ministries of Interior, Construction and Housing, Health, and Education), and Bedouin representatives of major patronymic groups who are appointed by the state. The fact that the same Israeli officials—who in the previous decade actively participated in the sometimes violent resettlement actions—were put in charge of the Bedouin towns as "experts on Bedouin affairs," created resentment and dissipated the possibility of trust and cooperation. The Bedouin representatives to the councils who find that they are frequently compromised and given little credence, are viewed by their constituencies as coopted by the state.[15] The police, the administrative staff, and even the employees of health clinics are predominantly Jewish. This reinforces the notion of domination. The licensing of the few businesses existing in the settlement (grocery stores and a gas station) is controlled by the administration. The Bedouin perceive an implicit threat of the loss of permits and government controlled resources should the community or individuals act in a fashion that the administration considers disloyal to the state. As a matter of fact, the administration knows that some of these small shops operate without a license. The randomness with which the state agencies act, just as in the case of the destruction of squatter hamlets, increases Bedouin insecurity. For example, before a demonstration against the expropriation of Arab lands, for which the organizers obtained permission, the owner of a grocery store warned his children not to participate because he did not have a license to run his store. Against the better judgment of his family, one of his sons attended the demonstration, was arrested, and released a few days later. After his arrest the young man did not even try to pursue the university application.

The Bedouin doubted that a full self-rule would ever be given to them. In 1987, using the statute that guarantees the right to an elected council to every town over 15,000 inhabitants, the local members of the New Communist Party (Rakah) supported by the national chapter brought a successful case before the Israeli Supreme Court. Rakah has very little following among the Bedouin but is politically active on their behalf. The court's order was delayed. The regional Negev council, using its prerogative of making judgment on the basis of the local situation, declared the area "unstable." At this time a dispute between two Bedouin *hamayel* (sing. *hamula,* a patronymic group) erupted and was followed by a violent confrontation that resulted in one death. The potential for such conflicts in Bedouin settlements is relatively high. Urban environment brought into close physical proximity groups of various social strata and origins that compete over the limited resources the settlement provides. Furthermore, the formerly dominant lineages do not want to relinquish control over their clients although the economic and political grounds allowing for such a relationship ceased to exist. All Bedouin, regardless of their previous status, had to obtain permission to use land from the government. Given these circumstances, the significance of the tribal structure became less relevant to the daily life of people in the settlement. The formerly dependent *hamayel* became sedentary and entered into the labor market earlier than did most Bedouin and in many instances were thus able to accumulate greater material wealth. They could afford to refuse client status, and thereby become an obstacle to the maintenance of the former power relations among Bedouin groups. A new source of conflict alliances based on social strata emerged in the settlement, along that of "bloodlines." This particular dispute occurred between one of the dominant lineages and the *'abid* (black descendants of slaves). The conflict was exploited by the regional administration and used as the argument for not holding election to the local council.[16]

Through political and economic submission the state created dependence, rather than integration, of the Bedouin with the Israeli society. The land policy and the resulting sedentarization constituted the basis for the transformation of the Bedouin economic and social foundations. This had a pronounced effect on their identity formulations. The policies and the manner of their enforcement diluted the potential for forming opposition against the state, thus eliminating the Bedouin as a political threat and preventing crystallization of a common Arab front.

THE POLITICS OF SEPARATION

The repressive measures taken by the Israeli state alienated the Bedouin. At the same time, by applying its persistent politics of separation in dealing with the Israeli Arabs, the Israeli state was able to prevent the Bedouin from joining the opposition.

The major wedge inserted by the state among the various Arab groups in Israel concerned military service. Although members of all these groups are Israeli citizens their relation to the Israeli Defence Forces (IDF) differs. The Druze are by law drafted into the IDF, the Bedouin can serve on a voluntary basis, and the rest of the Arab population is exempted from it. This effectively muddled the issue of loyalty and pitched the three groups against one another. Serving in the IDF carries practical benefits. For example, in recognition of their service the Druze were exempted from having to obtain travel permits at the time of military administration and during curfews (Jiryis 1976). People who serve in the IDF are granted university tuition waivers and educational loans. However, the problem of who is and who is not allowed to serve in the Israeli forces is of greater ideological and symbolic significance than pragmatic. There are very few Bedouin who do serve in the military forces, and their willingness to do so is hardly representative of the Bedouin population at large. The Arab political activists, however, never fail to point this out, creating a situation in which Bedouin are marginalized by other Arabs as well as the Israeli government.

The most acute problem for the Bedouin vis-à-vis the state was an equitable land settlement. In the hope of reaching agreement with the state with regard to the land issue, the Bedouin participated to a degree in the Israeli electoral political system. As one informant observed, however, the purpose of this limited participation was merely a strategy to convince the government of their "loyalty." The Israeli political parties, mostly Labor and Likud, lobbied the Bedouin intensely before every election but never kept their promises, and consequently drew little support. Although the parties campaigning in the Negev overtly tried to persuade the Bedouin to participate in the democratic process, their approach was aptly expressed through the argument that "the Bedouin should go where they are sent and not where they want to go" (Eloul 1985:3).

Those Bedouin who put their trust in the Israeli political process became greatly disillusioned with its effectiveness. In 1973 the Bedouin List (party) was established and succeeded in gaining one Knesset (Parliament) seat. Before the 1977 elections the List was merged with an Arab List and suffered from internal division among its constituent Arab groups. Following the 1979 assassination of its leader by the Druze opposition the list collapsed and was never revived (Eloul 1985:3). The failure to exert influence on issues that concerned them directly, particularly regarding land settlement, increased Bedouin alienation and disenfranchisement. They remained powerless to affect state policies, and ultimately their lives, in any significant way.

The Bedouin List was one among several steps taken by the state to institutionalize the Bedouin as a distinct group. Government ministries have either branches for Bedouin affairs or special liaison officers with the Bedouin. Recently a new position was opened for the Advisor to the Prime Minister on Bedouin Affairs (a parallel office exists for Arab Affairs). Despite the increasing similarity in life-style to the rest of the Israeli Arabs, the Bedouin appear in all statistics as a separate group.

Although the state failed to convince the Bedouin to be its ally, it effectively enlarged the gulf between them and other Arabs. The emphasis on differences between the Jews and the Arabs and within the Arab population is an essential component of state control (Lustick 1980).

The threefold division employed in the analysis of group relations in the Middle East, the so-called Middle Eastern trilogy, consists of pastoral nomads (Bedouin), peasants (*fellahin*), and urban-dwellers. It corresponded to ecological niches and reflected the occupational and social structure of the Middle Eastern society. Although these three categories were never rigid, generally their populations remained stable over time (Barth 1969). Economically interdependent, each of these groups derived its own identity from the distinct practices of everyday life, a loyalty to traditions, and ultimately from social class (De Vos and Romanucci-Ross 1975). Both the *fellahin* and the urbanites consider the Bedouin to be of a lower stratum in the Arab society, although this does not correspond to the image the Bedouin hold of themselves. The upper strata of the Arab society believe the Bedouin to be illiterate, nominal Muslims with a questionable piety; simple, but brave and respectable, although dangerous in their devotion to honor. Their view represents a nostalgic longing for the simplicity and purity in life. The Bedouin dialect is widely believed to be the purest form of the language the Prophet Muhammad spoke. Still, the plethora of jokes about the Bedouin points to their incompatibility with progress and pictures "people whom time have left behind."

Fredrik Barth's (1969:10) work on "the social organization of cultural difference" emphasized the importance of boundary definition in the maintenance of identities. "Entailed in boundary maintenance are also situations of social contact between persons of different cultures." A closer interpersonal contact on a regular basis between the Bedouin and other Arabs served to reinforce the perception of difference. Owing to the acute shortage of Bedouin teachers, the schools are staffed by northern Arabs who, after completing the necessary degree, are sent to the Negev by the Ministry of Education on a rotational basis. Removed from their own environment these teachers consider their jobs and the life-style imposed on them a severe hardship. Differences in dialects lead to lack of comprehension while differences in socialization, everyday practices and expectations about schooling lead to occasional conflicts between the teachers and their students and families and, by extension, the community. Because of the teachers' youth and lack of experience, the Bedouin are reluctant to award the recognition usually granted to this highly esteemed profession. Consequently, the Arab teachers remain isolated, choose to live in Beer Sheva, and rarely socialize with the Bedouin.

The sources of apprehension that exist between Israeli Arabs and the Bedouin lay mainly in the political sphere. The Bedouin did not embrace Palestinian nationalism and remained uncommitted politically, rarely expressing sentiments toward any political entity. Because Bedouin serve in the Israeli military forces, they are perceived as sometimes collaborating with Israeli politicians,[17] and of lacking interest and support in organizing demonstrations promoting Arab causes. Arabs often mistrust their motives, effectively enlarging the gulf between the groups, all to the advantage of the state.

For example, the Land Day (Youm al-'ard) initiated by Israeli Arabs in 1975 to protest land expropriations and express Arab unity drew very little participation from the Bedouin. The National Committee for the Defence of Arab Lands, formed by Rakah, declared March 30th of each year a day of general strike and called on all Israeli Arabs to take part in demonstrations. This initiative was generally successful in all Arab-inhabited areas, with the exception of the Negev. The first such demonstration in the Negev was organized by political activists from northern Israel in 1982. It was attended in small numbers, mostly by the youth, and was followed by a police action, detention of suspected leaders, house searches, and random arrests of participants. The show of police force intimidated the Bedouin and even smaller numbers participated in the demonstration the following year. The call for a general strike was ignored. The Bedouin reacted in the same way to the call for protest actions on the "Day of Equality" instituted on June 24, 1987 by the countrywide Committee of Heads of Arab Local Councils in Israel, which demanded parity in municipal budget with Jewish towns.

None of this means that Bedouin are not sympathetic to the plight of other Palestinians. The 1982 invasion of Lebanon by the Israeli forces and the consequent massacres of Palestinian camps caused grief and brought a sense of common cause. Children born that year were given names with nationalist meaning—Sabra, Shatilla (names of the massacred Palestinian camps), Fadi (from *fedayeen*, freedom fighter)—and some openly wore T-shirts with Palestinian symbols. A PLO (Palestine Liberation Organization) cell uncovered by the Israeli security in the summer of 1986 indicated a significant departure from the Bedouin role of passive sympathizer. It was the first such cell discovered among the Bedouin. It caused a great deal of concern among the Israelis and received wide media coverage. Its members were relatively young—an indication of the general discontent felt by the generation of the Bedouin born and raised in the state of Israel.

The majority of young people have for practical purposes forgone hopes for the return of their land. The urban communities have experienced a demographic explosion—over 75 percent of inhabitants are below fifteen years of age. Restrictions on new construction in the settlements, the increasing price of building plots, and the severely limited job opportunities beyond that of wage labor provide little prospect for the future. The arrested have not, however, become cultural heroes. In spite of political radicalization of a fraction of Bedouin youth drawn into the mainstream Arab and Palestinian politics, the Bedouin remained uncommitted and inactive.

MARGINALITY AS RESISTANCE

For the reasons elaborated above the Bedouin became alienated from the Israeli state and disillusioned by its political process. At the same time they only tangentially participated in the Palestinian nationalist movement. The settled Bedouin withdrew from the direct political contest between the Israeli and the Palestinian nationalisms. In resisting identity forged and imposed on them by outside forces the Bedouin took an active part in reclaiming their culture. Although the roots of resistance are grounded in the socioeconomic sphere, in counteracting an identity constructed from outside Bedouin draw on their own cultural traditions. This can be detected in their strive for economic independence through self-employment, reliance on customary law and institutions rather than the state judicial system for conflict resolution, and civic community activism with the *hamula* as its core element. The Bedouin rejected a proposal advanced by the state administrators to open a tourist industry in the settlement to capitalize on the exotic. Commercialization of Bedouin heritage was perceived by them as an attempt to dispense with it, and consequently the marketing of "Bedouinness" failed.

Ironically, religion became a prominent means of reclaiming cultural identity, despite the fact that in the Islamic world the Bedouin were known for their questionable religious observance. Religious practices received little attention during the early stages of Bedouin settlement. There was only one small mosque in a town of 15,000. It did not attract many faithful, even for the Friday prayers. Ramadan, the month of fasting, was observed by few, few practiced daily prayers, and even fewer made the pilgrimage to Mecca, although opportunities for doing so already existed. Within the last six years, however, a tremendous change has occurred in the realm of religious practice and meaning. In 1987 there were seven mosques and more were planned for. Nonobservance of Ramadan has become a deviant behavior; children were fasting and women were receiving instruction in prayers. Most elderly men and women have made the pilgrimage to Mecca despite the high cost.

Most importantly, religion has acquired a different social significance. Struggling with the question of identity—Bedouin, Arab, Palestinian— Bedouin give preference to the Muslim framework of self-expression and reference. The new leaders in the settlement present themselves as pious Muslims. They encourage community sponsored and financed projects, such as a neighborhood child care center and a youth club, through which they hope to minimize dependence on the resources provided by the state. These acts constitute incremental steps on the path to self-rule on the local level. Religion serves to disguise social action that might be perceived as hostile to the Israeli state and induces greater self-reliance by creating an alternative structure to the one promoted by the state. Nonetheless the Bedouin retain their apolitical stance with regard to the Israeli-Palestinian conflict. For example, a preacher brought from Gaza was quickly dismissed for the overly explicit political tone of his sermons. The revival of Islam is, of course, not confined to the Bedouin. However, for them the religious Muslim construction overarches the present political alignments. Islam came to serve as the base cultural identity marker. In a context in which competing factions sought to impose an identity on the Bedouin—one consistent with the discourse of the Israeli-Palestinian discourse—the Bedouin resolved to become "good Muslims," thus rejecting the outwardly imposed identity.

The politics of the Israeli state perpetuates ethnic divisions of pre-1948 Palestine through juxtaposing the Jewish and the Palestinian interests. The process of consolidation of their respective national identities resulted in marginalization of the Bedouin. In the battle over economic and political domination the state enforced a systematic and relentless policy of settlement that neutralized the Bedouin as a potential enemy.

Conflict elucidates cultural differences and creates space for their management, and ethnicity, being an elusive concept, renders itself to manipulation by political actors. Group identities bend and shape themselves under the pressure of political change (Isaacs 1989). Processes of ethnicity are linked to, and expressive of, the state as hegemonic power. They do not necessarily, however, correspond to identity formulation. As I have argued, for the Bedouin of Israel ethnicity and identity are cognitively distinct, one representing political domination; the other, cultural self-representation. In fighting the ethnic construction imposed on them, the Bedouin explore and employ mechanisms derived from their own cultural traditions.

ACKNOWLEDGMENTS

Materials for this chapter were gathered during fieldwork carried out from October 1981 through June 1983. My research in the spring of 1986 was sponsored by the Sapir Foundation for Social Research of Tel Aviv University, while the fellowship from the American School of Oriental Research supported my research in the summer of 1987. I am grateful to both institutions.

NOTES

1. Throughout the text I use the collective term *Bedouin* to refer to all former nomadic pastoralists, now mostly sedentarized, in the Negev Desert. Although culturally homogeneous to a remarkable extent, the Bedouin do not constitute a corporate political entity.

2. J. B. Barron, *Palestine; Report and General Abstracts of the Census of 1922* (Jerusalem, 1923).

3. Beer Sheva is at present the capital of the Negev, its main administrative and industrial center.

4. This classification corresponds roughly to the Cyrenaica Bedouins' division into aristocratic landowning Bedouin and clients with no right to land and water who can use these resources only with the permission of their owners. The clients, like the *fellahin* in the Negev, were not admitted into the agnatic political groups of the aristocratic Bedouin. They were, however, in distinction to the Negev *fellahin,* allowed to intermarry with the Bedouin. Such affinal ties did not entitle them to membership in the corporate organization that held the right to the territory (Peters 1968).

5. I refer to the Druze, Christians, and Muslims as religious groups; and the Bedouin, *fellahin,* and urbanites as occupational groups.

6. Anthropological literature is replete with examples illustrating the manipulation of segmentary lineage structure by the colonial administration (Fernea 1970; Levy 1989; etc.).

7. According to the oral history recounted by a Bedouin informant, "when the government [Turkish government officials] came and asked our grandfathers to pay taxes they said they would, but the smart ones left the next day and the government could never catch up with them."

8. The charter of the World Zionist Organization requires that the Israeli government transfer land to the Jewish National Fund. In this way land becomes the inalienable property of the Jewish people and cannot revert to non-Jewish

ownership. Although it is not technically correct, I will use "state" instead of "Jewish National Fund" with regard to the question of land ownership.

9. Abu Lughod (1986) regards autonomy as the defining feature of Bedouin identity. The Bedouin of Western Desert in Egypt adapted to the changed economic conditions without adverse affect on their identity formulations. Their adaptation, including partial settlement, was conducted on a *voluntary* basis.

10. Lancaster (1981) and Levy (1989) address the issue of pastoral nomads, distinguishing between two types of power—the state and the tribal government—and therefore having two types of sheikhs with different degrees of legitimacy.

11. The actions of the "Green Patrol" continued into the 1980s.

12. The first settlement for the Bedouin in the Negev was constructed in 1968. It was designed for 1,200 families, of which only 25 settled there by 1974 (Lewando-Hundt 1979). Among the various explanations for its failure was the erroneous architectural design (small, preconstructed houses), the continuing dispute over landownership, and the lack of recognition for the cultural preference of the Bedouin, which at the time called for retaining physical distance between the various social groups.

13. One *dunam* equals one-fourth acre.

14. The survey I conducted in one settlement as to the distribution of sources of income shows the following employment: construction 30 percent, trucking 18 percent, other wage labor 25 percent, store owners 15 percent, teachers 15 percent, unemployed 12 percent.

15. The person who fired shots at the demonstration in a Bedouin settlement, which is discussed later in the text, was a Bedouin sheikh appointed by the Israeli administration. All Arab leaders appointed by the government have the right to carry weapons. This right is denied to other Arab inhabitants in Israel, although granted to the Jewish citizens.

16. The elections were held in the spring of 1989. One may speculate that the uprising in the occupied territories of the West Bank and the Gaza Strip added the incentive for allowing a form of self-rule on the local level and curbed the potential for the opposition in the Negev. Indeed, the Bedouin did not participate in staging the support strikes. Also, none of the large lineages supported by the government won significant positions in the town council. This points to the failure of the state to manipulate the Bedouin lineage structure in the changing political arena in the settlement.

17. This refers to an incident in which Bedouin sheikhs ceremonially received Ariel Sharon, then the Minister of Agriculture and later Minister of Defence, which met with a wide disapproval among Israeli Arabs.

REFERENCES

Abu Lughod, Lila
    1986   *Veiled Sentiments. Honor and Poetry in a Bedouin Society.* Berkeley, Los Angeles, London: University of California Press.

Barron, J. B.
 1923   *Palestine; Report and General Abstracts of the Census of 1922.* Jerusalem.
Barth, Fredrik
 1961   *Nomads of South Persia.* New York: Humanities Press.
 1969   Ed. *Ethnic Groups and Boundaries.* Boston: Little, Brown and Company.
De Vos, George, and Lola Romanucci-Ross, eds.
 1975   *Ethnic Identity. Cultural Continuities and Change.* Palo Alto: Mayfield Publishing Co.
Eloul, Rohn
 1985   "The Rise and Fall of the Bedouin List: A Study of Jewish Politics in the Arab Sector." Paper delivered at the American Anthropological Association, Washington, D.C.
Fernea, Robert
 1970   *Shaykh and Effendi: Changing Patterns of Authority among the El-Shabana of Southern Iraq.* Cambridge: Harvard University Press.
Granot, A.
 1952   *The Land System in Palestine: History and Structure.* London: Eyre and Spottiswoode.
Issacs, Harold
 1989   *Idols of the Tribe. Group Identity and Political Change.* Cambridge: Harvard University Press.
Jakubowska, Longina
 1985   "Urban Bedouin: Social Change in a Settled Environment." Ph.D. dissertation, State University of New York at Stony Brook.
Jiryis, Sabri
 1976   *The Arabs in Israel.* New York: Monthly Review Press.
Lancaster, William
 1981   *The Rwala Bedouin Today.* Cambridge: Cambridge University Press.
Levy, Smadar
 1989   "When Leadership Becomes Allegory: Mzeina Sheikhs and the Experience of Military Occupation." *Cultural Anthropology* 4(2):99–136.
Lewando-Hundt, Gillian
 1979   "Tel Sheva—A Planned Bedouin Village." In *The Lands of the Negev*, A. Shmueli and Y. Gradus, eds. Tel Aviv: Ministry of Defence Publishing House.
Lustick, Ian
 1980   *Arabs in the Jewish State. Israel's Control of a National Minority.* Austin: University of Texas Press.
Marx, Emanuel
 1967   *Bedouin of the Negev.* New York: Praeger.
Marx, Emanuel, and Moshe Sela'
 N.d.   "Matzavam Shel Bedouy haNegev" (in Hebrew). Mimeographed.
Peters, Emrys
 1968   "The Tied and the Free: An Account of Patron-Client Relationships

among the Bedouin of Cyrenaica." In *Contributions to Mediterranean Sociology*, J. G. Peristiany, ed. The Hague: Mouton.

Rosen, Steven
  N.d.   *Notes on the Origin of Pastoral Nomadism: A Case Study from the Negev Desert and Sinai.* Unpublished manuscript.

Salzman, Philip
  1980   *When Nomads Settle. Processes of Sedentarization as Adaptation and Response.* New York: Frederick A. Praeger.

SIX

Hyenas on the Border

Edgar Winans

Wild beast of the forest.
Stands on the far hill.
Forest, boma, sorghum field,
Sees all, devours all,
From the place of the mounds of skulls,
To the herds of fat cattle in the West.
(Praise poem to Mkwawa, king of Uhehe)

THE POWER OF BEASTS AND KINGS

The power of the beasts of the forest is a familiar motif in the thought of the Hehe people. The praise poem that forms an epigraph for this essay is one of many likening Hehe kings and princes to wild beasts. A common praise name for the warrior-king Mkwawa of the late nineteenth century was *likoko*: wild beast. Kings create order through their violence when it is controlled and directed on behalf of their people, but by the same logic, they themselves are not ruled by this order. It is their power to create order, and thus also, chaos.

The identification of the powers of rulers and their families with the beasts of the forest is a familiar aspect of the iconography of kingship in Africa. Many authors have discussed the titles associated with offices and the animals these invoke, descriptions of rituals of enthronement, renewal, and death, and examples of praise songs and poems that utilize metaphors of wild and powerful beasts to represent the power of princes. However, it is important to recognize that the ritual practices that so many authors discuss are viewed by the people not only as metaphors but also as real transformations. For instance, in Ankole the Queen Mother becomes a leopard after her death, and dead kings become lions.

Transformations of humans into wild creatures is often an element of the conceptualization of the vitality of the whole kingdom as it is in the Ankole cosmology, but it is also often associated with closely related concepts of power, danger, and death as well. Thus, it is not princes alone who may be wild beasts. Others, too, may take on animal form, control animals through supernatural powers, or behave like animals even when maintaining the appearance of humans. In all these various conceptions, the individuals involved are transformed. The changes are often temporary, and the individuals may transmogrify frequently, and at will. Such transformations are neither easy, nor without hazard. Usually, there is a great cost involved, the details of which are as varied as are the other details of the cosmology in question, but the power is as great as are the costs.

In the "Author's Note" of his recent book, Michael Taussig attempts to indicate to the reader some fundamental aspects of his thinking about power, "That is why my subject is not the truth of being but the social being of truth, not whether facts are real but what the politics of their interpretation and representation are." He goes on to say that, "With Walter Benjamin my aim is to release what he noted as the enormous energy of history. . . . I choose to work with a different conflation of modernism and the primitivism it conjures into life—namely the carrying over into history of the principle of montage, as I learned that principle not only from terror, but from Putumayo shaminism" (1987:10). The power of a Hehe praise poem lies in the montage of images of man-made history and forces of nature that it evokes in the listener. In just this fashion, the Ankole express the terrible powers of the king and their connections with the procreative powers of his mother. The powers of kings unite man and nature in these images.

In a classic monograph on the Ankole kingdom John Roscoe (1923) conveys very clearly the symbolism of power and status accorded the Mugabe (king) and members of his family. In a chapter dealing with the mother and sister of the Mugabe, he explains inter alia, "When the Mugabe's mother fell ill . . . the Mugabe was sent for . . . should he consider the illness serious, he communicated with the medicine-man, who mixed the royal poison and gave it to him. He handed it to his mother, who drank it and died at once." After suitable preparation, fluid from her stomach was mixed with milk and kept in a pot until it became full of grubs, "when one of them was taken into the forest and was said to become a leopard" (1923:60–61). He goes on to describe how the sister of the king is transformed into a python after death, and the king himself becomes a lion.

Scattered, although numerous, descriptions of such phenomena have entered the literature in the detailed reports of rituals on enthronement and mourning for rulers and their families as well as under the rubric of a belief in "leopard-men." There are related bodies of literature dealing with "man-eating lions," "cults" of cannibals, and terrorist movements, right up to the present. Perhaps the best-known examples of this genre are such popular books of the early twentieth century as *The Man-Eaters of Tsavo* (Paterson: 1912), and *Le Juge et le sorcier* (Jadot and De Lannoy 1934).

There is a strong continuity of thought between these images of princely power and the depredations of "hyenas" in the midtwentieth century. Yet it is no small step from the kings and chiefs with their wars of conquest and plunder, their contending clans, powerful oracles and sorcerers consulted by king and commoner alike, to colonial overrule, police, courts, markets, money, and finally, the approach of independence for the contemporary nations of Africa.

Our concern in the analysis that follows is a series of violent killings of cattle that I witnessed during 1960/61 in Iringa District of Tanzania (then Tanganyika). The killings were attributed to hyenas, but the people made it clear to me that the hyenas were not ordinary animals. They were witches, people in the shape of hyenas who killed cattle, but did not eat them. They were said to kill people whom they ripped apart, but did not eat. Indeed, people said the hyenas had killed one man recently, but I was never able to confirm that assertion. The killings caused widespread fear and entreaties for action by the government, but it was the eve of independence and the authorities seemed unable to act.

Nor was it clear what the authorities should do. No accusations were made against any specific individuals. In fact, people were careful not to accuse anyone by name. By the same token, the steps they took to protect their cattle and themselves appeared to me so limited as to be ineffectual. They set traps around their cattle kraals but undertook no hunts for the hyenas who could be heard every night in the bush surrounding the houses, fields, and kraals. They didn't even set any night watches, which I knew they did when Baraguyu raiders were in the area. It was as though they were powerless to control the threat of the hyenas in their midst.

In a study of the distribution of beliefs in leopard-men, Birger Lindskog found an imagery of rulers, their families, and other people of power from many parts of Africa that parallels what Roscoe describes for the Ankole (1954:144–178). Lindskog himself links symbolism of dangerous beasts not only to rulers and other powerful people but also to secret societies, cults of leopard-men or lion-men, witches, sorcerers, and brigands who are also sometimes cannibals. The beliefs and images are clearly widespread, old, and often connected to the ideology of power and its forms and uses.

Lindskog draws our attention to issues of change and continuity in the ideology of power and authority and directly challenges the assumption of government officials of the colonial era who saw these as manifestations of what might at best be called criminal opposition. I am concerned not only with the form and content of these images of power but also with their relation to action.

In his analysis of Bashu thought, Randall Packard has made a major contribution to this issue of change in ideology (1980:237–267). Packard here considers the formulation offered by Evans-Pritchard in his justly famous study of Zande thought (1937), and the subsequent efforts of Bohannan (1958) and Ardener (1971) to give it an historical dynamic.

Although Evans-Pritchard's functionalist formulation implied a dynamic for change, there was no processual mechanism. Both Bohannan and Ardener sought to overcome this static conception of ideology, but neither went far enough. Indeed, Bohannan specifically extracted ideology from the workings of history, while Ardener argued from his Bakweri data that ideology is similar to a template which may be reordered over time, but nothing is lost or gained (Ardener 1971:156).

Packard, drawing on Ardener, writes, "such a symbolic transformation . . . is occurring among the Bashu and . . . Ardener's template model needs to be modified to allow for long-term conceptual change which represents something new and not just a rehashing of previous concepts" (1980:241). Packard places the emergence of belief in female witches firmly in the context of changes induced by market penetration. However, the male-female duality contained in the accusations against women is ancient and connected to a bush-homestead or nature-culture contrast in Bashu thought. Furthermore, the exorcism rituals introduced by men to combat female witches have been opposed by the Christian churches and the national government. This has introduced yet further new elements in the ideology of power.

Subsequently, women have successfully utilized the fear of female witches to induce men to share the cash returns from market-oriented activities; precisely one of the points of conflict out of which the male accusations of female witchcraft and the necessity of its control first arose. Packard concludes by observing that the world of the homestead is becoming like the world of the bush in the eyes of Bashu men. These men view women as rejecting the old order of the homestead by becoming witches. Furthermore, some men are now becoming witches, first as assistants to women, and then as full-fledged witches themselves. To Packard this represents a breakup of a basic dichotomy of Bashu thought: men who are conceived as the bearers of culture are acting like creatures of the bush. "We must therefore ask if [the old dual-

ity] . . . must not eventually give way to a new ordering of social experience, an ordering which will take the new values and patterns of
behavior which are causing disruption and transpose them into the
realm of the socially acceptable" (1980:261–262).

Several tools useful for understanding local political action in contemporary Africa emerge from this. A critical dimension of political action
is competition for the vocabulary in which conflicting interests will be
articulated. Hegemonic groups are able to define such a vocabulary, an
ability that enables them to identify opposition and protest as witchcraft,
banditry, and terrorism. In the Bashu case, Packard shows how market
penetration created ecological conditions in which power allocations
were opened to gender competition. Male hegemony was well established and thus sufficiently strong to frame the challenge from women
as witchcraft. To put it another way, men were able to construe opposition as illicit within the context of local political meanings.

The utility of Packard's formulation lies in demonstrating the manner
in which this very labeling of women's protests concedes to them a power
that continued to grow because the conditions of market exchange and
the elaboration of institutions of the state and of the church also continued to grow. This interaction between social organization and ideology is generating a new structure of meanings in which men as well as
women are witches and the identification of men with order and women
with danger and disorder no longer holds.

In a recent paper Simeon Mesaki has argued that accusations of
witchcraft, resort to witch hunters, and the killing of persons suspected
of being witches is widely prevalent in contemporary Tanzania (Mesaki
1988). He links this to current state—society relations, as well as the persistence of older ideology. To understand such linkages, we must
examine events at the local level. The transition from direct colonial administration to an independent successor government entails enormous
continuity, and must often look very familiar to local people grown
accustomed to colonial rule.

WITCH KILLINGS IN THE RUAHA BASIN

I turn now to a consideration of some case data collected nearly thirty
years ago in the Ruaha Basin of what was then the British-administered
Trust Territory of Tanganyika, now the independent nation of Tanzania. The date is important to my understanding, because it was the
eve of independence.

In many ways, daily life appeared undisturbed by the approach of independence, yet there could scarcely have been a person in the whole country who was unaware that independence from British rule was near. There had been intense political activity at the local level in many parts of the country, and a major effort at the national level stemming from the formation of the Tanganyika African National Union (TANU) in July 1954. The people who formed TANU were already involved in an earlier organization—the Tanganyika African Association (TAA). But TAA was weak in several ways. It was largely urban in membership, and its efforts to extend into the countryside had brought it into competition with the numerous tribal unions and with the traditional chiefs who acted as agents of the British Administration under the policy of indirect rule then followed in Britain's African colonies (Bienen 1967:21–25). Its most critical weakness, however, was felt to be a lack of strong communication and coordination between its branches.

By late 1953 the time to seek a more unified effort appeared to be at hand, and TAA was failing in its action. The president of the Meru Citizens Union had traveled to New York to address a sympathetic United Nations on the issue of land alienation in Arusha District in 1952, and, as Cliffe (1964) has shown, there was widespread and bitter opposition to Agricultural Ordinances introduced by the Colonial Administration after the end of World War II. Further, European action aimed at a political union of Tanganyika with Kenya and Uganda had greatly alarmed TAA members. The formation of a more strongly centralized instrument of political action was not easily attained, however. In order to grow, TANU absorbed existing organizations of all sorts: tribal unions, cooperative societies, even football clubs. These disparate entities were all in opposition to British overrule, but often had little else in common. TANU was opposed at the district level in many places by the newly formed Local Councils, multiracial elective bodies that the government was promoting (Taylor 1963). Over seventy such local councils were then officially recognized. The multiplicity of "tribes" recognized by the administration, the diversity of their organization and the omnibus nature of TANU made it difficult for anyone to gain a clear view of issues and candidates when elections were held. This was sharply evident in the general elections of 1960 that were designed to usher in "responsible self-government." TANU received 83 percent of the votes cast, but as Bienen pointed out in his analysis of the outcome, only about 100,000 people out of the 800,000 who were registered actually voted (1967:55–56).

In Iringa District, where the Ruaha Basin forms the northern border, the traditional Hehe king continued to enjoy British support, as did the traditional lords who ruled under him. However, among the people there was also a welter of loyalties to local clans that had been conquered by the Hehe kings in the nineteenth century. Nevertheless, in my dealings with people, very little resentment of the king surfaced, despite TANU's position that such rulers were collaborators. I found TANU members in the district, but many were living in town, and many were from other parts of Tanzania.

The attention of the people seemed focused on other matters. Cash cropping was expanding rapidly, and there was hope that the weak demand for agricultural products manifested by low local prices would soon turn around. Despite these price conditions, a struggle for land was under way in locations favorable to market-oriented agriculture. Bitter competition for market access, for lands suitable for cash crops such as tobacco and peas, and for cattle herds was evident everywhere but was controlled by the great stress placed on public decorum and personal self-control.

As my work progressed I became aware of violence and witchcraft accusation in the district. Indeed, it was pervasive, and was addressed at the time in an article that I wrote jointly with my colleague, Robert Edgerton (Winans and Edgerton 1964). At the time, we saw such action as a major aspect of Hehe interpersonal relations, and considered it in the broader context of oaths, sorcery, law, and social control. In many respects I continue to agree with that interpretation. However, we were overly concerned with the configuration of Hehe culture, and I now believe that we did not sufficiently consider the wider setting of government ordinances, competition for market access, cash, and employment, and the bitter struggle between government officers and local farmers and herders over how their small holdings and herds would be managed.

From the vantage point of the Ruaha Basin, on the very edge of Iringa District, even the efforts of TANU to mobilize the people seemed remote and mostly the subject of a never-ending flow of rumors. Elections were approaching and it was crucial to the party that there be a strong showing at the polls if they were to have a powerful mandate at independence. In *Pawaga,* as the Ruaha Basin is called in the Kihehe language, the subchief repeatedly assured the people that TANU was unimportant and that nothing would change, but nobody believed him. They knew change was coming, but they did not know of what it would consist. Their eyes were on the removal of what they considered capricious local ordinances prohibiting cutting and burning of trees, prohibiting killing of game, prohibiting movement of stock into the adjacent highlands without dipping for ticks, and dozens of other similar regulations. They also wanted permission to move stock across district boundaries, the right to sell hides and skins freely and a road into their area to replace the seasonal track over which goods and people then moved. They knew of Mwalimu Julius Nyerere, President of TANU, and newly elected Chief Minister, but they knew little of what he might do, or how his government might differ from that which preceded it. They had hopes and desires, but little feeling that channels were about to open within the administration, which would enable them to achieve these goals.

There wasn't even a visit from a district officer on tour, although that had been a regular aspect of administration throughout the 1950s. This may well have been a consequence of a severe drought in 1959/60, but the local chief didn't know that, or didn't explain it to the people. In any case, the drought was followed by extraordinary rains in 1960/61 and there was severe flooding on the Ruaha River. Food was very short, cattle suffered from hoof rot because of the standing water and mud, and malaria and dysentery were much worse than usual.

The Ruaha Valley had not always been a backwater (Winans 1986). It has long been a contact zone for people speaking several different languages, and in the nineteenth century it was an important leg on one of the caravan routes leading from the Indian Ocean Coast to the eastern part of the Zaire Basin. Thus, the control of Pawaga had been a real economic and political prize in the past. In 1961 it did not appear that the government regarded it as a prize of any sort. One elderly subchief and six village headmen represented the local government. There was one dry-weather track and a single mobile police post. Evidence of British efforts to develop the area was a derelict generator house meant to run a cream separator for a milk and ghee scheme that failed because of variable milk delivery in the hot, dry lowlands. There was also a flood-ravaged diversion canal along the river that had been intended to serve an irrigated paddy scheme. Conflicts over access to land that could be irrigated, combined with annual flooding and silting, reduced this plan to a few subsistence cultivators who attempted to grow wet rice in swampy spots without irrigation. The powerful men of Pawaga were the owners of large herds. They grazed their animals over a large region during the rains and concentrated them near the river in the long dry season.

These stock-owners were engaged in a never-ending conflict for water and grazing lands with people who had no animals and cultivated near the river. Fields were of several types ranging from intensively culti-

vated, irrigated land on the riverbanks to dry fields cleared by fire and
bush knife for a single season of rain-fed cultivation. All were fenced to
keep out stock and wild animals; even slash and burn required heavy
labor inputs. The issue of access to water locked stock-owners and cultivators in bitter and ongoing contention. Yet stock-owners and cultivators were equally bound in economic dependence on each other. Stock
lending and joint herding were necessary to large owners if animals were
to be safely managed. While wage labor was almost the only means of
acquiring cash open to poor men, only the large herders ever had sufficient money to even consider hiring outside help.

Men with hundreds of head of cattle and equally large numbers of
sheep and goats could not possibly handle their herds alone, and some
had too few children to accomplish the task. Families with single millet
fields of about a hectare often faced starvation in an arid zone that had
a history of rain failure as often as once every three years, a single river,
and limited land along its banks. Farmers and herders formed a larger
social and economic unity, but one not noted for its amicable relations.
There were cross-cutting divisions of language and traditional tribal affiliation left from the old days of the caravan trade, yet all were united
by the need to protect themselves from stock raids by the Baraguyu, a
Masai-speaking, herding people who came long distances for the water
and forage afforded by the Ruaha River in years so dry that other
sources of water failed. For many of the local people, the Hehe chiefs
and the government police seemed as much enemies as the Baraguyu
since they constantly arrested and fined people for contravention of
local ordinances governing agricultural practices. Nevertheless, for most
of the population, the large stock-owners were by far the most powerful
figures in the region. They were at once a source of stock lent to be
herded, and thus of milk and manure, and also a source of potential
wage employment if animals were to be driven long distances.

They were also practically the only source of animals necessary to pay
a proper bridewealth. Most people viewed these large herders as arbitrary and capricious in their dealings, and constantly sought alliances
with them that would somehow control them. The inequalities with
which they were concerned were very great. My surveys indicated that
men whose herds numbered 100 or more cattle controlled about 80 percent of all stock. The remaining 20 percent of animals were distributed widely among the 96 percent of households owning less than 100
animals.

Such inequalities in control of resources were a major source of fric-
tion, yet at the same time, the complexities of interrelationship based on

stock exchanges for marriage, blood brotherhood, lineage obligations, and mourning of the dead mitigated the hardships of the people without animals. In such inequality long continued there is opportunity for clients as well as patrons. Beyond this, cattle had meanings connected to all these social acts. In Uhehe, cattle have names and genealogies just as people do. These are often deep and go back to gains and losses resulting from war in the late nineteenth century. To the people of Pawaga, the genealogy of a cow paid in bridewealth was as important as was its condition, age, and color. To own 500 cattle was to be wealthy in the sense of the control of productive resources, but it was also meaningful in social and historical terms reaching well beyond outputs of milk, blood, meat, and manure. Men and women stood and simply gazed at cattle in the same fashion people gaze at beautiful things in all societies. They were always willing to engage me in discussion of the relative beauty of different breeds and to identify for me the geographic provenience of any particular type.

Despite this shared appreciation, the big herders complained about the carelessness of the young men on whom they depended for labor in herding. These men entered into traditional agreements by which they received milk from the herds they tended as well as rather vague promises of a goat or sheep if herds grew. Tradition had shifted sufficiently by the 1960s that they also got small sums of money irregularly. These young men sometimes engaged in ivory smuggling and game poaching to stretch the meager yields from small fields of millet and from their herding. They had little hope of ever completing bridewealth payments and thus remained indebted to their fathers-in-law as well as to the herders from whom they sought cattle for such payments.

A daylight cattle raid by a group of Baraguyu warriors directly into the community in which I was working focused my attention on demands that I had heard repeatedly from the cattle owners, but that had seemed of less concern to me than the conflicts between herders and cultivators. Nearly every owner of stock had complained to me about the paucity of police protection for their herds. The daring raid certainly demonstrated to me that there was a need. However, in an interview with a large herder two days after the raid I found what I thought was a surprising set of concerns. He said he had lost cattle to the Baraguyu over the years, usually one or two at a time out of his kraals at night. Once, years before, he had lost twelve head in a single raid. The recent raid he thought very unusual because it had occurred in the middle of the day, right near the chief's court. He thought the raiders were probably drunk on brandy.

Usually a relatively quiet man, he went on in some excitement on this occasion. He told me there was much more danger from wild animals than from the Baraguyu. Hyenas had tried to get into his kraals just the night before, he said. He took me to see a dead hyena and showed me numerous wire traps he had arranged around his three kraals. I was duly impressed, for I had heard the hyenas on many nights. I had also heard lions from time to time and I simply inserted notes in my journal about the heavy population of game, surmising that the dry season concentrated animals of all kinds near the river.

I never saw another stock raid in Pawaga, but I heard hyenas almost every night, and I heard plenty of talk of their danger to herds, and possibly to herders as well. Finally, I heard a story that gave it all a new shape for me.

One evening, at my field camp, I had several local men as my dinner companions. The talk was very informal and lively. I had been in this field location for a rather long time, and the men were less formal than they had been earlier in my stay. They had known me for at least a year, although I was working in several locations and had not lived in this area continuously. There were numerous topics of conversation, but we inevitably turned to cattle. There were two men in the group who owned large herds, and both complained about the lack of police protection. I assumed this was connected to the recent cattle raid. Nothing could have been further from their minds.

The actual topic emerged as another guest began a story. He was a game scout, a local man who was an employee of the Department of Wildlife. We were on the edge of a very large game reserve, and this was his sector.

He was a fine storyteller: a quiet man of indeterminant age with years of experience and a vast knowledge of plants and animals. He told us that he had been on his way home from a long circuit of his region in the Reserve a few days before. Because he had been in the bush for some time, he was anxious to get home and continued to walk into the evening. It would be a moonlit night, and he figured to get home before the moon set. His plans were disrupted by a totally unexpected turn of events.

Just after nightfall he encountered a large pack of hyenas. There were many of them, and they came after him. He said, "There were too many to shoot, my friends, so I ran to climb a tree. As I climbed in a big thorn tree with low branches, I dropped my rifle and there I was sitting in the thorns, my body bleeding from the thorns, my rifle on the ground, the hyenas looking at me. I thought to myself, they will soon continue their safari and I shall get down from this accursed tree, but then I saw their leader. She was young, you may not know this my friend, but hyenas travel in packs and their leaders are always females," he said, explaining to me what I supposed the others already knew:

> Now, they did not go as I expected, but continued to watch me in my tree. The moon was above the hills now, and I could see them very clearly. Their leader ran amongst them and came close to the tree and jumped, but could not reach the limbs to climb up with me. I could then see that she had beads around her neck: many fine strands, and gold earrings in her ears. She was not a true hyena, but a witch: a woman who could become a hyena and speak the language of those beasts. She wanted me. They stayed the whole night. I was very cold in my tree, but still they watched me from the ground, and would not leave. Only when the night was over and it was light, did they leave. I stayed up in my tree until the sun was well up. You cannot know with witches. Perhaps she was still there hiding in the bush and waiting for me. When the sun had been in the sky for time enough to make my aching body warm, I came down and found my rifle where I had dropped it. I came home then; very quickly. I have been sleeping with my rifle since then, I have not walked out at night without friends. These hyenas who are witches, they continue after you once they have started.

The end of the story was followed by a short silence from all of us, but before I could find my voice to ask questions, there was a chorus of agreement that witches in the form of hyenas were the scourge of Pawaga at just this time. They were around every night, and were killing cattle by getting into kraals; something one would not expect a hyena could do. No real hyena could open a kraal, and besides, these hyenas did not eat the cattle, they only killed them. There was a lion who lived on a ridge above my camp, about a mile away. The men now told me that he was a witch as well. "The father of all these hyenas," one man said. They condemned the police as useless, unwilling to help with the hyenas. They blamed the government for the lack of petrol that marooned the mobile police post. They left without explaining why the witches were so active, why they took the form of hyenas, what they wanted the police to do, or what they intended to do themselves.

I already had casebooks full of witch accusations drawn from other parts of Uhehe. Divination techniques of several sorts appeared in such cases, and I had collected a large array of counteractions that could be used to combat the evil intentions of witches. I knew some witches could fly. I now added to my data on witches that some could assume animal form. I also added explicit warnings from my guests of the evening that

I myself was not immune from hyenas and I should walk at night only with a group of other people.

A few days later a cow was lost by a herdsman while the whole herd was grazing. Although a search was conducted, it was not found by nightfall. That night we heard plenty of hyenas. The remains of the lost cow were found the next morning, not far from the millet fields of the village. Trampled dry grass, lots of tracks and most of the carcass were what I could see. The animal remains were plentiful, and I was surprised that all those hyenas had not finished them off. When I said so, the men commented that the hyenas were just not hungry. They urged that I get on with the tasks of the day since there was nothing to be done.

That same evening a group of men visited my camp to talk of the uselessness of the chief and the fact that the police had no petrol and could run neither their Land Rover nor the generator that powered their police radio. There was no protection in Pawaga, they said, and when they tried to cultivate, the police arrested them for burning cuttings in order to clear fields. They asked me about the elections, and they said that the large herders had argued against anyone standing for election in the local council elections that had been held previously.

I offered to loan petrol from my drum so the police could get some from Iringa themselves, and I offered rides to Iringa and the District Office to any men who might want to find out about the upcoming elections scheduled for November. No one took up my offers. A day or two later I had a visit from a big herder who asked me if I would intercede with the police in Iringa to obtain a permanent police post in Pawaga to control raiding and burning. He said he also wanted the hyenas controlled and told me that he had lost an animal to the hyenas on the previous night. More police and a younger chief for Pawaga would control all these troubles, if Iringa would just give them. He departed with complaints that the government was not protecting the people, and that there was no government anymore so far as could be seen from all the losses he and others were suffering.

Nobody in Pawaga thought there was any government. The police offered only petty harassment. The hyenas killed the cattle, the rains flooded the fields, the road was impassable, and when there was discussion of a future African government, nobody had any facts. There was repression for which people could see no purpose, and the things that did seem important to them were things that could not be directly discussed with the European officers.

It had taken a long time for people to say directly to me that the hyenas were witches and not animals. There are doubtless many reasons for this. They did not know me well because I was a newcomer in their midst. I might easily be a witch myself. Just a few months earlier a government geologist had been killed in neighboring Dodoma District for behaving like a witch as he spent day after day walking backward through the bush doing geological mapping. I might also be a government officer for all anyone knew, however, despite the fact that I had said I wasn't. This was a serious danger since the maze of ordinances was regularly infringed by nearly everyone. Minor matters might be of little interest to a European officer, but some offenses were not minor matters. Elephant poaching was one such offense, and accusations that someone was a witch was another.

Tanganyika, like many other British African territories, had a witchcraft ordinance. This law is based on the premise that witchcraft does not exist, thus witches cannot. Under this ordinance, it is the accusation of witchcraft that is an evil. Malicious individuals make accusations of witchcraft against others to intimidate, isolate, or even destroy them. In this same line of reasoning, the "witchdoctor" or "witchfinder" is thus a charlatan who encourages such accusation, profits from it, and preys on the ignorant and superstitious. Accusations and practices of witch eradication, even if nonviolent, are offenses punished by fines and/or imprisonment. I shall return to this issue, but in the current context it is worth noting that the Tanganyika Witchcraft Ordinance of 1928 did not actually make reference to "witchdoctors," but simply specified punishment for anyone making a pretense to "occult power or knowledge."

The primary concern before us at this point is the lack of a proper government in the eyes of the people of Pawaga. There were certainly government agents: police and chiefs, veterinary assistants, game scouts, and dressers at the dispensary. The trouble was that they did not do anything the people wanted or needed, and to make matters even more baffling, they did do a variety of things which were unresponsive to people's needs. Can such a situation constitute government? As the local population saw it, it could not. There was talk of elections and independence, but no evidence that anything was actually changing. The local chiefs were still in office and still insisting that there would be no change, but rumors certainly promised otherwise. If this is coupled with the drought followed by floods, sickness, and death, the threat of Baraguyu raids, and losses of stock to sickness from the terrible weather, then there were ample grounds for a dramatic heightening of local tensions.

The visits I received from poor farmers and powerful herders seem to me to constitute strong evidence for such an interpretation of local views on the situation. All the people of Pawaga asked the same things of me: that I convey their requests for police and a young and vigorous chief to the District Office in Iringa. It was simply not the case that the wealthy sought protections and the poor, elections. Neither group accused the other of being the witches, at least to me. Their reasons could simply have been their uncertainty as to my real status, but in any case, they all voiced fear of the hyenas, conviction that the hyenas were really humans, and an unwillingness to directly accuse any specific individuals.

Some aspects of this situation bear striking resemblance to the circumstances discussed by Allen Roberts in an essay dealing with the Tabwa (1986). He discusses episodes of lion-related deaths among the Tabwa living on the western foreshore of Lake Tanganyika at the time of the first missionary activity in the late nineteenth century. The missionaries ridiculed the "superstitions" of the "heathen," who said that the lions were men. The most any of them would admit was the possibility of old lions no longer able to hunt normal game who had become "man-eaters." They accused the Tabwa of fomenting evil rumors. The logic is very similar to that which animates the Tanganyika Witchcraft Ordinance of 1928 discussed above. Any reference to man-lions was malicious, inspired by the Devil, and subject to severe punishment by the White Fathers.

Although the Tabwa are not a great distance from Uhehe, there is an even closer occurrence in Singida District of Tanzania, which has been the subject of two essays by Harold Schneider (1962:124–128; 1982:95–109). These essays discuss the occurrence of man-lions in that area from the 1920s through the early 1950s (1982:96). Between 1946 and 1948, over 100 killings were attributed to the lion-men in Singida District, and the authorities investigated them officially.

A point of interest to us in the Schneider analysis is his mention that the government was operating on two theories concerning the lion-men during the outbreak of killings that took place in 1946 until 1948. Like the White Fathers among the Tabwa, they considered the possibility of "man-eating lions" and went so far as to hire professional hunters to shoot the lions that could be found in Singida (Wyatt 1950). However, they also took the view of the Belgian authorities of the 1930s whom Roberts reports as having hanged several lion-men. The British explored the possibility that these might be men dressed in lion skins committing murders for what the authorities thought might be political reasons. Following up on this possibility, they asked the then government sociologist, Hans Cory, to investigate. Cory recommended that, "the political structures in various parts of the country could be better supported" (quoted in Schneider 1982:97).

INTERPRETATION

We opened this essay with two important ways in which African kings have expressed their power: a praise poem to a great Hehe king and the elaborate ritual killing of an Ankole Queen Mother. In both these enactments, the power of nature that these personages possess is expressed through the metaphor of a dangerous beast. The Ankole are specific: the Queen Mother becomes a leopard; the king, a lion. In the hands of a Hehe poet, the metaphor of king as a natural force is rendered in a somewhat less literal fashion: wild beast of the forest who sees and knows all in his kingdom. The references in the poem to "place of the mounds of skulls" and "fat cattle in the West" deal with important victories won by Mkwawa against major opponents on his borders. The poetry is not simply flight of fancy that metaphorically expresses the qualities of kings; it is full of specific and detailed references to a very real history. The witnesses to the recitals are well aware of the realities expressed. The life of Mkwawa, and the events mentioned in the poem were more than fifty years in the past when I heard the poem recited, but even my young assistant and the boys who were loitering in the shade near my informant knew the events it chronicles. The power of the king is expressed with great precision. He may kill or confiscate, banish or reward as he chooses. Although the powers of the king surpass those of a normal man, every man enjoys power. "The lioness hunts daily, but the old lion eats first," says a Hehe proverb. Any Hehe woman or child can tell you that fathers and grandfathers enjoy many privileges, and that all of these are very precisely defined, carefully protected, and meticulously observed.

It is in the details that power resides. Like the king himself, every clan elder must count and guard his privileges daily and in even the most mundane interaction. No Hehe, young or old, will countenance a failure in the forms, and thus in the substance of privilege. Because kings can "see" and "hear" in a fashion not given to others except sorcerers and witches, they are particularly on guard against infringements.

In reading descriptions of leopard-men by diverse authors one is struck by the painstaking attention to detail, not of the authors, but of the leopard-men themselves. Lindskog's book illustrates iron claws, some set in "paws," terrible to look at, and even more terrible to read about in use (1954: chaps. II, III). There are carved feet of the beast used painstakingly to create a proper appearance to the ground around a body. There are masks and capes and plain skins worn by the men. It is sometimes reported that the animal ran on all fours when carrying out an attack. Bodies of victims are often reported as having been dragged about, sometimes for long distances, as a leopard is known to do. Growls, roars, and screams are reported from the killers, "intended to make people uneasy" (1954:37). Lindskog also gleaned numerous reports, some very detailed, of the cannibalism of the leopard-men, but he does not attempt to assess the authenticity of these, and they are not a universal aspect of the accounts. In the case of my own data, there is no claim to cannibalism, nor could I see any evidence that the hyena-men even ate the cattle they had killed.

Like the attention to detail of the leopard-men, there is an equal attention by the witnesses. If one returns to the account of the game scout, it is full of details. He even told us what kind of tree it was that he climbed, and how he found his rifle on the following morning, and especially, small details of the hyenas. Most striking, of course, was his description of the leader, a young female adorned with necklaces and earrings. He returned to this several times in his account: it was the crucial detail. No "normal" hyena would wear necklaces and earrings, and although a man might wear earplugs, and a Baraguyu man might also wear a strand of beads around his neck, it is women who wear the kind of small gold earrings and the multiple strands of beads of which he spoke. This was a man skilled in bush craft. I believe the detail is extremely important to the complex of activities and the effect they achieve, just as it is in the enormously intricate symbolism of power and terror surrounding kings and chiefs.

I do not mean to imply that the sex of the leader has an ideological significance similar to the analysis made by Packard, who argued that the imputation of witch power to women in Bashu society emerged out of earlier cosmological ideas about women in Bashu thought. Packard asserts that "women are potential sources of misfortune because of their innate association with the forces of the bush" (1980:260). Packard is not arguing that Bashu men manipulate their ideas consciously so as to keep women subordinated. Far from it; complexity and detail emerge in their unconscious associations, and it is precisely this that leads to the power that accrued to Bashu women who might be witches. This power made Bashu men fear them and concede privileges to them that men had seen as their own by right of the creation of the cultural world. It is this same logic that responds to the further penetrations of the capitalist economy by construing disorder within the Bashu homestead as a consequence of witch-women "infecting" men with their witch power and thereby transforming them. When men act like "creatures of the bush" can the old duality of bush and homestead, so central to Bashu thought, be maintained, asks Packard (1980:262). Such conclusions by Bashu men rest on the details of their experience, in the light of their cosmology. I am arguing that the Hehe, like the Bashu, view themselves as making inferences of the most general kind from the most meticulous observations.

The failure of the ancient powers of the chiefs was clear. Now the Europeans who had usurped the chiefs were withdrawing, leaving behind an unresponsive bureaucracy. It enforced roles imposed by the Europeans for which people could see no reason, and refused to act as the chiefs would once have done when hyena-men threatened. Hehe kings and chiefs had once stood athwart a duality of forest and cultivated field; nature and culture. They were of the forest, but created order with their power. In this ideology, hyena-men destroy that order, but in 1961 no prince stopped them.

In Pawaga in 1961 cattle were the primary victims of the murderous activities of the hyenas. It's not that humans were immune, but rather that they were almost incidental: a nameless herder, the game scout who escaped, others if they should get in the way. In the subtle conflict of meanings under way in Pawaga cattle were crucial. They were often the single assurance that one would survive in a bad year. They were also the only thing of value that the capitalist world conceded to Pawaga. Cattle were also beautiful, and the primary metaphor for women, for the continuity of the lineage, and for the bonds of friendship. Above all, cattle are not beasts of the forest, but rather a part of the world of the homestead. They are a crucial evidence of the human ability to control nature and to transform it into friendship, kinship, and marriage.

Earlier, I noted that cattle genealogies are important in Uhehe. Some breeding lines are less susceptible to diseases endemic to the region, some possess pleasing colors or markings, some have horn forms that are thought particularly beautiful, and some are better milk cows. People have a great deal of this sort of knowledge and are very concerned with it. However, other concerns, which lie in the world of human relations, are held equally important. Lineage linkages are contained in human genealogies, of course, but are equally contained in the genealogies of cattle. A herd is a living testimony to marriage pacts, bond friendships, debts owed, and debts collected. Cattle are the central means for the creation and severing of social relations. From this point of view marriage requires not only a man of one lineage and a woman of another but also cattle to be transferred from the man's lineage to the woman's, and then within her lineage, to various members. Without such transfers, there may be cohabitation, but there is no marriage with its capacity to produce children who have proper social identities, legitimate claims to membership and inheritance, and obligations to parents and to parents' siblings.

The market economy has had a pervasive influence on this whole structure of meanings since it introduces a monetary valuation of animals determined from outside the system. The penetration of market relations began in Pawaga a century or more ago. There has been ample time for market values in money to become deeply embedded, yet people are uneasy about keeping cattle simply as a market commodity. It is possible to achieve a proper marriage through the substitution of monetary equivalences for the animals required. It is often done, and it is even seen as clever by some younger and well-traveled men who take advantage of government regulations that set a standard value for animals used in bride payment. This value is often lower than the actual market price of an animal, and thus allows a market-wise negotiator to substitute money for animals and make a profit on a marriage. Older people are uneasy about such actions, and fathers find they have lost control of sons who conduct their own negotiations, and pay monetary equivalents from earnings. Brides may also suffer in this arrangement because there is no group of animals in their fathers' herds that represents them, and their own sons may find no support from their mother's lineages at marriage negotiations a generation later.

People were clearly ambivalent about all these changes, but there was almost no ambivalence about the difficulties of actually marketing stock. Government regulations surrounded almost every aspect of formal sale. Permits were required for moving stock across a district boundary, for moving stock from lowlands to highlands, and for selling stock at a gazetted auction. There was also a tax on stock sales, and thus a form was required that reported a sale and served as a receipt for the payment of the tax. Of course, these and other regulations could be evaded, and often were. However, such evasion defeats the longer-term purpose of creating evidence for an important transaction. Stock loses its crucial social meaning in these circumstances, while also failing to fully gain the advantages that accrue from free market exchange with its minimal social extensions.

The killing of cattle seems to me to reflect all of this. It is a rejection of the demystification of cattle that has resulted from their commodification. At the same time, it is a rejection of the endless qualifications and hedges on commodification that the colonial authorities had invented to "protect" the market in stock from "low-grade animals," epidemics, and "unscrupulous" traders who would supposedly take advantage of

naive herders who were not conversant with price variations across the
territory.

CONCLUSION

There are two strands to the analysis of hyena-men in Pawaga. On one
hand, I am concerned with the appearance of the hyenas, and I link that
to the failing efficacy of the chiefs and the inability of TANU, the party
of national independence, to project itself into the local circumstances
of the region as the British authorities withdrew. On the other hand, I
have argued that understanding of the events rests in close attention to
the local details. In these terms, I have asked why cattle rather than
humans died at the hands of the hyenas. In the accounts of other areas
afflicted with terrorism of this sort, there is no mention of the killing of
stock. Of course, this is no proof that it does not occur, only that the
accounts do not mention it. In Pawaga, it was central and intolerable.
The people were accustomed to cattle raiding, but this was different.
Killing the animals was a negation of traditional meaning, a recognition
that cattle were becoming simply an item in the market and that even
that market was largely out of reach since the government that created
it had also created conditions in which marketing was on such adverse
terms that its only attraction was the lack of any alternative source of
cash.

There is a substantial and penetrating body of literature that has
attempted to reexamine a great variety of violence and criminality in its
historical context. Engels was not the last to argue that theft is a form
of social protest (1969). The work of Hobsbawm (1959) has been the
proximate source of a great deal of the recent work in this vein. Terence
Ranger, working in this tradition, has produced a long series of powerful analyses that have sought to reinterpret many activities that the authorities in East and Central Africa have attempted to suppress (see
Ranger [1967, 1970] and the fine book on African social protest edited
by Donald Crummey [1986]). If this literature has a shortcoming, however, it is in insufficient concern with the internal dynamic of change in
ideology at the local level. The greatest power in most of these analyses
has been concentrated in the contradiction between the extension of
capitalism and the local structure of production. In this, it has given
meaning to resistance that the authorities had been able to conceptualize
as primitive, and thus irrational, violence.

I have been concerned with demonstrating that violence, killing, and terror must also yield meaning in a close analysis of the idioms of local understandings. In recent years we have become accustomed to governments and resistance leaders explaining and labeling attacks on villages, railways, and bridges. What is less familiar is the struggle over meanings where it is witches and sorcerers, diviners, and witchfinders who occupy the stage and no guerrilla spokespersons exist. In these confrontations death seems to come to victims who have no apparent connection to either government or opposition. Often the perpetrators remain not only nameless but also seemingly classless. Indeed, as in this case, they may be something both more than and less than human. It was not the government in a concrete sense that was the target of the hyena attacks; rather, it was the success of the colonial government in undermining the old order, in promoting the cash economy, in protecting its exploitative conditions, and then in simply appearing to withdraw its powers while leaving behind its forms.

The powers of witches have not failed as a consequence of the successful transition from British overrule to Tanzanian independence. We have already noted Simeon Mesaki's survey of Uchawi (witchcraft) in contemporary Tanzania, and his conclusion that it is more prevalent than it was at independence. His survey reveals how varied this witchcraft is, however. It is hardly the case that it takes the form of hyenas or lions everywhere. Nevertheless, this form remains powerful in certain regions. In the period since 1987 there have been numerous killings by "lions" in Tunduru District to the south of Iringa District. The newspapers in Tanzania have reported these killings, and I have discussed them with Tanzanian friends. There has been official inquiry into the deaths that have occurred even on the outskirts of towns and in broad daylight. There is no official figure for the number of victims, but the widely held belief is that they number over 100 persons. The killing continues, and I note, without surprise, that officials are organizing hunts to rid the area of old, isolated, man-eating lions.

Horace Campbell has written recently (1987) on the Sungu Sungu movement in Shinyanga, Mwanza, and Tabora Districts. In this region the members of the movement have accused many elderly women of being witches. The movement differs in many ways from the cases of transformations into beasts which we have considered. There is a similarity as well, despite these many contrasts. All of these movements have occurred in times of extreme economic and political pressure. In each case the authorities are locally perceived as having failed to meet crucial needs of the people. Not only state power but also local authority simply has not been responsive to local distress and has often exacerbated the situation through a failure to even recognize that there is distress. The power of the authorities to extract goods and services from the people is not matched by any semblance of a return, yet the state is so distant that it offers no target for local action.

With Michael Taussig, I see this as a time of terror, a time in which things are disordered and remade. Such remaking entails powerful forces and terrible risks. The reforging of meanings inhering in the daily acts of a people may involve simply discarding long-held views, but the evidence seems to me to indicate that people seldom do any such thing. Their lives have changed, but the clash over these changes is still difficult to resolve.

The question of how cattle were to be used was far from settled within Pawaga in 1961. The identity of the hyenas was less urgent to the people of Pawaga than was the fact that they were members of the community and were destroying its central resource. People neither identified particular perpetrators nor asked that they be arrested. They demanded protection, which I take to have meant police patrols, and a subchief who would give moral leadership. As the people saw it, the external failure allowed an internal failure to occur.

The beasts of the forest were destroying one of the few things that had meaning in both the old and new orders. How could people even continue to live in Pawaga under such circumstances, would seem to me to have been the unstated question before them at the time. In the years that have passed since the crises of drought, political turmoil, and local terror, an answer has emerged. Irrigated agriculture has come to the Ruaha Basin, and large areas have been brought into production. The hyenas were correct, cattle herding was no longer to be a central source of meaning and sustenance in Pawaga. Moreover, the main reason for its loss of meaning has been the loss of a local economy only loosely connected to the larger market system. Irrigation agriculture links Pawaga to the world economy by ties far more immediate than the trade in livestock ever did. This is not the first such linkage of the Ruaha Basin to the world system. I suspect that in the extension of the caravan routes along the Ruaha River, there was also violence and conflict. Indeed, it was in this time that Pawaga first became a part of the Hehe Empire and experienced the power of *likoko*: a king who is a Beast of the Forest.

REFERENCES

Ardener, Edwin
1971   "Witchcraft, Economics and the Continuity of Belief." In *Witchcraft, Confessions and Accusations,* Mary Douglas, ed. London: Tavistock.

Bienen, Henry
 1967   *Tanzania: Party Transformation and Economic Development.* Princeton: Princeton University Press.
Bohannan, Paul
 1958   "Extra-Processual Events in Tiv Political Institutions." *American Anthropologist* 60:1–12.
Campbell, Horace
 1987   "Popular Resistance in Tanzania: Lessons from the Sungu Sungu." *History Research Seminar Series.* Dar es Salaam: University of Dar es Salaam.
Cliffe, Lionel
 1964   "Nationalism and the Reaction to Enforced Agricultural Change in Tanganyika During the Colonial Period." Kampala: EAISR Annual Conference.
Engels, Friedrich
 1969   *The Condition of the Working Class in England.* E. Hobsbawm, ed. London: Panther Books.
Evans-Pritchard, Edward Evan
 1937   *Witchcraft, Oracles and Magic among the Azande.* London: Oxford University Press.
Hobsbawm, Eric
 1959   *Primitive Rebels: Studies in Archaic Forms of Social Movement in the 19th and 20th Centuries.* Manchester: Manchester University Press.
Jadot, J., and L. De Lannoy
 1934   "Le Juge et le sorcier." Brussels: Conference du Jeune Barreau de Bruxelles.
Lindskog, Berger
 1954   *African Leopard Men. Studia Ethnographica Upsaliensia, VII.* Uppsala: Almqvist and Wiksells.
Mesaki, Simeon
 1988   "Uchawi and Ujamaa: Witchcraft, Sorcery and Magic in 'Socialist' Tanzania." Chicago: African Studies Association Annual Meeting.
Packard, Randall M.
 1980   "Social Change and the History of Misfortune Among the Bashu of Eastern Zaire." In *Explorations in African Systems of Thought,* I. Karp and C. S. Bird, eds. Bloomington: Indiana University Press.
Patterson, J. H.
 1912   *The Man-Eaters of Tsavo.* London: Macmillan.
Ranger, Terence O.
 1967   *Revolt in Southern Rhodesia 1896–7. A Study in African Resistance.* London: Heinemann.
 1970   *The African Voice in Southern Rhodesia 1898–1930.* London: Heinemann.

1986 "Bandits and Guerrillas: The Case of Zimbabwe." In *Bandits, Rebellion and Social Protest in Africa*, Donald Crummey, ed. London: Currey.

Roberts, Allen F.
1986 "Like a roaring lion: Tabwa terrorism in the late nineteenth century." In *Banditry, Rebellion and Social Protest in Africa*, Donald Crummey, ed. London: Heinemann.

Roscoe, John
1923 *The Banyankole*. Cambridge: Cambridge University Press.

Schneider, Harold
1962 "The Lion Men of Singida: A Reappraisal." *Tanganyika Notes and Records* 58/59.
1982 "Male-Female Conflict and Lion Men of Singida." In *African Religious Groups and Beliefs*, S. Ottenberg, ed. Meerut, India: Arcana for Folklore Institute, Berkeley, Calif.

Taussig, Michael
1987 *Shamanism, Colonialism, and the Wild Man*. Chicago: University of Chicago Press.

Taylor, J. Clagett
1963 *Political Development in Tanganyika*. Stanford: Stanford University Press.

Winans, Edgar
1986 "Violence and External Pressure in Tanzania." Philadelphia: American Anthropological Association Annual Meeting.

Winans, Edgar, and Robert Edgerton
1964 "Hehe Magical Justice." *American Anthropologist* 66(4), pt. 1.

Wyatt, A. W.
1950 "The Lion-Men of Singida." *Tanganyika Notes and Records* 28.

PART TWO

Resistance

Pl. 2. "Pancho Villa's wife during the Mexican Revolution" on display in El Palacio de Cortez, Cuernavaca, Mexico.

SEVEN

Ideas on Philippine Violence: Assertions, Negations, and Narrations

Jean-Paul Dumont

One of the problems with violence is that we all know intuitively and experientially what it means. It is immediately obvious and commonsensical, and this is clearly why it is problematic. In his attempt to answer the question, "is an ethnography of violence possible?" Jean Jamin (1984: 17 [my trans.]) with perhaps even too much assurance and certitude—for doubt itself must be doubted—makes this remark: "The notion of violence concerns phenomena that are sufficiently heterogeneous to make them sociologically inoperational; its proteiform and polysemic character almost prevents anyone from defining it" (Jamin 1984:17 [my trans.]).[1]

And thus I shall not attempt to define what escapes definition. In a minimalist vein, however, I understand the word to refer perhaps to the use of, and always to the abuse of force. Because violence remains hopelessly entangled with the issue of legitimacy, it is fair and necessary to state, once more, that I have no pretension to objectivity. There are villains in my biased story, and I shall let them wear the black hats. This said, my concern here is limited to documenting violence in a specific context, although I shall focus less on the real thing than on the concept of violence, its virtuality.

If actual violence is necessarily the manifestation of a conflict, understanding such conflict and violence cannot be achieved without placing them in their cultural context. Anthropologists can assume that much. Violence is expressive. Violence is also expressed. It is at once representation and represented, at once manipulative and manipulated. It is the strength of such a manipulation that I would like to emphasize here, by reflecting on my ethnographic experience of the Philippines. Limited though it may be, it will allow me to be at once minute and concrete—in short, to be attentive to details that might otherwise escape the attention of those who focus too narrowly on actual events alone or exclusively on sociopolitical institutions. The thicker, fuller, or denser the description, presumably the rounder the hermeneutic yield.

What historically passes for the first encounter between the West and the Philippines—Magellan's arrival in Cebu in 1521—was violent from the onset. Humabon who ruled on Cebu was hastily converted to Christianity and encouraged to recognize the suzerainty of the Spanish Crown, or else. And Magellan never finished the first circumnavigation for which he is nonetheless credited, as he was defeated by Lapu-Lapu who ruled on the neighboring island of Mactan and thus became the first nationalist hero of the Philippines.

I might as well jump to Marcos's dictatorship since the history of the Philippines is nothing but an incessant succession of political conflicts and uncontrolled violence: piracy, abductions, revolts, revolutions, occupation, and resistance succeed one another. Ferdinand Marcos, elected President in 1965, declared martial law in 1972 and thus seized power until "people power" and the "revolution" of February 1986 brought him and his administration down, with Corazon Aquino's democratic but frail triumph.

To evoke the notion of violence when speaking of the Philippines seemed to me, in my fieldworking experience at the end of the Marcos regime and before the assassination of Benigno Aquino on August 21, 1983,[2] a little farfetched. Of course, I knew of the historical forces that had shaped the present Philippines. From Magellan's arrival and his demise in 1521[3] to the imposition of martial law by Ferdinand Marcos in 1972 and thereafter, a quasi-uninterrupted succession of violent political turmoils had given to the Philippines its identity and orginality. The Moro raids,[4] the Dagohoy revolt,[5] the revolution of 1896,[6] the Japanese occupation,[7] the Huk rebellion,[8] or, today, the confrontation between the NPA[9] and the MNLF[10] on one hand and the troops of the regime on the other hand, were all sufficient reminders of a situation that year after year had been tense, if not explosive.

And yet, between such an abstract knowledge and my concrete experience of the Philippines as I lived it, there was a great deal of distance, a fundamental discrepancy. Certainly there were private armed and uniformed guards almost everywhere in the cities of Manila and Cebu, and I could not pretend to ignore them, even though there were hardly any on the small and altogether out-of-the-way province-island of Siquijor. And in front of my very own eyes, school children were regularly involved in elaborate and compulsory paramilitary exercises. But, at once, the posting of uniformed guards as well as the martial training of the young appeared to be undertaken with a substantial amount of bonhomie—with good humor and a sense of humor—which seemed to guarantee that presumably things would not get out of hand. After all, even the Philippine Constabulary Officer who had come to check on my wife and myself about a week after our installation had paid to us what he called "only a courtesy call." I perceived then and there little tension. Troubles were or seemed to be elsewhere. In this general social and political atmosphere, "martial law, Philippine style" was a phrase, the popularity of which was in tune with the famous or infamous concept of "smooth interpersonal relationship."[11] And most of my informants displayed the expected and proper modesty and shyness amidst a profusion of endless smiles.

In the isolation that our insularity guaranteed, it was all too easy to forget that perhaps our hosts' smiles, their suavity, their pretense to be light and merry, real as all this might have been, deliberately obfuscated a contrary aspect of their culture. All happened as if the Siquijorians made a special effort to impress on us that erratic violence was, if it had ever been anything else, a thing of the past. And indeed people, in town as well as in the *barangay*,[12] seemed to emphasize the same theme: "On this island of ours"—some 75,000 persons, more than 80 percent of them Roman Catholics and more than 99 percent Cebuano native speakers, inhabited its 350 square kilometers—"harmony is in order." It was a matter of *angay*, which signified the evenness of treatment between people, their equality. As a verb, this word connoted "agreement" and also referred to the tuning of musical instruments. It was in addition a matter of *uyun*. As an adjective, the word meant "parallel." In the present derivative sense, it referred to "getting along with," to "adjusting to each other." Both *angay* and *uyun* were concepts that implied a sentiment of achieved equality between people.

But the metaphor that people preferred to use for our benefit was slightly different. In fact, it was almost exclusively, but repeatedly, expressed in English, in one single stock phrase that suffered little variation: "Here we form one big, happy family." This was said in English not only because those who uttered it wanted to make sure that we understood their message but also because being uttered in the prestige language—Tagalog, the language of Manila, or Pilipino, the official national language of the nation-state, conveyed less prestige—the phrase acquired a special resonance that amplified its meaning and augmented its rhetorical suasion.[13]

In and of itself, the statement would have had little to attract attention, had it not been asserted over and over again, in a manner that could only beg for deconstruction. When I realized that my informants were not merely expressing their personal feelings, but repeating a stock phrase learned at school, I became enticed to prod further into the meaning of the phrase. When I asked my informants to gloss the same phrase in Cebuano, they did not retranslate literally the word *family* (I would have expected *kabayanan* or the Spanish, borrowing *pamilya*). Instead, they said "Dinhi sa Siquijor, madaiton mi" or "malinawon mi," that is, "here on the island of Siquijor, we are peaceful" or "we are at peace." The verb *dait* means "to have good personal relations" and has thus strictly positive and social connotations. The adjective *linaw*, often used to describe the state of the sea, means "calm," and therefore connotes the continuity between natural environment and social milieu.

But that imputed harmony, as I came to realize, had in fact a triple aspect: (1) a descriptive or referential one (as it reflected the way in which Siquijorians tended to perceive their society), (2) a programmatic one (as it formulated the way in which they wished their society to be), and (3) even a performative one (as it also purported to bring about such an idyllic order). As a consequence, allusions to or mention of violence were more or less eschewed from conversations with me, since it did not fit the model of self-presentation that the Siquijorians wanted to impress on us. In the same way, different informants made an all-out effort to protect, not to say overprotect us from any mishaps to which we might have been exposed. The first time I was about to witness a brawl between two inebriated adult males, I was quickly ushered away from the scene and sheltered "for my own good." Thereafter, not only was it difficult for me to get directly any detail about this incident, but its very occurrence was even questioned, if not flatly denied.

Nonetheless, such an illusory eradication of violence could only achieve its opposite effect: the displayed and proclaimed absence of violence could only point at its absconded presence. If violence was so forcefully denied, did it not reveal its importance in that particular cultural setting? Hidden as violence was, where and at which level did it enter into the praxis of villagers and townspeople of Siquijor?

It was commonsensical to explore the ways in which Siquijorians perceived the occurrence of death. Inasmuch as it was rarely, if ever, considered as simply natural, it was always, in part or in whole, a violent occurrence, brought about by someone else's evil will. Except perhaps for the very old, no one died exclusively of what we would call natural causes; nor were such causes ignored. Because there were two systems of reference—a traditional one to which the world of spirits, of witch-craft, or syncretic Catholicism belongs and another one to which West-ern medicine belongs—it was clear to everyone that Tasio had indeed died of old age (*kay tigulan na siya*), while "high blood" was responsible for Carla's demise. But there was something else, too, something "sup-plementary" to use a Derridian vocabulary.[14] "Kidney failure followed by cardiac arrest" may have been good enough to obtain a bona fide death certificate for Tasio, but the hacking of a chicken, followed by the examination of its entrails, revealed to his immediate family that some spirits had visited his liver. As for Carla, whose demise was untimely, high blood pressure may have led to a fatal stroke, but "someone" (*usa ka tawo*) whose identity I learned only later from a reluctant informant, had borne a grudge against one of her close relatives. This person had been seen—I was told—roaming around Carla's home a few days before the fatal stroke and was thus strongly suspected of witchcraft. As a mat-ter of fact, was not her death the last episode in a feud to which two close relatives of her husband had already and prematurely fallen vic-tims? In other words, neither Carla nor Tasio—albeit to differing ex-tents—had just died. Each one had been killed: he by unspecified (and so vague as to be almost generic) spirits and she by the magical power of a jealous or revengeful, powerful and nasty, neighborly affine.

Although in my understanding neither death resulted from any act of violence, the villagers obviously saw it differently. Similarly, they tended to perceive the presence of the spiritual world among them with such acumen that it tended to blur—without completely eradicating—the difference to which I, for one, preferred to hold, namely, the differ-ence between natural occurrence and supernatural intervention. When Zikil blew off his arm while fishing with a stick of dynamite, that was—and everyone agreed—a *disgrasya* (i.e., just an accident). But when Senio disappeared at sea, he had not just drowned in a fishing accident but had been the victim of a *kataw*, of a siren who had seduced him, kid-napped him, and ultimately killed him.

But most cases of violent death are highly ambiguous and susceptible to a wide variety of contradictory, yet equally accepted explanations. For instance, when Ime died quite prematurely in what seemed to me a straightforward accident—the teenager drowned while skin diving when he became entangled in a fishing net—no one denied the immediate cause of his death. In addition, however, some had supplementary thoughts: the fishing net had been bewitched, another diver had done him in, and the irate spirit of a neglected relative had longed to see him in the beyond—all of the above and more.

What should become obvious by now is that the world surrounding the Siquijorians could not be and indeed was not as harmonious as they pretended it to be. Within their very cultural constructions, they had wrapped themselves into constant potential aggression. They had to contend not only with natural problems such as typhoons and the all too banal intrusion of death but also with the supernatural world that they had constructed. The latter was full of undesirable beings, each one more eager than the next to bring harm and doom to human beings.

Furthermore, the ordinary and mundane tensions that life in a village or in a neighborhood necessarily entail may lead to accusations and suspicions of witchcraft, the utmost manifestation of an unspoken, silent, if not secretive aggression. Beyond direct physical aggression and beyond the more subtle manipulations of witchcraft, acts of violence could still be perpetrated between living human beings even in absentia.

One day, as I inquired about the cause of a young man's death in the *barangay* where we lived, I was told that he had been killed, that his body had just been brought back to the village from Mindanao. He had been killed by his enemies; they killed him during his sleep. Were there any bad wounds on his body? None whatsoever. You are telling me that his enemies killed him in his bed and that his body bears no mark? But then, how do you know he was killed? Because he was fighting. But I thought he was asleep. Yes, asleep and fighting. I was puzzled, indeed. How do you know he was fighting? Because of the picture. Did I want to see it? The immediate family had in its possession a snapshot that had been taken, as I understood, by the police who investigated the case. The body, half-naked, lay on its deathbed, presumably in the exact position in which death had taken him. You see, he was fighting. I could see no such thing. Can't you see, the room is in great disorder, his arms are folded, his fists are tight, his legs spread. It began to dawn on me that, had he been in an upright position, he would be in a fighting posture. More explanation came about. While asleep, souls[15] can take a stroll (*suroy-suroy*); this is why one can see others in one's dreams. The soul leaves the body and in fact goes and visits others, and normally returns to join the body just before the person wakes up. While he was asleep, he picked a fight with his enemies in his dream. They overpowered him, and this is how he got killed. This was obvious to everyone but me, although finding the murderer was a more formidable task, entirely left to the domain of speculation and suspicion.

In interpreting this particular death as the result of a deliberate and mischievous act of violence, the Siquijorians continued to project the fear that violence inspired in them. But, in the instances that I have presented so far, violence does not appear in action, nor even as a process. It is more of a passion, something to which they may be subjected rather than something that they may inflict. Moreover, they consider themselves more readily as its victims than as its perpetrators. In other words, violence is of greater concern to them than they are inclined to admit.

This ideological perception of violence reflects in part the different experiences of colonial and neocolonial dominations to which the Siquijorians have been submitted. About the dark aspects of their historical past, the Siquijorian social memory seemed to have been selective. Time had not softened but perhaps even amplified the Spaniards' misdeeds of the nineteenth century as well as the particular rigors of the Japanese occupation in World War II. For instance, I was told several times by informants who had not been immediate witnesses to such atrocities that Japanese soldiers in town had abducted at least several babies from their mother's arms, tossed them in the air so as to catch them better with their bayonets. Not only is this a story that, as I discovered later, has currency practically everywhere in the Philippines; no informant could be any more specific as to the identity of any such victim, nor could I find any evidence of such event in the death register of the local parish. My point here is not to deny, even less to justify, the occurrence of Japanese atrocities, but to underline that ideology can never be a mere reflection of experience. The experience of violence had structured the ideology of experience in such a way that the ideology, in turn, structured the experience.

This structured and structuring aspect of ideology and experience comes to the fore as soon as an example of proclaimed and enacted violence is introduced. This became apparent in a story that I was told at first in bits and pieces, although publicly and without any inhibition.

Toward the end of World War II, as the context indicates, a Japanese fighter pilot bailed out of his Zero, well in sight of the coastline. He swam ashore. And there he was safe and sound and hiding on Crocodile Point. Partisans had seen his parachute descent, looked for him, and picked him up without much difficulty. This was most unfortunate for the airman. They brought him back to town. He was fastened to a post in front of the Municipal Building, and without any water to drink, he stayed there, exposed to the wrath of the local population for three days according to some, for seven days according to others. After this, somehow still alive, he was brought back to the shore where he had landed. There was among them a woman who was so angry at what the Japanese had done in the Philippines that she took a *bolo* (a heavy weeding cutlass), opened up his belly, and ate his liver *kinilaw* (i.e., raw or seasoned only with coconut vinegar). Oh, yes, I could ask her if I wanted to, but she may not want to talk about it.

In many respects, it was a collective but piecemeal recitation as it had been purportedly a collective and spontaneous deed. The accuracy of the deed itself, its truth value, I could never establish because the successive narrators were not the participants, whose identity were always left in a blurred distance, save for the main character of the story. She lived somewhere in a neighboring *barangay*. But, discouragingly, she was much too old, too deaf, too unwilling to talk to be interviewed. I had been warned. I attempted several times to reach her but never could, as I was always at once encouraged and discouraged to pursue her testimony.

Amidst the conviction, suspicion, presumption of a revealed and unverifiable truth, a narrative experience of violence remained. It pointed at the Siquijorian preoccupation with, inclination toward, and justification of violence. Beyond the lost truth value of the event that it relates, and which structured the narration, the narrative, in turn, is bound to structure any possible future violence, giving it its value as argument. As such, English-speakers would say that it goes directly to the heart of the matter. For Cebuano-speakers, the heart of the matter is, in fact, a different organ, since the seat of emotions is the *atay*, the liver.

To take here a brief pause and bring to a temporary closure one panel of my diptych on Philippine violence, it seems manifest that violence in effect permeated the entire society. Despite assertions to the contrary, or perhaps because of such a denial, violence was omnipresent, at the very least as a forged memory, in everyone's consciousness. Time after time, and without much restraint, all forms of political authority had been able to manipulate to their own advantage the structuring value of its coercive argument, thus keeping the Siquijorians in line in their isolated insularity, fearful of their own nightmares and daydreaming of smooth interpersonal interaction.

When I first became interested in the Philippines, at least in Siquijor, one of the 7,109 islands that constitute the archipelago, the nation was under martial law. In my limited experience of the world, the mere utterance of the phrase "martial law," in and of itself, is sufficient to conjure images of great unpleasantness, with heel-clicking sounds, public executions, and other Orwellian horrors. I thus braced myself for the worst.

On arrival, I was surprised—I must confess—that the martial law atmosphere, pervasive as it may have been, was more diffused than I had anticipated. A province-island[16] in the central Visayas, Siquijor was poor, indeed. It was also small and isolated. Its homogeneity from any viewpoint was spectacular. And the KBL,[17] Marcos's party, had such a firm grip on the island that everyone and everything was calm, the peasantry complying, the bourgeoisie profiteering, and the political opposition either silent or under control. There was perhaps no great reason for the regime to exert an excessive surveillance, even though within a week of our arrival the Philippine Constabulary Commander paid me and my wife the visit of courtesy to which I have alluded above and thus welcomed us to the island.

Soon after, however, while in the market of the nearby town, I was approached by a drunkard who addressed me with insistence. What did I think of the political situation in his country? Eager to resist committing myself on this matter with someone I did not know, and unable to disengage myself, I felt I could at least learn something by returning the question. What did he think of it? I could not repeat here his exact words without being offensive. Suffice it to say that they were not entirely laudatory for the chief of state, and perhaps even less for his uxorial Minister of Human Settlements and Governor of Metro-Manila.[18]

When four men drifted from a nearby coffee-shop table to ours, I expected trouble rather than their echoing, albeit sotto voce, my imbibing and original interlocutor. "You are not afraid of being arrested in saying that of Marcos?" I asked. "Oh, no," someone replied, "this is martial law, Philippine style." As an outside observer, I could not help being struck by the paradox of a statement that affirmed and refuted itself, its own validity, as well as its very legitimacy in a modern—perhaps even postmodern in that it seemed to have been more parodic than ironic—display of disingenuous sophistry reminiscent of the lying Cretans.

This was indeed a curious phrase, which I was to hear again and again, from many different quarters, until January 1981, when Mr. Marcos saw fit to lift martial law, a strictly pro forma maneuver, meant almost exclusively for American consumption. The political life of the country remained as stonewalled as ever and "Now it is democracy, Philippine style" began its career as a cynical replacement. Prior to that, however, "martial law, Philippine style" was in fact a cliché that everyone employed incessantly, and sometimes for no apparent reason, as if it were—and it probably was—perfectly commonsensical and transparent to anyone. Even in the most rural *barangays,* where most people did not have any real command of English, they would utter that expression with the same eagerness as they would repeat, to the great merriment of their audience, this other English joke: "Family planning? No, family planting!" Clearly, if the two expressions were constantly repeated with an apparently inexhaustible appeal, they must have meant something to those who uttered them.

In effect, both phrases functioned as narratives. Perhaps they were rudimentary ones, but this did not diminish in any way their saliency. Nor did their obligatory brevity, owing to the locutors' general lack of competence in English, make them stylistically any less crisp. On the contrary, they could have functioned rigidly, that is, in a formulaic way. They could have been uttered as statements, but they were not susceptible of any variation, other than contextual ones, of course, and even that was very limited.

In addition, such formulae were used almost as quotes. They were in fact often preceded by the particle *kono* (i.e., "they say, one says, it is said that"). In using this particle, Cebuano-speakers disengage themselves and thrust on a third party the responsibility of what they portend only to report. Such a lack of assertiveness is perhaps in step with a value system that pretends to favor smooth interpersonal relations (Lynch 1973), but it was also a rejection. It allowed speakers to place a distance between themselves as speaking subjects and the reference of their discourse.

This distancing was also a political disengagement that justified and revealed, vis-à-vis the government and its programs, a marvelously militant passivity. Being militant, this disengagement was thus paradoxically a form of resistance to the government, and therefore it was, indeed, a form of engagement, one of *The Weapons of the Weak* that James C. Scott (1985) has discussed with such lucidity in the Malaysian context. To the use and abuse of force by the government, the Visayan peasants could at least resist with irony, which was precisely the (only) rhetorical device that they chose and/or that was left to them. The rhetorical device that was used was manifestly ironical, because no other avenue was open to them who were not convinced, but forced into obedience and acceptance. To family planning, the peasantry objected—and still does—as government interference in their private life, although they were unwilling or unable to state it. They never went as far as rejecting it openly. They never accepted it, either. And so, instead, they turned it into ridicule. As for martial law, need I say that they were never consulted?

In evoking (or is it invoking?) a "martial law, Philippine style," they did not have the power—nor, of course, the determination—to resist it.

But, once more, I should be prudent in this assertion. Even though it was not a joke, but an expression that was presented as a mere description, it was not—one would have guessed—a neutral, objective one. To start with, martial law is an interesting oxymoron, since it refers to the law of exception par excellence, that is, to the law that abolishes the law, to a sort of legal scuttling. Adding to it a style, be it a Filipino one, was a way of taking exception with the exception, without reverting to the status quo ante. It could only be a funny way of mellowing down the martial law and its rigors. But in so doing, it necessarily added the arbitrariness of a cultural flavor to the arbitrariness of the exception. And thus, turning to irony, the phrase at once underlined and ridiculed the imposed submission from which the speakers could not escape. Using English, a tool with which they feel at once familiar and clumsy (see Dumont [in press]), the *barangay* people did not miss the pun, something they had not invented but were just repeating. Turning martial law into derision, they defused it, and thus passively disengaged themselves from its grip.

Yet, at the same time it should be abundantly clear that it was also wishful thinking, a mere invocation whereby passive resistance remained short of active rebellion. In fact, this also reflected a deep depolitization of the rural masses, who, with a sense of powerless despair, tended to satisfy themselves with turning everything into mockery, that is with the *simulacra* of their liberation, since either they pretended not to submit to martial law or they denied its rigor and thus its very existence. And thus all happened as if violence as abuse of power had no, or little, grip on the peasants of Siquijor.

This was 1980.

Let me jump to the end of 1985 and to the very beginning of 1986, and allow me the license of a little detour through Great Britain, Cambodia, and Hollywood.

The Killing Fields was a historicopolitical film in which the British film-maker Roland Joffé presented his interpretation of two separate but related series of events, the American intervention in Cambodia in the early 1970s and the subsequent takeover of that country by Pol Pot's Khmer Rouges in 1975.[19] The two events were unmistakably distinct and yet clearly linked in *The Killing Fields*. The film condemned both events for their horrible and senseless violence. The depiction of such violence was so graphic that the film was rated "R." Part of its emotional appeal derived from the fact that the star of the film was a man who had no previous acting experience and who, in effect, played himself in it. Although a feature film, it aimed at truthfulness and at truth; and thus, without pretending to be a documentary, it had documentary qualities.

Any resemblance between the Cambodian tragedy and the turmoil that the Philippines had undergone in the mid-1980s does not seem a priori very compelling. Surely, the Philippines have suffered their share of violence. Popular uprisings and their repressions have run across the entire history of the archipelago. Still in the mid-1980s, the carryover of the Huk rebellion in central Luzon, of an Islamic nationalistic insurrection in Mindanao, and of a rural proletarian agitation in the Visayas—without mentioning the seeming itchiness of some segments of the military—tended to indicate that everything was not totally smooth in the islands. In addition, according to the Association against Detention and for Amnesty, or Selda, quoted in the *New York Times* on November 10, 1986 (p. 8, col. 3), "there [we]re 70,000 former political prisoners, 35,000 of whom suffered some form of torture" and "400 remaining political prisoners." At the risk of appearing cynical, I would have to say that, on the horror scale to which we have become accustomed, these numbers are almost low.

And yet, for anyone concerned with violence and its anthropological interpretation, there is a parallel that must be drawn, or at least sketched. Interpretive prudence commands it, since too many a Southeast Asian scholar was (should I say embarrassingly?) taken by surprise by the Khmer Rouges's violence. It ran so much against the grain of what any student of the area had learned and could normally expect from the Khmer ethos. History, with the might of its contingency, painfully shattered images of all-smiling, easygoing people, gentle in their manners and smooth in their social interactions. Somehow, Norodom Sihanouk's princely and debonnaire image too had been deposed. And thus, despite all that which separates Cambodia, historically and culturally, from the Philippines, it seems reasonable to wonder—which, of course, we have already begun doing—whether the latter's front of social ease, emphasis on smooth interpersonal relations, and the like does not, in fact, hide a latent, and thus far repressed, sense of violence that, given the proper context, could burst forth any moment.

But there is also, perhaps, an even more compelling reason to mention *The Killing Fields* when speaking of the recent past of the Philippines. During the brief but intense electoral campaign in preparation for the elections of February 7, 1986, which, in the end, were to bring about Ferdinand Marcos's fall, violence came to the very fore of actuality. I am not referring here to the real thing, neither to the "goons"[20]—

as they have come to be known—nor to their exactions, but to an altogether different machination, the manipulation of the idea of violence. This is something that was manipulated over and over again in the Philippines throughout the mid-1980s, with the intemperate speeches of Juan Ponce Enrile,[21] with the real and imaginary, at any rate rumored and repeated, threats of military coup at each absence of President Corazon Aquino, and with the sort of permanent suspense that it created in Filipino affairs. Even though I have no special wisdom that allows me to foresee the future (neither to anticipate the loyalty of the armed forces nor to predict a military coup), I cannot help but perceive the strength that the idea of violence—the idea of it and its ideology—possessed and continues to possess throughout the Philippines.

At any rate, it was certainly an innovation on the part of the Marcos's campaign management to bolster his political appeal by presenting *The Killing Fields* to the electoral masses. It was not shown as mere entertainment so as to capture the attention of an audience before the advent of a political speaker. It was meant by Marcos's political machine as an element of its propaganda, as demonstrated by the deliberate effort on the part of the KBL—Marcos's party—to give it a maximum of public exposure. Undoubtedly, this effort was facilitated by the fact that the film was recent, that it had a mass-audience appeal and that it had just arrived on the Philippine market.

In addition to these preconditions intrinsic to the film, there were others that were intrinsic to the Philippine situation itself, in the multiplicity of its local variants. For the sake of electoral efficiency, the film had to be shown almost everywhere and to almost everyone. The film was shown not only in Manila and other cities throughout the archipelago but also even in remote localities still without electricity or theaters where it was necessary to organize special runs on privately owned battery-operated videocassette recorders (VCRs).

This was, indeed, the case on Siquijor. On this impoverished island where electricity had barely arrived to the town centers, the political machine of the KBL party was in full swing. Its effort to deliver, by hook or by crook, as usual, impeccable electoral returns, in line with the wishes of Malacañang Palace,[22] included the screening of the film. This was made possible by militant VCR owners who, by virtue of being part of a relatively wealthy bourgeoisie, had evidently quite a bit at stake in the process. The wealthiest KBL members and the most active Marcos supporters certainly had something to lose were Marcos not returned to office, not the least of which included their grip on local power, their total dominance and control of the local economy, and their social glamor. They were also the ones who were the most likely to own a VCR. In effect, the local bourgeoisie being as entrepreneurial as could be expected, had already begun to exploit for commercial purpose the possibilities offered by the VCR. As early as 1984, one person ran a video show on large screen every Saturday night, using a generator-operated VCR. The passage from a commercial use to a political one was as easy and painless as the passage from recreational to commercial had been.

It may not be immediately obvious to everyone why or how such a film could possibly bring grist to Mr. Marcos's political mill. The convoluted reasoning behind this ran something like this.

The first part of the film, which focused on the American entanglement, was not considered to be more than preambular. Even though its importance was played down, it still made—just in case someone paid real attention to it—two astute but not so subtle points. On one hand, it (not so much the film itself, but its electoral manipulation) was directed against the Americans. They had practically forced the issue of an election in the Philippines and were reminded that their previous interference in the domestic affairs of another Southeast Asian country had been ill-fated. On the other hand, it could not fail to strike, for domestic consumption, an anti-American note, and thus a nationalistic one, destined to resound as an ideologically perfect chord in the ears of the Philippine electorate.

But the ideological pièce de résistance was to be found in the second part of the film as it depicted in full colors the gore and horrors of the communist takeover. Here the dialectic of electoral representation and fictional representation reached quasi-perfection. For, in a fabulous ellipse, it stated that given the Cambodian precedent, a vote for any form of opposition whatsoever was an endorsement of the communists, who— no doubt, and the entertained electorate was encouraged to entertain no doubt whatsoever about that—would do here what they had done there, and, therefore, Marcos and Marcos only (with the help of his party, the KBL) could save the Philippines from total disaster. The film, in this particular context, had the merit of brandishing a highly simplistic but immediately identifiable scarecrow. The alternatives could not be clearer. It was to be either the vague promises offered by the KBL or the suggested certitude of a bloodbath, that is either Marcos's bliss or the Reds' blitz. Of course, this was never specifically stated, since obviously the film made no such claim, but this was precisely the strength of this form of propaganda, its indirectness, to say nothing of its insidiousness.

In the end, I gather that it backfired, or at the very least that it remained too inefficient an argument to have swayed enough votes in the hoped for direction, since Mr. Marcos lost. In the *barangay*, the threat of violence had not been entirely lost. Perhaps the subtleties of the plot had been missed by many spectators who, because of their lack of education and political sophistication, knew precious little about Cambodia. But the fact that the film was manipulated for political ends and that it contained a veiled threat had not escaped their attention. Once more they reacted passively to the film, which had neither mobilized them politically nor demobilized them. Instead, they turned to another solution, one with which we are now familiar, namely, derision. And, indeed, as late as September 1986, when I revisited Siquijor briefly, one of the young men who had gathered together for the slaughtering, plucking, and further preparation of a chicken in my honor pointed at the bloodstain on the ground, at the scattered feathers and at the dead bird, invited me, laughingly, with an ample movement of the arm, to contemplate "the killing fields."

Of course, a complete study of violence would require an in-depth examination not only of the threats—that is, of the virtuality of violence—but also of its actuality, as the *barangay* peasants experience it. In addition to the all-too-human murders and assassinations, the supernatural world—which brings its toll of deaths, which causes sicknesses and accidents, which allows curses and bewitchings of all sorts—would have to be scrutinized.

In the ethnographic case that I have documented above with several examples, I believe I have shown that the mere threat of violence, "always already,"[23] stands beyond its mere virtuality, as it is itself a form and a use of violence. In that sense, threat is necessarily a use (and more often than not, an abuse) of force, because it is always given, that is imposed from a political above to a political below, and because it contrasts immediately with the persuasion to which a discussion between equals could pretend.

If martial law, birth control, and the political manipulation of *The Killing Fields* constituted, in the experience of the Visayan peasants, different—if not disparate—threats made by "the government," all three also represented instances of violence. Violence, in this case, was not seen as the exercise of force, but as its abuse. And it was experienced as an abuse not so much for any intrinsic quality that it might have—since, in a real but circular way, each activity was well within the law—but because the legitimacy of the power from which it emanated had begun to wane. Interestingly, threats necessarily index the weaknesses of a present

and refer to the promise of a future. Martial law was decreed in order
to end a political turmoil, and promised a "new society" that the KBL
was to deliver. Family planning was a response to a population explosion
and was to be a solution to overpopulation and poverty. And the screening of *The Killing Fields* indicated a political danger and forewarned of
total destruction. But if threats also entail the carrot as well as the stick,
they cannot convince. A decree is not an argument.

Confronted with such violence, the Visayan peasants responded like
most peasants do, that is, neither with enthusiasm nor with rebellion but
with increased passivity, cynicisms, and witticisms included. And this
may be why, at least in the *barangay* I know best, those who a few months
before could speak of "Our beloved President Marcos" could, as early
as September 1986, and without batting an eye, call upon the smiles of
"Our President Cory." And yet, in the same breath, the same people, as
depoliticized as ever, could answer my "What has changed since my last
visit?" with a smile and these words: "Sigi gihapon, pinobre tanan" (it
goes on, we're still poor).

In order to analyze the distinctive character of violence in a specific
Philippine province, I have carefully avoided what I would like to call
the "frontal attack" method. If I have not produced a mugshot imagery,
if I have not exhibited the dreadful evidence of battered or mutilated
bodies, if I have not focused on the lamentable results of violence, it is
because these images—powerful as they might be on occasion—beg for
a systematically deferred interpretation of what they illustrate. Instead
of looking deliberately for actual instances of conflicts and violence, I
have chosen to draw from my daily experiences on the island of Siquijor.
The notes and memories that I have kept of the encounter were sufficient, I believe, to document the general social, historical, and cultural
context in which conflicts and its resolutions—violent or not—emerge.

Following the dominant Visayan mode of behavior, I have thus preferred to be indirect in my treatment of violence, and to focus on its setting, that is, on the general conditions for its genesis. On one hand, I
have presented the negations and narrations whereby violence presents
itself as a pervasive condition of existence on the island. On the other
hand, I have documented the experience that the islanders have acquired of an idea of political violence, its trace—a mental scar—as they
carry it in their heads.

Ideas and deeds exist only in dialectical relationship. So does violence,
which is a habitus in the sense that Bourdieu (1977:passim) gave to this
phrase, at once structured and structuring: structured because the idea

of violence results from historical events, stored as the memory of past deeds, of past encounters, of past frustrations; and structuring because the idea of violence informs human actions, determines the acceptability, even the banality of violence, if not the ability to erase the scandal of its occurrence. A solid grasp on current events and the institutional analysis of sociopolitical structures are, indeed, necessary to explain, or better to interpret, the occurrence of violence. Yet, as the case of Siquijor illustrates, this remains insufficient because violence is represented, manifested, and manipulated on many different levels and in many different arenas, and because violence is informed and con-structed by a variety of factors that transcend the hic et nunc of its occurrence.

ACKNOWLEDGMENTS

Earlier versions of the two main parts of this chapter were written independently and presented at two different symposia organized by Dr. Carolyn Nordstrom on the theme of communal violence: in December 1986 in Philadelphia, Pennsylvania, at the 85th Annual Meetings of the American Anthropological Association and in Phoenix, Arizona, at the 87th Annual Meetings of that association.

Field research in the Philippines was made possible in 1979 by a Summer Grant from the Graduate School Research Fund of the University of Washington (Seattle) and in 1980/81 by a Fulbright-Hayes Research Fellowship administered by the Philippine-American Education Foundation (Manila), while I was affiliated with the Department of Sociology and Anthropology, Silliman University (Dumaguete) and with the Cebuano Studies Center, University of San Carlos (Cebu City). Ethnohistorical research in the archives of Spain, the Vatican, and the Philippines was supported in 1982/83 by two consecutive grants respectively from the Social Science Research Council and from the Spanish-American Friendship Treaty as well as by a leave of absence with pay from the University of Washington. I revisited the Philippines, all too briefly to my taste, in the summers of 1983 and 1986 to attend conferences organized by the Joint Committee on Southeast Asia of the Social Science Research Council. Substantial revisions to these papers were made during 1987/ 88, while I was a member of the School of Social Science at the Institute for Advanced Study in Princeton, New Jersey, under a fellowship from the National Endowment for the Humanities. To all these institutions, I express my gratitude.

Finally, I wish to thank Jean Comaroff, Michael Cullinane, E. Valentine Daniel, Elinor Dumont, Reynaldo C. Ileto, Charles F. Keyes,

Dorinne Kondo, JoAnn Martin, Resil B. Mojares, Carolyn Nordstrom, Sally A. Ness, and Edgar V. Winans for their critical comments.

NOTES

1. Jamin's words flow better of course in the original, which reads as follows: "L'hétérogénéité des phénomènes auxquels se rapporte la notion de violence suffit à démontrer qu'elle n'est pas un concept sociologiquement opératoire; son caractère protéiforme et polysémique la rend presque indéfinissable."

2. Returning from several years as a political expatriate in the United States, Benigno "Ninoy" Aquino, Jr., an opposition leader, was murdered on August 21, 1983 while under the "protection" of government security personnel, as he stepped down from the plane that had brought him back to Manila International Airport. This incident marked the beginning of a crisis that precipitated the end of the Marcos regime in February 1986. It also allowed against all odds for the coming to power of "Ninoy"'s charismatic widow, Corazon Aquino, as President of the Republic of the Philippines.

3. Magellan never completed the first navigation of the globe. He let himself be dragged into a local conflict between Humabon, who ruled on the island of Cebu—he converted quickly to Christianity and furthermore had recognized the suzerainty of the Spanish king—and his enemy Lapu-Lapu, who ruled on the neighboring island of Mactan. Magellan and a number of his companions died in the ensuing engagement.

4. Muslim piracy and the pillaging of coastal towns under Spanish control was particularly active during the eighteenth to nineteenth century. On this topic, the interested reader could profitably consult Warren (1981).

5. In 1744, on the island of Bohol in the central Visayas, a Spanish friar refused to bury a police constable on consecrated ground. His brother, Francisco Dagohoy, led against the Spaniards a rebellion that was to give Bohol a practically independent regime until 1829. Unfortunately, there is, to my knowledge, no book-length treatment of the Dagohoy rebellion.

6. The nationalist revolt that broke out in August 1896 marks the beginning of the Philippine armed struggle against Spain's rule.

7. In the course of World War II, the Japanese occupied Manila as early as January 2, 1942. General MacArthur landed on the island of Leyte place on October 20, 1944, but fighting in the Philippines went on until the surrender of Japan on September 22, 1945 (Agoncillo 1965; Hartendorp 1967).

8. *Huk* is an abbreviation of *Hukbalahap*, itself an abbreviation of the Tagalog phrase, *Hukbong Bayan Laban sa Hapon* (People's Anti-Japanese Army). Founded in 1942, it was a guerrilla force. In 1946, it was renamed *Hukbong Mapagpalaya ng Bayan* (People's Liberation Army). The best source on this topic is Kerkvliet (1977).

9. The New People's Army (NPA) is a Marxist-Leninist revolutionary guerrilla movement operating in the northern Philippines (mainly Luzon, but also

some of the Visayas; Negros, for instance). On the topic of Philippine insurgency, the interested reader may wish to consult Kessler (1989).

10. The Moro National Liberation Front (MNLF) created in 1969 is essentially a Muslim armed movement operating in the southern Philippines (Mindanao, Sulu, and Palawan) and reacting to the Christian encroachment of territories traditionally held by Muslims.

11. In a well-known but now often decried study of Philippine values originally written in 1960, Lynch was the first to identify "smoothness of interpersonal relations (or SIR)." He defined it in the following way (1984:31):

> SIR may be defined as a facility at getting along with others in such a way as to avoid outward signs of conflict: glum or sour looks, harsh words, open disagreement, or physical violence. It connotes the smile, the friendly lift of the eyebrow, the pat on the back, the squeeze of the arm, the word of praise or friendly concern. It means being agreeable, even under difficult circumstances, and of keeping quiet or out of sight when discretion passes the word. It means a sensitivity to what other people feel at any given moment, and a willingness and ability to change tack (if not direction) to catch the lightest favoring breeze.

12. Philippine municipalities are made up of several *barangay* or dispersed villages and one *poblacion,* designated as "town" in the local English usage.

13. On the issue of language, see my forthcoming article (Dumont in press).

14. The supplement is but the trace of the operation of *differance* (see Derrida 1973, passim).

15. On Visayan souls, see Dumont (1987).

16. In the administrative lingo of the Philippines, province-islands are islands that are large enough to have the status of a province and small enough to constitute only one province. Among the Visayas, Siquijor, Bohol, and Cebu are province-islands, but not Negros, which is divided into two provinces: Negros Occidental and Negros Oriental. Siquijor was inaugurated as a province on January 8, 1972.

17. The Declaration of Martial Law on September 21, 1972 had brought political life to a halt. Shortly before the election of April 7, 1978, Marcos organized his own political grouping, the *Kilusang Bagong Lipunan* (KBL), or in Tagalog, lit. new society movement.

18. Imelda Romualdez Marcos was appointed Governor of the newly created Metro Manila Region on November 6, 1975. By the autumn of 1978, she cumulated the latter function with the newly created cabinet post of Minister of Human Settlements.

19. King of Cambodia from 1941 to 1955, head of state from 1960 to 1970, Prince Norodom Sihanouk was deposed by the pro-American Premier Lon Nol and formed a government in exile in Beijing, after which war raged between the Lon Nol forces and Pol Pot's Khmer Rouges, who captured Phnom Penh on April 17, 1975. Over a million people were to lose their lives in executions and enforced hardships under Pol Pot's regime.

20. Goon squads, presumably under unacknowledged yet precise orders, carried out a number of political assassinations of a number of opponents to the

regime in addition to creating a general sentiment of physical insecurity for political dissenters.

21. Juan Ponce Enrile was for years Marcos's Defense Secretary. A staged attempt against his life had been the pretext chosen by Marcos to declare martial law on September 21, 1972. Enrile's defection on February 22, 1986 played a crucial role in the collapse of the Marcos regime and in the installation of Ms. Aquino on February 25, 1986, in whose cabinet he kept his post as Defense Secretary until November 23, 1986 in the aftermath of a failed coup that he allegedly engineered. On August 28, 1987 a military rebellion led by one of Enrile's protégés, Colonel Gregorio B. ("Gringo") Honasan, erupted and was crushed the next day. Among the now enormous albeit uneven literature that relates the February 1986 events in the Philippines, I have found the account given by Fenton (1986) lucidly written and particularly helpful.

22. In Manila, Malacañang Palace is the official residence of the head of state.

23. I borrow freely this "always already" from Derrida (1977, passim).

REFERENCES

Agoncillo, Teodoro A.
  1965   *The Fateful Years: Japan's Adventures in the Philippines, 1941–45*, 2 vols. Quezon City: R. P. Garcia Publishing Company.
Bourdieu, Pierre
  1977   *Outline of a Theory of Practice*. Trans. R. Nice. Cambridge and London: Cambridge University Press.
Derrida, Jacques
  1973   *Speech and Phenomena*. Trans. D. Allison. Evanston, Ill.: Northwestern University Press.
  1977   *Writing and Difference*. Trans. A. Bass. Chicago: The University of Chicago Press.
Dumont, Jean-Paul
  1987   "A Sheaf of Souls: Siquijor Reinterpretations." Paper presented at the Symposium on Soul in East and Southeast Asian Folk Religions, 39th Annual Meetings of the Association for Asian Studies in Boston, Mass., April 10–12, 1987.
  In press "Language and Learning in a Visayan Rural Community." In *Reshaping Local Worlds: Formal Education and Cultural Change in Rural Southeast Asia*. C. F. Keyes, J. Keyes, and N. Donnelly, eds. New Haven: Yale University, Southeast Asia Studies.
Fenton, James
  1986   "The Snap Revolution," *Granta* 18:33–169.
Hartendorp, A. V. H.
  1967   *The Japanese Occupation of the Philippines*, 2 vols. Manila: Bookmark.
Jamin, Jean
  1984   "Une ethnographie de la violence est-elle possible?" *Etudes Rurales* 95–96:16–21.

Kerkvliet, Benedict J.
1977   *The Huk Rebellion: A Study of Peasant Revolt in the Philippines.* Berkeley, Los Angeles, London: University of California Press.
Kessler, Richard J.
1989   *Rebellion and Repression in the Philippines.* New Haven and London: Yale University Press.
Lynch, Frank
1973   "Social Acceptance Reconsidered." In *Four Readings on Philippine Values,* F. Lynch and A. de Guzman, eds., IPC Papers no. 2, 4th ed., revised and enlarged, pp. 1–68. Quezon City: Ateneo de Manila University Press.
1984   "Social Acceptance Reconsidered." In *Philippine Society and the Individual: Selected Essays of Frank Lynch, 1949–1976,* A. A. Yengoyan and P. Q. Makil, eds., Michigan Papers on South and Southeast Asia, no. 24, pp. 23–91. Ann Arbor: The University of Michigan, Center for South and Southeast Asian Studies.
Scott, James C.
1985   *Weapons of the Weak: Everyday Forms of Peasant Resistance.* New Haven and London: Yale University Press.
Warren, James Francis
1981   *The Sulu Zone, 1768–1898: The Dynamics of External Trade, Slavery, and Ethnicity in the Transformation of a Southeast Asian Maritime State.* Singapore: Singapore University Press.

EIGHT

Time and Irony in
Manila Squatter Movements

Philip C. Parnell

Students of oppression and resistance may enrich their study through awareness of their own expectations of how conflicts can and should develop. This is a necessary step in the ethnography of resistance, for oppression can exist in the culturally grounded perceptual frameworks of those who view and assess the values of resistance. These frameworks, or structures of evaluation, have a multitude of components, but one of their primary elements is time. For example, the relationship between the means and ends of resistance has a temporal component derived from the perception of resistors. Resistors use time to organize their actions. If the analysis of resistance uses temporal frameworks that differ from those of resistors, however, the relationship between the means and ends of resistance may be obscured, or appear perverse. The analyst could be like the play-goer who leaves the theater at intermission, and then criticizes the playwright for constructing a lousy ending.

To understand the ways in which time gives meaning to the actions of resistors, outsiders—as analysts—need to shake loose the bonds of their own temporal frameworks and use time as resistors use it. Toward that end, this chapter discusses a list of suggestions for studying oppression and resistance, with a focus on finding the role of time. The list is a product of the evolution of my own understanding of how resistors in another culture, in this case squatters in Metropolitan Manila, the Philippines, view the goals and strategies of their reform movement. The list and its explication may be of value to other researchers. Where I originally saw failure in the urban-poor reform movement, I can now see accomplishments, and a practical wisdom born of challenging the problems of life and poverty in Manila.

Over a period of eleven months during 1987/88, I lived among leaders of the reform movement in a large squatter settlement known as Commonwealth, with approximately 100,000 inhabitants and 1,100 acres. The squatters were instigating governmental projects to bring land and housing to urban-poor residents of Manila; and, within the projects, they were attempting to negotiate a new partnership between squatters and governmental agencies in the reconstruction of urban-poor settlements. Yet, as squatters argued their version of planned change, their actions appeared to bring together and into confrontation the myriad forces that opposed and sought to prevent land and housing reform. Ironically, forces of disorganization seemed to be growing daily as a result of the movement by the poor to organize urban change. It was also possible that I was, through continued research, increasing my knowledge of the depth of disorganization that characterized relationships among squatters and between squatters and governmental organizations.

Disorganization also appeared to be imminent elsewhere within Philippine politics and society. Reports of impending coup attempts against Corazon Aquino, President of the Philippines, were frequent, as were "red alerts." (The communist New People's Army is mounting an attack on Manila!) National and metropolitan politicians were slicing up their parties and forming new coalitions, and squatter organizations were, similarly, developing new oppositions and alliances among themselves. So many groups were involved in the shifting field of conflicts over the use of land in Commonwealth that I found it difficult to imagine how the squatters and their allies in the Aquino government and the Catholic Church (mostly Jesuit organizations were involved in the reform movement) could find time to parcel out settlement land and begin the task of installing sewers and creating infrastructures for the new urban-poor development. Then, in the midst of confusion born of too much organization, the reform movement expanded. It moved into another large settlement near Commonwealth (Payatas Estate, with 3,296 acres), and then among the poor along the main thoroughfare that ran through Commonwealth, settlement by settlement toward the heart of the Philippine capital.

Sama Sama, the largest squatter organization in Commonwealth, had been a catalyst for formation of a coalition of governmental housing and land agencies to plan and guide urban land reform. Women residents

of Commonwealth represent the leadership and most of the membership of Sama Sama, which claims 18,000 member families. Sama Sama,
working with governmental agencies, constructed a unique approach to
development of Commonwealth, one in which the government and
Sama Sama were equal partners in planning and implementing the project. However, as the project in Commonwealth was supposed to be proceeding, I frequently saw the heads of housing agencies visiting the new
squatter settlements that Sama Sama was beginning to organize. I wondered how the agencies, so short of time and resources to create change,
could afford to expand their involvement into new settlements and additional projects.

Plans for reform grew astronomically, ending with the goal suggested
by Sama Sama and adopted by federal housing agencies to move all of
Metropolitan Manila's approximately three million squatters across the
street from Commonwealth, where the Philippine Congress was located.
If completed, this massive city of the poor would surround the Congress.
Although the political symbolism of the housing plan was elegant, some
members of Congress responded by mounting an effort to relocate the
Congress on another side of the city.

My research had begun in August 1987, and through December, I
spent most of my time conducting interviews in the settlement and at-
tending meetings between Sama Sama and governmental organizations
(the National Housing and Urban Development Coordinating Council,
the Housing and Land Use Regulatory Board, the Department of Public
Works and Highways, the President's Commission on the Urban Poor,
and other development agencies). I followed the growth of Sama Sama
and its intensifying conflicts with other squatter groups who opposed
Sama Sama's approach to reform. These conflicts led me into the study
of Sama Sama's formidable opponents within the settlement. Largest
among these were the multitentacled Philippine land syndicates. The
syndicates have their hands in many enterprises, including mining, government, law, and import businesses, but within squatter settlements
they are landlords over large regions of the poor.

The largest land syndicates in the Philippines operate within Commonwealth and Payatas Estate. They are the most successful groups in
providing land and security to the urban poor. All syndicate heads claim
to be heirs to Spanish land titles, which the United States government
decided to honor in 1902. In practice, neither the government nor federal courts now recognize any Spanish heir as the owner of land in the
region. However, the inheritance cases are still under appeal. The alleged heirs use court case documents to convince the squatters they own

the land. As long as the legal cases are in progress, syndicate leaders can obtain injunctions against government-based or private efforts at demolition of homes on the land.

The syndicates provide land and sometimes homes to squatters newly arrived in Manila from the countryside or other cities, and to those whose homes have been demolished in other settlements. They are the most effective groups in the Philippines in providing shelter to the urban poor. They also provide shelter to military, police, lawyers, and politicians who, at times, have used influence and arms to protect homes on syndicate land from demolition. Squatters and syndicate friends and allies, once settled, help the syndicates maintain control over their land. Syndicate leaders profit from fees paid by squatter families, and some build relatively elaborate homes on the land, which they sell for profits higher than those provided by shanties. Syndicates attempt to strike bargains with the government, at times seeking more valuable commercial property owned by the government in exchange for the larger plots occupied by squatters. Although many squatters find that the syndicates provide them with services the government has not been able to provide, the syndicates appear to be primarily businesses rather than political movements.

During the first stages of my research I had attended a meeting called by one of the syndicate's enterprising corporate satellites. The gathering was between the satellite, which sold prefabricated concrete housing from Korea (cleverly called the Cory House; President Aquino is affectionately called "Cory"), a few leaders of Sama Sama, and leaders of a small settlement (about 150 houses) in Payatas Estate. Residents of the small settlement had recently resisted demolition of their homes by a real estate developer, and Sama Sama had found a new ally by joining them at their barricades. The meeting, which was held in an office building in a fashionable section of Metropolitan Manila, had ostensibly been called in response to their problems. During the discussion, the importers attempted to sell Sama Sama the idea of using Cory Houses in the development of their settlement. The idea was ludicrous, for if there is anything Manila does not lack it is concrete, and Sama Sama interpreted the suggestion as a revelation and warning that syndicates wanted a piece of the reform movement.

In addition to controlling much of the land in the Commonwealth region that the Aquino government had set aside for Sama Sama's development project, the syndicates were expanding their control over new portions of urban regions near Commonwealth. The government appeared to have limited knowledge of the syndicates and their well-placed connections. The President's Commission on the Urban Poor and I separately began to study the syndicates. Two actions that affected Commonwealth as a result of governmental study were the stationing of a contingent of Philippine Marines on land near Commonwealth and a request from housing authorities that President Aquino form a blue-ribbon military unit to demolish homes on syndicate-controlled land.

At about the same time, in the spring of 1988, several of the highest ranking leaders of the Philippine Communist Party and its military arm, the New People's Army (NPA), were arrested in a housing development that bordered Commonwealth. Then, in July 1988, governmental military forces raided what they claimed were over twenty NPA safehouses in a settlement area that Sama Sama represented, although without knowledge of an NPA presence. Ironically, only a few months earlier, the head of a conservative syndicate who claimed loyalty to the United States had told me that she controlled the same settlement area. Sama Sama's community organizers were embarrassed by the raid. For a group like Sama Sama, identification with communist forces can endanger governmental and church-based alliances.

Manila is a city of rumors (some college students form rumor brigades). Sama Sama's daily attempts to expand its alliances among squatter organizations in Commonwealth and nearby regions, and within governmental agencies, generated a constant flow of new information about urban-poor politics. The squatters, with new discoveries about their settlements, generated speculation and theories about urban-poor organizations and alliances. One of the more interesting explanations suggested to me by veterans of battles for low-cost housing was that land syndicates were actually being supported by the Aquino government. According to this theory, the dense settlements controlled by anticommunist syndicates would serve as a buffer to attack from the southern Luzon brigades of the NPA. The syndicates certainly had allies in the government, from judges to chiefs of police. I attended the birthday party of one of the two most powerful and visible syndicate leaders and found myself consuming several large roasted pigs with municipal prosecutors, heads of Veterans of Foreign Wars organizations, police, lawyers, and other syndicate leaders.

When I heard this rationale for the relatively unchallenged growth of land syndicates, I was eager to find an explanation for the contradictions that were proliferating within my knowledge of squatter organizations. Although the plan appeared a bit ludicrous—it united the politically plural squatters of Commonwealth and Payatas Estate, liberal leaders in the Catholic Church, and land syndicates in a master plan to resist the storming of Manila—I considered it seriously. Why else were syndicates tunneling through mountainsides near Payatas Estate (they said in search of gold)? Why did the syndicates claim alliance with the United States? Why were they so successful at using the legal system to maintain control over land they did not legally own, and which others so desperately wanted? How were they able to make so many allies among politicized squatters in the syndicate struggle against the Aquino government to gain control over land and the allegiances of millions of urban poor? Were the syndicates oppressors, or leaders of a form of squatter resistance against the government's failure in land reform?

After January 1988, as my research on Sama Sama, the land reform movement, and the Syndicates continued, each interview I conducted encouraged me to look further for a larger system into which the interweaving dynamics of conflicts and disputes over land reform would fit. At the same time, I realized that I was failing in my own attempts to generate plausible hypotheses that could straighten out the twisting and erratic routes Sama Sama and its government allies appeared to be following to reach the destination of land reform. I knew of studies of the world system of trade and resource capture that maintained Third World poverty. Many of the dynamics outlined for Latin American squatter settlements, which are part of such a system (Castells 1983) appeared to apply to the Philippines and the lives of its urban poor.

However, the leaders of Sama Sama were also aware of the same systems, and they were not pessimistic about the chances for their success in achieving ownership of land and houses. They presented their project to the larger public as a prototype for urban land reform. As Philippine senators were lamenting the values of Filipinos who could not mount development miracles like other Southeast Asian nations (Taiwan, South Korea, and emerging Thailand), my poor Philippine neighbors were optimistically constructing change. However, at that point, to me, the members of Sama Sama and their allies in government were part of expanding disputes that appeared petty in relation to the larger goal of bringing affordable land and housing to the urban poor. My impressions were shared by some Philippine politicians who argued that urban-poor squabbles and resistance were barriers to national economic development.

I was concerned about the difference between my perspective and that of Sama Sama. Members of Sama Sama appeared to be astute students of American culture, and they frequently dropped hints about their opinions of my views. Most often they talked to me about the nature of time, something I would come to understand much later. As we talked about the Commonwealth housing project, or discussed plans for meetings in the settlement or at governmental agencies, I often asked "When?" and rarely received a clear answer or one that did not change several times. Although the women of Sama Sama had dedicated their lives to the future, they maintained a future that appeared to be amorphous. To teach me about time, leaders of Sama Sama sent me to a new schoolhouse that the metropolitan government had constructed and asked me to find the toilets. There were none. They told me about "Cubeta (toilet) City," a settlement where the National Housing Authority had constructed sewers and placed toilets for squatter houses, but where the houses were never built. The head of a government agency suggested I go to the new schoolhouse to find out if there was any electricity. There was none. I proffered a contribution toward toilets and electricity. They refused my offer. I seemed to be running senseless errands that, through my willingness to do them, appeared meaningful.

Sama Sama took me to almost weekly meetings with governmental and private development agencies where we viewed maps, project blueprints, and aerial photographs of Commonwealth. After the meetings, during our long rides back to Commonwealth, and at many other times when we gathered in the settlement, members of Sama Sama asked my advice on their conflicts with other groups. I most often suggested that they negotiate, the same advice that President Aquino's Commission on the Urban Poor frequently gave to Sama Sama and other squatter organizations. The squatter leaders considered negotiating with their opponents in the settlement, even discussed it at leadership meetings, but always decided against it. The increasing conflicts and disputes led me to believe that, even if the Aquino government found money to fund reform in Commonwealth and Payatas Estate, and it seemed the funds would never appear, implementation would be impossible, if not bloody. I envisioned a community that, through its reform project, would institutionalize the divisions and conflicts among Sama Sama, the land syndicates, and the many squatter groups that opposed its plan for reform. At the worst of times, I considered the harm that could visit the many women of Sama Sama who were dedicating their lives to reform, and I wondered if their vision of Commonwealth merited the dangers that were brewing.

After months of uneasy nights, and numerous disappointing mornings when the only changes in the settlement seemed to be in the moods of my neighbors, the messages Sama Sama conveyed to me through their stories began to weaken the filters of my perception. They had repeatedly stated that the government could not build houses for the poor that the poor would care to own. However, the fact that Sama Sama had spent so much time enlisting government support and participation in their housing project had clouded this message for me. I thought that Sama Sama was placing new trust in the Aquino government, but I was wrong. Through holding fast to Sama Sama's basic assumption that the use of potentially successful means for creating housing for the poor and government planning of housing projects had always been incompatible, I began to see a plan that brought new meaning to the actions and optimistic persistence of Sama Sama in a project that had appeared to contradict the knowledge of the urban poor.

The Sama Sama, the blueprints and plans of development agencies and firms were part of a fiction that Sama Sama helped the government weave and embellish. Municipal planners and politicians dreamed of constructing large-scale communities to be inhabited by millions of urban poor, they imagined projects to serve as prototypes for Southeast Asia, and they sought the creation of military garrisons to confront their opponents. For those who think of cities as projects completed, or in terms of ends rather than processes, such fantasies represent the construction of success.

In contrast, the women of Sama Sama were involved in the construction of time. They sought time to build homes that would be expressions of their lives. To accomplish this, they needed to aid the government in conceptualizing a housing project that appealed to values held in development bureaucracies, and they had to prevent the government from implementing its project. The end of Sama Sama's reform movement was the construction of time to build their own community.

Within this goal of grassroots development, Sama Sama also sought a heterogeneous rather than homogeneous community. Governmental projects for the poor, in the planning stages and under the Aquino government, tended to identify clients as the lower strata of the urban poor. However, a mixed community of the employed and unemployed, the connected and the powerless, is more beneficial to the poor. As residents network within the heterogeneous community through development of friendships, families extended through religious godparenthood, and voluntary associations, they develop ties that carry knowledge about and access to jobs and other economic opportunities and strategies. Development projects exclusively for the poor tend to have a leveling effect on economic opportunity. They institutionalize poverty.

That an abundance of time—years rather than moments—could even be constructed; and that such amounts of time could be constructed rather than passed, used, saved, wasted, or done, was a subtle revelation that changed my perspective on Commonwealth. When I met with other Americans conducting research in Manila, we commented on the poor quality of life there: the pollution, crowding, corruption, traffic, and fortress mentality that was pervasive across businesses, from restaurants to banks. Manila seemed to be moving along the pessimistic evolutionary line presented in movies—*Blade Runner, Brazil*—in which the marginal and formerly successful in the urban economy found symbiosis through chaos. Urban deterioration was a force so immense that no group could hope to control it. Eventually I realized that the women of Sama Sama did not seek to be a part of the overburdened city, but planned to change it. Success within the city as it existed was Sama Sama's primary foe.

The shared temporal framework of the women of Sama Sama was derived from the common experiences of change in communities where they lived, rather than from the bureaucratic context of project planning. Through recognizing that framework I was able to use it in my analysis of Sama Sama's conflicts and other actions. From this experience, in which I was perhaps similar to an alcoholic who eventually recognizes that he is drinking, I have developed a brief list of suggestions for studying oppression and resistance. The list is primarily for the Western reader. It is possible that researchers who follow some of my suggestions will stumble on components of the perceptual frameworks of resistors. I explain the following suggestions through examples drawn from the actions of Sama Sama:

> Don't find fault, don't place blame;
> Look for the slowest resistors;
> Look for resistors resisting each other.
> That is redundant resistance, and could be very effective;
> If the government is intervening on behalf of resistors, it could be
>   co-opted, but only if its intervention fails;
> Compare the activities in which resistors involve you, and the way they
>   involve you, with the activities they provide the oppressors.

DON'T FIND FAULT, DON'T PLACE BLAME

The goals people seek through getting involved in conflicts vary across cultures. For example, a common goal of Americans as they solve problems is to place blame. Placing blame is sometimes confused with identifying the source of a problem. Although finding sources of problems can be an inherently valuable exercise, many of us who look for sources don't know what to do with them once we think we have found them. This is especially true of complex, dynamic sources of problems, such as the world market system or governments enmired in layers of personalism.

Placing blame, affixing guilt, and enacting rituals that impose negative identities on the guilty are activities of the U.S. legal system, which, to date, has not met with success in controlling what it identifies as social problems. Felstiner et al. (1980–1981) have argued that the processes of naming, blaming, and claiming are common components of dispute settlement in the United States. U.S.-based adjudication is today primarily a process for locating guilt and punishing the guilty. We generally do not use specialized legal institutions to eliminate problems through constructing change.

The members of Sama Sama provide a good example of the benefits of moving beyond placing blame. They identify the National Housing Authority (NHA), as it existed under the presidency of Ferdinand Marcos, as responsible for the Philippine government's failure to provide affordable and desirable housing for the poor. Sama Sama cites two major shortcomings of the NHA: (1) it completed few projects and (2) its low-cost housing projects, once completed, were too expensive for the poor.

Sama Sama, in its negotiations for land and a housing project with the National Housing and Urban Development Coordinating Council (HUDCC, a new housing agency established by the Aquino government) insisted on excluding NHA from the development of Commonwealth. The NHA was seeking to become self-supporting through its housing projects—the development of one squatter settlement would pay for the development of the next through squatter purchase of land and homes. This mission, coupled with the fact that many squatters had no reliable source of income or collateral, promised to once again hinder NHA's success in providing affordable housing to the poor.

But placing the blame for past housing failures on NHA, and excluding it from the Commonwealth project, was only Sama Sama's first step in controlling the housing bureaucracy. Personalistic Philippine governmental bureaucracies are infused with the entrepreneurial spirit. In relation to housing, it is apparent that Philippine bureaucracies do not now recognize an overarching policy; rather, they compete with each other. In addition, during the first years of the Aquino government, reorganization of housing bureaucracies was still in a state of flux. Jockeying for domains among them was intensified by the uncertainty of funding from the World Bank and other sources of aid.

Sama Sama moved beyond creation of a culprit identity for NHA by generating work for the agency in nearby Payatas Estate. With the help of HUDCC and the Catholic Church, Sama Sama carved a coalition out of the numerous independent squatter groups in Payatas Estate, and then led these organizations in a lobbying effort to convince the Aquino government to develop a housing project in this neighboring settlement. Following the suggestions of Sama Sama, HUDCC initiated that project in the spring of 1988. HUDCC placed NHA in charge of developing Payatas Estate. Sama Sama and its sponsors then suggested that NHA should attempt to move all of Metropolitan Manila's squatters to Payatas Estate.

Sama Sama, through forming a coalition among squatter organizations in Payatas Estate and, through its constant lobbying efforts to speed NHA's development of that area, was able to provide NHA with the greater involvement in urban reform projects that it sought, while at the same time securing NHA's exclusion from the Commonwealth project. Sama Sama went beyond placing blame on NHA for prior housing failures, created a successful diversion for NHA's attention, and, in Payatas Estate, provided the frequently criticized agency with an opportunity to clear its name.

Bringing NHA under control was, however, only one of Sama Sama's political challenges. The women who formed the leadership of Sama Sama supported President Aquino. They kept vigil over ballot boxes during the election, which led to Aquino's political triumph, and they had been active participants in the "People Power" revolution of 1986, which led to Ferdinand Marcos's flight to Hawaii. Sama Sama's sponsors within the Catholic Church also supported Aquino. This created a political dilemma.

Sama Sama's members knew that Aquino needed to make progress on land reform and squatter issues in order to maintain political support from both allies and opponents of squatters, as well as to prevent defections by squatters to those who were mounting violent challenges to her government. At the same time, members of Sama Sama knew from many previous lessons that the government could not construct housing for the poor, or poor communities. Sama Sama therefore needed to (1) construct time that was needed for the squatters of Commonwealth to continue building their homes and an infrastructure for the settlement, a task that would involve squatter labor and include the development of community-based jobs for squatters and (2) aid the Aquino government in the development of its own housing project for the settlement without allowing the government to implement the project. This dilemma leads to the next suggestion for studying resistance.

LOOK FOR THE SLOWEST RESISTORS

Rapid change in settlements can be detrimental to their future survival. Yet, in cities, change often seems to occur swiftly, through either growth or deterioration. In the West, many houses are constructed and completed as total operating units within a few months. Massive urban renewal is plotted for completion over the short period of a few years. Yet, if the seeds of oppression lie within the political and economic structures and systems of a nation and its ties to more powerful nations, removal of today's oppressors may not remove oppression. Certainly, at times, there are good reasons to desire the coupling of speed and resistance. Some harm and danger were part of everyday life in Commonwealth. Degrees of malnutrition, poor sanitation, and the tensions and disappointments of poverty and unemployment are a daily part of settlement life.

The urban poor, talking about change, offer the example of rural land reform in which tenant farmers are able to buy land. They purchase the land, but then must, on their own, find the means and knowledge to make it productive. They must purchase imported fertilizer and imported machines and use imported agricultural technology. They can afford none of these, and so are forced to sell their land and, once again, become tenant farmers. Thus the farmers, after much effort, have lost two battles rather than one.

Successful farmers, in contrast, first become self-sufficient through learning to use the resources that their own environment provides to render the land productive. They seek control of the land only after constructing a symbiotic relationship with it. In this way, they avoid moving from one uncontrollable relationship of dependence to another.

Farmers, however, face another challenge. Once they learn how to use the land and gain control over it, they must find ways to prevent others from taking it away. Like the successful farmer, the women of Sama Sama knew how to construct a community from scratch through materials that become available over time, but they also needed to develop strategies to maintain control over the settlement. Farmers may succeed in keeping their land if they can convince those who want it that there is better land available elsewhere. Similarly, Sama Sama busied the government with a development project that appealed to its vision of housing for the poor. At the same time, Sama Sama continued its slower but controllable and predictable process of building homes and creating a community infrastructure.

When it comes to finding and using resources, most members of Sama

Sama are nationalistic. In addition to arguing that Philippine land belongs to the Filipino, they are opposed to the sometimes harmful effects of using Philippine resources for the development of goods produced and marketed by foreign corporations. They also argue against the harmful effects of using foreign resources to develop Philippine land. In this sense, their movement is an indigenous one. It is based on the principle that since Philippine squatters are best suited to chart the development of their own communities, they should be given, or take, responsibility for land reform. Since they know how to develop the land in the context of poverty rather than dependence, they, not the government, can build communities without losing control over the process of development.

The ideal of indigenous development created a problem for those who supported the Aquino government. Leaders of housing agencies told members of Sama Sama that funding for the Commonwealth project would become available only through a loan from the World Bank. At the least, only foreign aid would make it possible for them to purchase land and housing at low costs and through acquiring low-interest loans. For Sama Sama, at least three problems were inherent to possible dependence on funding from external political groups: (1) foreign aid had been a major source of Marcos's power and wealth; (2) a project dependent on foreign funding and tied to the national economy, rather than squatter participation, could end abruptly, like many previous projects—squatters would lose control of their neighborhoods and possibly their homes; and (3) acceptance of governmental aid would include political obligations.

The third problem was a pressing one for Sama Sama, for the settlement they sought to control was politically plural. Many squatters join groups in the same way they build their homes. They don't move from one group to another over time; rather, they accumulate group memberships. Groups, like houses, are a form of protection from hostile elements of the environment. That being a member of one group is ideologically incompatible with being a member of another group is of no greater consequence than mixing fiberboard and wood in constructing the wall of a home. Contradictory group memberships form a hedge against uncontrollable change and are a means of coping with an uncertain future. Creating a diverse political network is part of the process of surviving poverty. For example, both Commonwealth and Payatas Estate are mazeways of organizations and groups developed to take advantage of prior development policies and programs. When the policies and programs were changed or failed, the groups remained. These groups then continue to lobby for the return of those policies that formed their charters, or they seek new members through convincing uninformed squatters that the program that spawned the group still exists. Each group in Commonwealth, regardless of its politics or its stance in relation to Sama Sama, was of value to Sama Sama's plans through its contribution to the incremental development of the settlement's infrastructure. However, the political pluralism of the settlement rendered it an unlikely achiever in the development of a housing project financed and run by the government. However, if Sama Sama had presented housing agencies with a plan for a project that could have succeeded, the government certainly would have rejected it. That plan would have included the following goals:

1. Grassroots development of Commonwealth over a period of several years.
2. Exclusion of government involvement, and politically tied aid, from development.
3. Governmental participation in the form of protecting grassroots development, primarily through prevention of both private and governmental demolition of squatter homes.
4. The preservation of heterogeneity within Commonwealth, and settlements in general, which included protection of the homes of those who opposed the housing project that Sama Sama was developing with the government (for Sama Sama, a fiction).

To achieve these goals, Sama Sama needed to buy time for grassroots development (protection from demolition or externally controlled change) and direct government attention away from the incremental development occurring in Commonwealth (by discussing the future rather than the present). In this context Sama Sama faced several challenges:

1. It needed to help President Aquino appear to be succeeding in urban land reform.
2. It had to keep the housing project it planned with the government for Commonwealth alive while preventing its implementations.
3. It had to oppose those squatter groups who challenged the Commonwealth project without gaining control over them or causing their dissolution.
4. It had to avoid dependence on external funding for settlement development while at the same time developing a project that was dependent on external funding.

These challenges became Sama Sama's strategies in the construction of time during which squatters would develop Commonwealth through a process of indigenous social evolution. Sama Sama needed to show support for the Aquino government in order to receive its protection from private and municipal developers. At the same time, Sama Sama needed to prevent implementation of Aquino's housing policies in Commonwealth. One way in which Sama Sama succeeded in doing both was through achieving official governmental sponsorship of and involvement within ever-expanding housing projects for the poor. In this way, well-meaning governmental agencies and officials could spend their time constructively but with little impact on Commonwealth. All housing agencies, not just the National Housing Authority, became involved in an ever-expanding process of planning projects and negotiating with squatters who would be affected by those projects.

At the same time that Sama Sama slowly led housing agencies into increasingly elaborate and expanding courses of urban land reform, it needed to develop additional means of preventing or slowing implementation of the projects. However, Sama Sama could not appear to be working at cross-purposes. How Sama Sama accomplished this leads to the next suggestion for those who study resistance.

LOOK FOR RESISTORS RESISTING EACH OTHER. THAT IS REDUNDANT RESISTANCE, AND CAN BE VERY EFFECTIVE.

Diversification of approaches within a resistance movement may be effective through proliferating the work, and consuming the time, of oppressors. Consumption of oppressor time creates resistance time. In a diversified resistance movement, the targets of resistance cannot necessarily deal with all forms of resistance by dealing with one. Sama Sama had many opponents among squatter organizations. By escalating their disputes with their opponents, rather than acquiescing to or appealing to their common identities and problems, Sama Sama fomented the expansion of governmental plans for housing projects while at the same time decreasing the likelihood that the government would be able to implement those projects (as a result of increased squatter resistance). In other words, through actively engaging their squatter opponents in disputes, Sama Sama increased squatter participation in the movement to create time for the grassroots evolution of squatter communities.

How Sama Sama accomplished the expansion of their movement through disputes is illustrated in the expansion of a political conflict among squatters of Commonwealth and Payatas Estate that escalated during 1987 and 1988. As stated above, there are many types of squatter organizations and they, along with many nonsquatter organizations, including the government, claim ownership of land in both Commonwealth and Payatas Estate. The land syndicates, for example, have encouraged and organized scores of squatter homeowner associations that are united under the umbrella of syndicate-run corporations.

Other large groups include those that claim rights to the land as war veterans or their children. During the 1980s, the homes of several of these groups were demolished by the government. Surviving groups have created links to governmental agencies, primarily the Bureau of Forestry Development. Some of them linked up with land syndicates.

There are also large nonveteran groups that have formed around the past policies of the Bureau of Forestry Development (BFD), which claims all of the urban Payatas Estate area as unclassified public forest. In 1983 and 1984, the BFD awarded large rental plots to individuals who formed groups that distributed the land among their members. In 1984 the BFD was forced to abandon this policy, but the squatter groups it spawned continue to claim and sell plots of land to the poor. They lobby the government for return of the BFD policies and award governmental officials land in return for the promise of support.

There are numerous leader-focused homeowner (squatter) associations with links to municipal political leaders and national bureaucrats who occasionally find funds for group projects. Some homeowner associations were once funded by international aid agencies and then formed links to land syndicates when the funding dried up. One large homeowner association was originally linked to a rural land reform movement. Its leaders then gained influence and positions within local government. When that influence began to wain, the same leaders joined forces with a subdivision developer who claimed ownership of the land the squatters occupied and had ties to the municipal government. Now that the squatter-developer-municipal ties appear to be severed, the same leaders are forming ties to land syndicates and religious groups.

As a result of the actions of Sama Sama and its allies within the Catholic Church and governmental agencies (primarily HUDCC and the President's Commission on the Urban Poor), during 1987 and 1988 two large coalitions opposed to each other formed among syndicate, veteran, homeowner, and other groups in Commonwealth and Payatas Estate. Some of the groups allied with Sama Sama, while others allied with Sama Sama's major opponent among the Commonwealth urban poor. Although Commonwealth and Payatas Estate represent two different phases in coalition development, the coalitions in each region became linked to each other in 1988.

The coalitions are built on a history of settlement conflicts. Sama Sama, which represents one of these coalitions, in 1984 obtained strong leadership from a new priest assigned to the Catholic Church located in Commonwealth. At that time, the president of Sama Sama, Mrs. Vargas, had sought personal power and influence through forming links to the National Housing Authority, which proposed to move the squatters of Commonwealth to another region. The church, community organizers linked to the church, and most of the squatters opposed resettlement. In an election, they toppled Mrs. Vargas and elected their chosen candidate, Mrs. Herrera, president of Sama Sama.

Following the election, a division formed in the settlement. Mrs. Vargas and her supporters formed two new organizations: an economic cooperative that had the goal of buying land for resettlement and a coalition of groups who opposed Mrs. Herrera, the new priest, and the community organizers tied to the Catholic Church. Mrs. Vargas and the National Housing Authority became the focus of opposition for Sama Sama. Both continued to recruit new members: Mrs. Vargas on the theme of private land acquisition, and Mrs. Herrera on the theme of resisting demolition and resettlement and seeking on-site development.

Sama Sama also became involved in national politics and participated in the presidential campaign of Corazon Aquino and the "People Power" revolution of 1986. The Catholic sponsors of Mrs. Herrera's group had strong vertical ties to Aquino's supporters and many of the housing and land officials she appointed.

In August 1987 President Aquino set aside 371 acres of land within Commonwealth for on-site development. In February 1988 President Aquino recognized Sama Sama as the official representative of the squatters of Commonwealth in the planning and implementation of on-site development. Sama Sama would have an equal role with the government. Both moves by Aquino threatened those groups in Commonwealth who claimed control over and sold access to land. Some of those groups sought alignment with Mrs. Vargas.

After Aquino gained the Presidency, Mrs. Vargas lost her allies at the National Housing Authority. She then sought an ally in the head of a new land syndicate from whom her economic cooperative bought private land that bordered on Commonwealth. They began to move onto this land in January 1988. Mrs. Vargas remained in Commonwealth and continued to organize against Mrs. Herrera and her church-based supporters.

In December 1987 private developers attempted to demolish the homes of squatters who formed a small organization in Payatas Estate. Sama Sama joined them to create human barricades to resist the bulldozers. The community organizers who worked with Sama Sama then began to advise the small Payatas organization. More importantly, the organizers, together with other Payatas allies, brought together some Payatas squatters and government allies of Sama Sama to form a Payatas-based coalition to reform Payatas land use. Their goal was not just on-site development in Payatas, but also to use Payatas Estate as a resettlement site for squatters from all over Metropolitan Manila. Sama Sama became a strong threat to syndicates and private developers who claimed legal ownership of Payatas land.

As members of existing Payatas groups began to mutiny and join the new Sama Sama coalition, a coalition among the previously independent and often opposed Payatas groups began to form in opposition to Sama Sama and its patrons. Just as Sama Sama used opposition to these Payatas groups as an organizing force, those groups used opposition to Sama Sama and government takeover of the land to attract new members to their growing coalition.

Veterans groups, land syndicates, local government officials, and homeowner associations, some of which were allied with the Bureau of Forestry Development (which claimed control of all of Payatas Estate), joined forces to oppose Sama Sama and her government allies (HUDCC, the national Department of Public Works and Highways, the President's Commission on the Urban Poor, and the cabinet-level secretary of finance). Mrs. Vargas and her coalition in Commonwealth joined forces with this new Payatas coalition to oppose Sama Sama.

In April 1988 Philippine Marines demolished the new homes constructed by Mrs. Vargas's economic cooperative. Mrs. Vargas then sought an alliance with the largest land syndicate operating in the Philippines and Payatas Estate. With this alliance she brought the syndicate and its many allies into the coalition opposed to Sama Sama and linked Sama Sama's Commonwealth opponents to additional foes in Payatas Estate.

As the broad coalition in opposition to Sama Sama was forming in Payatas Estate, and as Sama Sama and its government allies were forming their own coalition there, the land syndicates of Payatas Estate began to build and sell houses on land in Commonwealth that President Aquino had set aside for on-site development. By July 1988, syndicates were advertising and selling plots of government-owned land in three large areas of Commonwealth. In response, government agencies that allied with Sama Sama presented to President Aquino a proposal to form a special military task force to demolish homes on syndicate-controlled land. Military, police, and squatters who lived on the syndicate land would certainly mount an armed resistance.

Leaders of the major land syndicates in Payatas Estate did not appear to be cowed by the proposal of military opposition. They suggested they would fight their battles in court (this was primarily a stalling strategy). The head of the largest syndicate claimed that only the lower echelon leaders within syndicate organizations would face demolition of their developments, and this would occur only if they defied the syndicate hierarchy.

Sama Sama's goal was not to gain dominance over all groups in Commonwealth and Payatas Estate. Through escalating disputes with these organizations, members of Sama Sama were catalysts for the formation of broader squatter coalitions. Squatter groups opposed to Sama Sama began to strengthen their ties to governmental organizations that opposed implementation of the Commonwealth project. Sama Sama's incitement of coalition building among its opponents became of little threat to Sama Sama after President Aquino had set aside the land of Commonwealth for squatter purchase and named Sama Sama as the group that represented the settlement's squatters.

Sama Sama's use of disputes to further the development of an opposition coalition had the primary effect of slowing implementation of the official housing project. It also increased and hastened participation by opposition squatter groups in the building of homes and community infrastructures. The expansion and escalation of disputes across squatter groups and coalitions also hastened the development of a heterogeneous community. Through generating the involvement of many types of groups in the struggle for development of Commonwealth and Payatas Estate, Sama Sama strengthened the commitment of those from a wide range of occupations, and with a wide range of social ties, to residency and participation in the future settlement.

The syndicates were among those most capable of providing diversity. Legitimate real estate developers treated squatters as enemies and sought demolition of their homes. Syndicates, however, built a variety of structures—they intermingled larger, finished, more expensive homes with the shanties that poorer squatters could afford. Through the syndicates, the unemployed, the newly arrived urban resident, the employed, and the socially and politically established became neighbors. And through such ties squatters were able to seek integration into urban opportunities.

Sama Sama's creation of a housing project in partnership with the government secured governmental protection of homes in Commonwealth. Sama Sama then developed strategies to turn that project into fiction, thus constructing time for indigenous development of the land. Sama Sama's success in creating relationships that expressed the group's perception of the future suggests the final two pieces of advice for those who study resistance:

> If the government is intervening on behalf of resistors, it could be coopted, but only if its intervention fails.
>
> Compare the activities in which resistors involve you, and the way they involve you, with the activities they provide the oppressors.

One often thinks of government coopting resistors through development projects. Sama Sama's reform movement shows that the tables can, at times, be turned. Knowledge was a strength of Sama Sama, and that gave the squatters the advantage they needed to coopt government agencies through partnering with them. This knowledge was based on Sama Sama's experience of both the strengths of squatters and the weaknesses of governmental projects. Such weaknesses were to be expected in the context of strident national political competition, national economic debt, and a national economy just escaping from some of the forces of dependence. Squatters constantly felt the effects of all of these national dynamics, and, over time, had developed strategies to deal with them.

Sama Sama's cooptation of government agencies was benign. The women of the squatter group shared goals with their allies in agencies— the alleviation of the troubles of squatters and success for the Aquino government. Rather than opposing the agencies, Sama Sama created a division of labor. The agencies could plan their reform project with the help of Sama Sama, and Sama Sama could carry out its own reform project with the protection of the governmental agencies. Although the two projects differed, their ends were the same.

Sama Sama's involvement of governmental agencies in the creation of official housing projects was an educational process for the new agency leaders. Sama Sama sought equal partnership in the official projects that it hoped would not be implemented. In the process of negotiating that partnership, Sama Sama informed governmental leaders, private developers, and technical experts about the nature of squatter life and the abilities and needs of squatters. They put forth their grassroots perspective for the government to take or leave. Grassroots politics had been a banner of Aquino's political challenge to Marcos, and the squatters hoped it would take hold and filter into official development policies. In the meanwhile, they produced the means to demonstrate its potential by constructing time, both for incremental development of their communities and, incidentally, for policymakers to look inward for effective use of Philippine resources.

The squatters easily forgave misunderstandings and sought to help their opponents while disputing with them. This pattern was evident throughout Philippine and settlement life in 1987 and 1988. Marcos and Aquino supporters formed relationships of cooperation within the settlement. Military forces who waged coup attempts against the Aquino government easily escaped their captors, some more than once. Captured NPA leaders were allowed to attend a birthday party, and escaped. The President's Commission for the Urban Poor met with syndicate leaders and asked for their advice.

Within Sama Sama's perceptual framework, my identity was similar to that of squatter allies within government agencies. Sama Sama considered me a benign outsider. But to many of the 100,000 residents of Commonwealth, I was a stranger in the settlement who could have represented any number of unwelcome groups or well-defined enemies. Nevertheless, I walked the settlement day and night without harm. Although my original perceptions of development were clearly different from those of Sama Sama, Sama Sama did not seek to set me straight through direct teaching. Rather, they involved me in their meetings in the same way they involved governmental agencies. They sent me on many meaningless errands (which were eventually meaningful) and insisted that I always speak Tagalog, rather than English (a component of their strong nationalism).

Sama Sama placed me in one of the settlement's smallest dwellings (suitable to the size of my family). They frequently sought my advice, and they never followed my advice. They involved me in a practice rather than an idea of development. The members of Sama Sama stated their primary message to me often, but always indirectly. They said, "We are poor, but we can give you time."

CONCLUSION

Like the irony of life, the irony of the Commonwealth housing project lies in time. Time is an important component in views of the city held by both Sama Sama and housing agencies. The Aquino government is pressed for time and, working from the top down, is focusing on leadership and law to generate rapid economic change. Faced with rampant factionalism among the powerful, it appears that the Aquino government is being asked by both supporters and opponents to act quickly. In relation to housing for the poor, some government planners want to replace communities that are evolving with a finished product. They are seeking a fait accompli. They have envisioned communities that are structured by centralized governmental planning. Through these communities they will bring under control the life-styles that squatters now represent. The finished products they imagine—houses, structured communities—will be symbols of accomplishment.

This view of urban development, although certainly not shared by all who work in housing agencies, appears to predominate in Philippine housing bureaucracies. However, it is a view borrowed from another time and place and is not realistic in the context of the Philippines today. It is an approach to urban change that in the past failed to produce housing for the poor that the poor would like, and which today is dependent on the availability of material resources that do not yet exist. It is certainly a view of development that would be an obvious fantasy were it not for Philippine ties of interdependence with wealthier nations. It assumes that the powerful cause change and that they can and will act swiftly. However, the resources necessary to realize this view of change may not become available.

This framework for change that moves from the top downward assumes that the source of power to affect and complete change is not time but material resources. In contrast, the foundation on which Sama Sama has built all its plans is the evolution of the home. The poor women of Sama Sama view the home, the family, and the community as processes rather than structures. A primary resource of process is time, and, although not successful at accumulating material resources, the women of Sama Sama were experts at constructing time. Time gave them the power to realize their views of the city and rights of access to land.

It is difficult to say where the truest view of reality lies, but certainly life itself is a process, and those who are shortest on time may experience most strongly the irony of living. The irony of the predominate bureaucratic vision of the city, a vision short on time and that could destroy the vitality of communities, provided Sama Sama the time it needed to continue its processes of community development. Sama Sama was able to create time out of the absence of synchronism between the nature of problems the government chose to address, the means it chose to manage them, and the resources available to put its plans into action.

The absence of synchronism between the problem-solving frameworks of those who govern and the problems of the governed may be common to culturally plural or stratified populations. If so, this source of irony may be a constant source of time, and therefore power, for the oppressed. Yet, to turn time into power, the oppressed must maintain as their constant reference point those processes that bring life to communities and make them vital and dynamic homes.

REFERENCES

Castells, Manuel
  1983   *The City and the Grassroots.* Berkeley, Los Angeles, London: University of California Press.
Felstiner, W., R. Abel, and A. Sarat
  1980–   "The Emergence and Transformation of Disputes: Naming, Blaming, and Claiming." *Law and Society Review* 15(3–4):631–654.
  1981

NINE

When the People Were Strong and United: Stories of the Past and the Transformation of Politics in a Mexican Community

JoAnn Martin

INTRODUCTION

For years anthropologists have mined the memories of Mexican peasants to understand the complex social and political factors that led to the years of turmoil that have become known as the Mexican Revolution. From Warman's (1980) description of tedious and uneventful mini-battles in which a handful of peasants exchanged gunfire with a local hacendado for hours, to Friedrich's (1977) portrayal of heroic agrarian leaders motivated by a complex interplay of personality and politics, to Doña Luz Jimenez's memories of confusion and fear as relayed by Fernando Horcasitas (1972), ethnographers have captured the rich and discordant experiences of peasants in the Mexican Revolution. In all these accounts, however, it is the past event that is highlighted in the ethnographer's account. This chapter shifts the focus from the revolutionary event itself to the stage on which revolutionary stories are told and to the processes of remembering and forgetting that underlie the telling of tales about the revolution. In short, I emphasize not the past, but the connection between past, present, and future which is established in the telling of tales of the revolution in the context of present day political struggles.

In Buena Vista, Morelos, Mexico, tales of the revolution lend a contrapuntal quality to the poetics of politics.[1] Rumors, stories, and everyday conversations render the practices that characterize the state bureaucracy—corruption and cooptation of opposition—meaningful at the local level. However, stories of previous revolutionary struggles also generate an impulse of resistance that is nurtured alongside power relationships. By "an impulse of resistance" I mean a tendency within a cultural form to view history as developing around struggles in which each generation is obliged to fulfill its role in an ongoing battle. The impulse emerges at the level of culture and exists side by side with many contradictory tendencies. Furthermore, since I am talking about an aspect of culture that is generated in the intersubjective creation of cultural meanings, the individuals who in fact create those cultural meanings may not be consciously committed to a strategy of resistance.

In 1984, when I first conducted research in Buena Vista, I paid little attention to this impulse of resistance, focusing instead on the structures of domination. By 1988, however, the impulse of resistance had become central to the development of a political movement in Buena Vista that challenged the legitimacy of Mexico's ruling party, the Institutional Revolutionary Party (PRI). The emergence of an opposition movement caused me to see the storytelling I had observed in 1984 in a new way. Like my informants, whose stories of the past changed in relationship to the present, I began to modify my previous understanding of power relationships as I observed and participated in the political struggles of 1988.

The power of Buena Vistan stories of the past lies in the aura of authenticity created when memory plays with the passage of time. The process of "remembering" history is always intimately tied to the needs of the present, and what has been forgotten may be resurrected or re-remembered as the anxieties of the present call to mind new dimensions of the past. But Buena Vistan storytellers do not rely on memory alone. They augment their memories of history with images and events borrowed from the "official history" that the government promotes in museums, statues, and television shows. Despite the borrowing, Buena Vistan storytellers maintain that their stories are authentic while government versions of history are not. The Buena Vistan concept of *autentico* emphasizes the creativity of a storyteller who draws on a plurality of times past and selects from official history to capture a "deep truth" that reinforces the connection between past, present, and future (Martin n.d.). Thus, the stories establish obligations between past, present, and future generations in which each generation is called to defend the struggles of previous ancestors and to fulfill an historic duty to the future (Benjamin 1969:254).

THE TECHNOLOGIES OF STATE POWER IN MORELOS

The state of Morelos was the home of some of the most tenacious fighters of the Mexican Revolution. Peasants in the state continued their struggle, which began in 1910 and continued until the early 1920s (Womack 1969). Their resolve must be traced to the long history of expropriation of land and exploitation of labor by the sugar haciendas and local caciques (Lewis 1960:80–97; Warman 1980; Womack 1969). Furthermore, in those days family names such as that of the revolutionary leader, Emiliano Zapata, inspired the kind of trust needed to sustain the long years of fighting. Zapata remained the leader of the revolutionary army of the south until government troops assassinated him on April 10, 1919.

When the revolution ended in Morelos, villagers benefited from a massive agrarian reform program that bore many similarities to Zapata's demands for land and liberty (Womack 1969). By 1927, 80 percent of Morelos villagers held provisional titles to land, much of it in the form of ejidos (Womack 1969). The law provided for expropriation and redistribution of land, but villagers often found their requests for land delayed by complicated legal procedures, and when they were finally given land it was never exactly in the form they had requested or in the amounts desired or needed (De la Pena 1981:96). Thus, agrarian reform was carried out as a gift from a benevolent state, not as a fulfillment of Zapatista demands for justice.

The agrarian bureaucracy quickly became an important tool for extending state power into Morelos villages. The power of the bureaucracy depended not on the ideals that government bureaucrats professed— these were often in line with Zapatista ideology—but on the practices that it promoted. These practices are embodied in the rituals of appeal to which peasants resort to resolve land problems. The rituals develop around the exchange of favors and payoffs, all of which take place against the backdrop of revolutionary ideology and its notions of justice.

In Buena Vista discussions of how to resolve problems begin with the search for *gente de confianza* (persons who can be trusted) within the bureaucracy: friends or relatives, or friends of friends or relatives who it is hoped will not ask too much in order to resolve the case. Such connections must be handled delicately because no one wants to imply that they would use those connections to circumvent the ideals of the revolution. In many cases these personal connections become the link through which bribes and payoffs are passed on to higher-level officials. Through their connections, Buena Vistans learn how much they are expected to pay to get a case resolved in their favor, to get a better job, or to get their children into a good school. The exchanges are protected by the notion of *confianza* (trust), which enables the connection to sympathize with the person forced to pay a bribe even while taking a little to compensate for the trouble.

In 1984 the most deleterious effect of these practices came from the mistrust and suspicion they generated in everyday social interactions. Knowledge of the intimate network of connections that linked the town to the state- and national-level bureaucracies was conveyed in everyday gossip and storytelling. Gossip did not rely on evidence to be believable in part because it drew on conceptions of the state that were already in place. Furthermore, gossip was a collective event that brought people together in a supportive atmosphere, and the demands of truth and factual evidence were subordinated to the need to demonstrate friendship and respect. Good friends built on one another's stories by providing further evidence or embellishing a theme, not by asking for evidence or arguing with interpretations.

The gossip focused not on the bureaucrats but on individual Buena Vistans who were also neighbors and kin. For Buena Vistans the corruption, which may ultimately be traceable to the political arena, had become endemic to all social relationships. The community's involvement in the politics of the state had, they believed, transformed honest citizens into corrupt politicians.

Tales of corrupt political leaders and of good community organizations gone bad rendered the structure of the Mexican political process intelligible to Buena Vistans and influenced their interpretations of the motives of political actors. In 1984, when I asked a woman about the movement to protect communal land, she commented,

> Yes, they say they are going to help, but I remember when José Martínez and his friends took over the ejidal land. At first everything was wonderful. Then they started selling ejido land. Now no one goes to their meetings and they just keep all the money for themselves.

Clifford Geertz (1973:313) has suggested that the analysis of political culture must reveal how all people get the politics they imagine. In 1984 many Buena Vistans could not imagine the development of a serious opposition to the PRI. Groups that formed to try to do something about land or water problems were quickly weakened by gossip, suggesting that their members engaged in corruption or were trying to obtain positions in the PRI. The gossip was not unrealistic or irrational given the history of the Mexican political system, but it made it difficult to trust any opposition movements.

The impact of Buena Vistans' conceptions of the state was a situation of widespread political alienation that repressed opposition movements far more effectively than did any directed government action. Foucault's (1980) conception of power as it is deployed from innumerable points through the construction of knowledge is far more helpful in trying to understand the failure of opposition groups in Buena Vista than those conceptions of power that seek to locate a central source in the state apparatus. However, if Buena Vista's political alienation can be better understood through a more amorphous conception of power, it is equally important to identify the points of resistance in the power network. Buena Vistans' stories of the past were central to the development of resistance.

In Buena Vista there are only a few people still alive who remember the revolution, but the ties of kinship and geographic locality reinforce Buena Vistans' willingness to see themselves in relationship to their revolutionary heritage. A woman described her daughter who worked with a movement to protect communal land, as following in her Zapatista father's footsteps. A man in his sixties whose father had died when he was a child explained his commitment to defend communal land as a result of his father's blood. His father, also, fought on the side of Zapata during the revolution.

The Mexican Revolution of 1910 provided a utopian vision of a past in which community unity prevailed and brave men and women stood in opposition to the government. The significance of the revolution for understanding the present far surpassed the ten-year period during which Buena Vistans struggled with the revolutionary leader, Emiliano Zapata, against the Mexican government. Unlike Ilongot headhunters, who Renato Rosaldo (1980) reports are fairly accurate in their dating of historical events, Buena Vistans' memories tend to defy chronological dating. The revolution is a marker that separates the past when the people were "strong and united" from the present when everyone is "afraid and weak." For insiders the physical features of the landscape are full of memories of the past. The mountains are where people hid not only themselves but also their wealth during the revolution. I often found that my informants would not tell me a story until we could "walk" through the story because to truly understand a story, one had to stand in the exact spot where the event took place. Likewise, one could not really know a person unless one knew their family and the role that family had played in the revolution.

Because of these connections with the past, Buena Vistans view themselves as the custodians of the memory of Zapata and the Zapatista fighters. They are particularly concerned with the authenticity of images of Zapata and the revolutionary fighters that the government uses to try to gain legitimacy. The issue of authenticity became important in the state of Morelos almost immediately after the assassination of Emiliano

Zapata. In 1926, six years after Zapata's death, Robert Redfield (1930: 203) recorded a corrido in Morelos that raised the question of whether the government troops killed the "real Zapata." The corrido ends, "It is certain and cannot be doubted, but they were deceived about Zapata, they cannot put Zapata down." In 1984 one of my informants questioned the authenticity of a picture—which hangs in the Palacio de Cortez in Cuernavaca—of Zapata dressed in a suit and silk scarf. Gazing at the picture, the man, a sixty-two-year-old peasant asked me, "Where do you think he borrowed that suit and tie? Zapata never owned a suit, he was a cowboy." He promised to show me an authentic Zapata.

When we returned to Buena Vista my informant invited me into his bedroom, where a banner protected by a clear plastic covering, hung on the wall. The image on the banner depicted Zapata on horseback looking down on a peasant dressed in white who gazed up at the revolutionary leader in admiration. Zapata's hand rested gently on the campesino's shoulder. The image is borrowed from a statue of Emiliano Zapata that was erected in Cautla, Morelos in 1932 when the Mexican government was trying to transform Zapata's image from that of a revolutionary to a paternalistic apostle of agrarianism. Ilene O'Malley, who has analyzed the Mexican government's use of revolutionary mythology, suggests that the image shows a relationship of "superior to inferior, father to child" (1986:60). But, my informant proudly announced, "This is the authentic Zapata who cared about the campesinos and listened to their problems. He was with the campesino." He told me that he had first seen this image of Zapata when the government had paid for him to attend a celebration in honor of Emiliano Zapata. Later he had found the dirty and dusty banner abandoned in the local municipal offices and the mayor had allowed him to take the banner home.

As the previous example illustrates Buena Vistans borrow freely from museum images, government statues, and official publications even as they proclaim that their images are authentic while those of the government are not. At issue when Buena Vistans talk about authenticity is not the image itself but the right of the descendants of those who fought and died in the Mexican Revolution to judge the "truth" of an image. For an image to be "authentic," it must be credible within the cultural context. But truth is more than just culturally credible; truth emerges in the deep structure of meaning created when Buena Vistan storytellers exercise poetic license to maintain the connection between past, present, and future.

Buena Vistan storytellers are usually the old people, the *ancianos*, who are widely respected for their wisdom about the past. In my research

with the movement to protect communal land, the ancianos would frequently interrupt meetings with a story about the past in which the plot
was developed around the problem at hand. Since the same tales were
told over and over again, but in response to different problems, the local
history when merged with the present retained a living quality.

Stories of the past often emphasized the subversion of the "everyday
practices" of making connections, pleading with bureaucratic officials,
and paying bribes. The actors in the stories get what they want not by
pleading, but by taking what they rightfully deserve. Furthermore, the
stories point to the significance of the little things that ordinary people
do in desperate situations.

In 1984 the gap between political alienation and remembered history
created a troublesome rupture between the past and the present that
reflected both a personal and a community-level crisis. Contradictory
passions plagued Buena Vistans. In the context of the legacy of the community's involvement in the Mexican Revolution and its long history of
defending its land and water, the inability of Buena Vistans to organize
themselves was a source of profound shame. Like their ancestors, Buena
Vistans hated the Mexican government and viewed the PRI as a corrupt,
opportunistic party. Unlike their ancestors, they were unable to unite.

POLITICAL PARTICIPATION

In 1988, I returned to Buena Vista to find a highly mobilized, activated
population that was engaged in a variety of political struggles against
the Mexican State at both the local and the national levels. At the local
level, the communal land movement had expanded into a *Coordinadora-
Democratica* with committees that dealt with communal land, ejido land,
health care, and water rights. Several Buena Vistans had become involved in the Cárdenas campaign as an open expression of their opposition to Mexico's ruling party, the PRI.

The emergence of new political leaders and new types of political
organizations enabled Buena Vistans to momentarily resolve the contradictions between their revolutionary heritage and the widespread
mistrust of politics. Whereas in 1984 stories of the past had seemed to
me to be merely an exercise in nostalgia, the politicization of 1988 reminded me that the practice of storytelling had kept alive the impulse
of resistance even during periods when people found it difficult to trust
their neighbors and friends. But to become effective in forming a widespread movement in the present day, the memories of the revolution

had to merge with some potential struggle. The campaign of Cuauhté-moc Cárdenas provided that justification for struggle.

Cuauhtémoc Cárdenas is the son of Lázaro Cárdenas, who was President of Mexico between 1934 and 1940. Lázaro Cárdenas is perhaps best known in the United States for his nationalization of Mexico's oil industry in 1938, a move that angered the U.S. government and foreign capitalists. In Mexico, however, he is admired by peasants and the working classes because he expropriated and redistributed land and protected the interests of labor.

Cuauhtémoc Cárdenas's name captured that merger of past, present, and future that was so central to nourishing the impulse of resistance in Buena Vista. In addition to his connection to his father, his namesake Cuauhtémoc, was ruler of the Aztec capital, Tenochtitlan, at the time of the conquest. According to some reports of the conquest, Cuauhtémoc—who was approximately twenty-one years old at the time—abandoned the city, but this version of the story is under dispute. In 1988 Cárdenas Campaign workers in Morelos told the story of how Cuauhtémoc, after having fought bravely against the superior power of the conquerors, stood before Cortez and declared, "I have done what I am obliged to do in defense of my city, and I stand before you as a prisoner, take the dagger from your belt and kill me with it."

Cuauhtémoc Cárdenas left the PRI in 1987, announcing that he would run for president as a candidate of a coalition of opposition parties. Mexico's progressive and radical parties, many of whom were deeply divided over political ideologies and strategies, quickly united behind Cárdenas. For the first time in postrevolutionary Mexican history the dominance of the PRI was challenged in a presidential campaign.

As election day drew closer, Buena Vistans spread rumors of PRI attempts to manipulate the election results by repressing those who supported Cárdenas. Stories that the PRI had demanded that all the teachers in the local school turn in their election credentials, that the PRI had asked each teacher in the school system to bring in the name of at least one other person who would vote for the PRI, or that those who failed to vote would lose their job gave Buena Vistans ready-made opportunities to demonstrate their bravery.

The desire to see a Cárdenas victory heightened when two of Cárdenas's top aides were killed in Mexico City only a few days before the July 6 election. The event touched off rumors that the military was being moved to different parts of the country to maintain control if Cárdenas won the election. One woman told me that no one would be allowed to leave the country on election day. Another claimed that PRI commercials used images of violence in El Salvador, Guatemala, and Nicaragua to threaten Mexican citizens who might vote for Cárdenas. A man who worked with the Cárdenas campaign confided in me that the military was divided and it was possible that there would be a coup before election day.

The images of repression, both actual and potential, gave Buena Vistans the opportunity to identify local opposition leaders. In 1984 Buena Vistans often interpreted opposition to the ruling party as a request for incorporation into the party, but in the context of the Cárdenas campaign Buena Vistans felt more confident that those who sided with Cárdenas were really opposed to the PRI. One man told me that they knew they could trust Cárdenas because given his father's position in the party he could easily have become the party's candidate if he had so desired.

In contrast to 1984, when tales of corruption dominated, in 1988 I participated in the collective telling of stories of bravery in the face of threats. The Maestro Miguel had been called to the governor's office and threatened with being sent to a small isolated community if he did not cease his organizing against government projects. He continued to be as vocal and as militant in his organizing. Another teacher involved in the Cárdenas campaign was told that he should not show a Cárdenas campaign film or he would lose his job. Hours later he was arranging to show the film in the community. A government employee became a local hero when he defaced a poster encouraging people to vote by adding the name Cárdenas before he hung the poster in his office as he was required to do by the government.

Once again Buena Vistans were taking part in the defense of the Mexican Revolution. Political speeches created the image of Cárdenas as a redeemer with roots in the long history of community struggles against repression. A young Cárdenas supporter explained to the people of Buena Vista who united in a political rally, "In order to speak of the Engineer Cuauhtémoc Cárdenas, as a candidate of the people, one must speak of the history of the people of Mexico." The speaker began with the conquest when Cárdenas's namesake Cuauhtémoc fought against the Spanish invaders and continued through the War of Independence, the Mexican Revolution, and the expropriation of the oil industry in 1938. Another speaker at a rally in Cuernavaca described Cárdenas as the candidate of the majority of Mexicans who had been exploited, and who had lost their land to those of money. Cuauhtémoc, he said, had come to save the country, "Like in the times when they had said Christ is coming and everyone said that it was not true, now Cuauhtémoc is returning after 500 years to defend the country."

The campaign of Cuauhtémoc Cárdenas encouraged Buena Vistans to re-create images of his father. Whereas in 1984 I found few people who remembered Lázaro Cárdenas, now people began to tell stories of his father. Older people began to reremember that they had been treated well by government bureaucrats during the time of Lázaro Cárdenas. Lázaro Cárdenas's stance against foreign domination of Mexico's oil industry became molded together with his son's promise to declare a moratorium on the payment of the debt if elected president. When I attended a Cárdenas political rally in which the candidate himself was to appear, Buena Vistans were very anxious that I record the event with my tape recorder. One man explained, "This is a historic opportunity for you. Lázaro Cárdenas had a very low voice so that no one could ever record his speeches. Now, you have the opportunity to record his son's voice."

On election day, Buena Vistans voted in large numbers for Cuauhtémoc Cárdenas, as did others in the state of Morelos, but they did so with ambivalence. Even within the Coordinadora no one saw the Cárdenas Campaign as a genuine solution to the community's problems. The Maestro Miguel made a strong argument in a meeting of the Coordinadora Democratica for abstention in the presidential elections, reminding people that elections would never resolve anything, and that it was far more important for the community to remain organized and fighting and free from any obligation to a political party. Another man argued against him, saying that abstention would be interpreted as support for the PRI and would make stuffing the ballot boxes easier. He did not argue, however, that Cárdenas was the solution to Buena Vista's problems. In the end Cárdenas won the election in Buena Vista, and the local mayor posted the results of the municipal elections in his office. Cárdenas won five votes for every one vote cast for the PRI candidate Carlos Salinas in Buena Vista. The fact that the mayor posted the election results signified to Buena Vistans the success of their own local-level organizing. For Buena Vistans Cárdenas's victory was important because it had been accomplished through the community united in a struggle to defend itself against a corrupt political system. In so doing, Buena Vistans had fulfilled their historic responsibility.

CONCLUSION

Resistance is often encoded in cultural forms rather than expressed in consciously organized social movements, with the result that the anthropologist is left to discern the elements of resistance in a culture of domination (Comaroff 1985; Ong 1987; Taussig 1980; Willis 1977). In Buena Vista, storytelling takes place within the framework of everyday life, and few Buena Vistans regard it as a form of resistance. Yet, an impulse of resistance is nurtured in the practice of storytelling and is reflected in the cultural knowledge produced in the stories. Through the stories of the ancianos, Buena Vistans learn that their situation is getting worse, not better; that once there was a time when problems were not solved through corruption; and that they are a people who have the capacity and the duty to struggle. In other conversations and stories, they learn, however, that neighbors, close friends, and kin act in much the same way as corrupt politicians, and that the state has the power to corrupt the good intentions of even the most admirable members of the community.

Local culture is thus constructed out of both the impulses to resistance and the relations of power, creating a situation in which both power and resistance are always being contested. In fact, it is this ever-present potential of a struggle that gives both domination and resistance its justification. In Buena Vista the constant manufacture of rumors of repression, of military coups, of vote fraud existed side by side with the creation of brave local leaders whose presence enabled the community to fulfill its mythical historical role. The talk about Cardenas and his campaign seized on every act of repression as evidence of the corrupt and brutal nature of the current government. The vote fraud and selective repression of the Cardenas campaign in 1988 became linked to Buena Vistans' "memories" of past revolutionary struggles, making it all the more important to defend the Cardenas campaign as their ancestors had once defended Zapata and his revolutionary struggle.

Why do stories of the Mexican Revolution draw the attention of both scholars and the local population? The power of storytelling comes from the way the narrative form moves the listener through the passage of time so that events in an individual's life are given greater meaning (Ricoeur 1983:54). Nowhere is this aspect clearer than in stories of the revolution. For many Buena Vistans the stories of the revolutionary years are narratives about their lives; their individual identity unfolds alongside the tales of their parents' and grandparents' involvement in the revolutionary struggle. More importantly, however, the revolutionary years mark a moment in the history of the community in which individual and community biographies became linked in a manner that affected the nation. Paradoxically, the power of this link has been preserved by both the state's revolutionary propaganda and the stories of the ancianos.

ACKNOWLEDGMENTS

This chapter has benefited from the advice and criticism of Laura Nader and Carolyn Nordstrom. I also would like to thank my friends in Buena Vista who spent so much of their valuable time teaching me about their culture and their history.

NOTE

1. Buena Vista is a pseudonym for the community in Morelos, Mexico, where I conducted research for this chapter.

REFERENCES

Benjamin, Walter
 1969   "Theses on the Philosophy of History." In *Illumination,* pp. 253–264, Hannah Arendt, ed. New York: Schocken Books.
Comaroff, Jean
 1985   *Body of Power Spirit of Resistance: The Culture and History of a South African People.* Chicago: University of Chicago Press.
De la Pena, Guillermo
 1981   *A Legacy of Promises: Agriculture, Politics and Ritual in the Morelos Highlands of Mexico.* Austin: University of Texas Press.
Foucault, Michel
 1980   *The History of Sexuality,* vol. 1. New York: Vintage Books.
Friedrich, Paul
 1977   *Agrarian Revolt in a Mexican Village.* Chicago and London: University of Chicago Press.
Geertz, Clifford
 1973   "The Politics of Meaning." In *The Interpretations of Cultures,* pp. 311–326, Clifford Geertz, ed. New York: Basic Books.
Horcasitas, Fernando
 1972   *Life and Death in Milpa Alta: A Nahuatl Chronicle of Díaz and Zapata.* Norman: University of Oklahoma Press.
Lewis, Oscar
 1960   *Tepoztlan: Village in Mexico.* New York: Holt, Rinehart and Winston.
Martin, JoAnn
 N.d.   "Authenticity and the Battle for History: A History of Competing Histories." Paper presented at the American Anthropology Meetings in Washington, D.C., November 15–19, 1989.
O'Malley, Ilene
 1986   *The Myth of the Revolution: Hero Cults and the Institutionalization of the Mexican State, 1920–1940.* Westport, Conn.: Greenwood Press.

Ong, Aihwa
1987   *Spirits of Resistance and Capitalist Discipline: Factory Women in Malaysia.* Albany: State University of New York Press.
Redfield, Robert
1930   *Tepoztlan, A Mexican Village: A Study of Folk Life.* Chicago: University of Chicago Press.
Ricoeur, Paul
1984   *Time and Narrative,* vol. 1. Chicago: University of Chicago Press.
Rosaldo, Renato
1980   *Ilongot Headhunting 1883–1974: A Study in Society and History.* Stanford: Stanford University Press.
Taussig, Michael
1980   *The Devil and Commodity Fetishism in South America.* Chapel Hill: The University of North Carolina Press.
Warman, Arturo
1980   *We Come to Object: The Peasants of Morelos and the National State.* Trans. Stephen K. Ault. Baltimore: The Johns Hopkins University Press.
Willis, Paul
1977   *Learning to Labor: How Working Class Kids Get Working Class Jobs.* New York: Columbia University Press.
Womack, John, Jr.
1969   *Zapata and the Mexican Revolution.* New York: Alfred A. Knopf.

TEN

The Politics of Painting:
Political Murals in Northern Ireland

Jeffrey A. Sluka

And now the music's playing and the writing's on the wall
And the dreams that you painted can be seen by one and all.
Now you've got them thinking and the future's just begun
For you sowed the seeds of freedom in your daughters and your sons.
(From the song "Your Daughters and Your Sons," by COLM SANDS;
cited in Rolston [1987])

INTRODUCTION

Political murals have become an important part of the political culture of Northern Ireland. They are important symbolic representations of the political conflict between the two ethnic communities; Catholic murals are an expression of the "culture of resistance," while Protestant murals are a reactionary product of a dominant or hegemonic culture. This chapter describes the evolution, political functions, and major themes represented in these murals and argues that they are both an expression of political culture and an interactive phenomenon in the ongoing process of political and ethnic conflict in Northern Ireland.

While today there are both Catholic and Protestant political murals in Northern Ireland, these murals have become particularly important in the Catholic ghettos. These murals emerged spontaneously as an important item of popular political culture during the Republican hunger strike in 1981. They were a popular response by young people—people in their teens and early twenties—to the political situation. However, since the end of the hunger strike—that is, since 1982—the painting of political murals has largely become assimilated into the organized Republican movement itself. This is because the movement recognizes the importance of propaganda that "raises the Nationalist peoples' morale, puts Ireland on the world stage and demoralizes the British government and its forces" (Republican Movement 1982), and they have come to recognize that murals are an effective and powerful form of visual propaganda.

190

If you were to visit Northern Ireland on a holiday and walk through the Catholic ghettos you would not see the resistance, or at least you would not see armed IRA guerrillas, riots, gun battles, or bomb explosions. What you would see is the British army and the paramilitary Northern Irish police (the Royal Ulster Constabulary [RUC]); the security measures like checkpoints, observation posts, fortified police and army barracks; and helicopters hovering overhead. What you would see is the military response to the resistance, but not the resistance itself. Nonetheless, you would know it was there; all you have to do is read "the writing on the wall." Political murals and graffiti are ubiquitous in the Catholic ghettos, and they are an unmistakable sign that the struggle is there. They are a sign of alienation and resistance, and they are a constant reminder that there is a guerrilla war going on—even if you cannot always see it.

Norman Mailer once referred to graffiti as "your presence on their presence." Political murals are like graffiti in this sense. In the Catholic ghettos they are an important means by which the popular resistance imposes its presence on your presence. The impact murals make on people can be conscious and obvious, but for those who live in the ghettos the murals are taken for granted and no one notices them much. But that does not mean that they do not have an important impact on their psyches. Because the murals are a constant presence, their impact becomes almost subliminal.

The functions served by political murals and graffiti in Northern Ireland are both internal and external—that is, they are directed both at "us" and "them"—at one's own community and the outside world. They are directed inward at the community in that they are meant to educate and elicit support, and to keep the struggle in the mind's eye. They may also be intended to fulfill a political socialization function, as implied in the quotation at the beginning of this chapter from Colm Sands's song "Your Daughters and Your Sons."

Their meaning is directed toward the outside world in that they are intended to express the community's alienation, their political views and aspirations, and their resistance. The Republican movement uses murals and graffiti quite consciously in this way. An aspect of murals that make them a particularly effective form of propaganda is that they are highly photogenic. There is a constant stream of journalists passing through the Catholic ghettos—the major "war zones" in Northern Ireland—and the pictures they take are circulated around the world. The Republican movement can therefore communicate with the world through the murals and graffiti captured in these photographs and film clips. Other "outside" audiences that are being communicated with include the authorities, for example, the British government and the security forces, and the Protestant-Unionist community. What they are saying is that they are not weak or passive. They are saying to the Loyalists that they can and will defend themselves, and they are saying to the authorities that they reject them and will resist domination, oppression, and injustice. A good example of this is the impact the murals and graffiti have on the British soldiers who patrol these ghettos. When a patrol rounds a corner and comes face to face with graffiti like "You are in Provo Land," or a mural with a life-size guerrilla armed with an automatic rifle or a rocket launcher, with a caption like "Victory to the IRA," you see in a very direct way how graffiti and murals allow the Nationalist resistance to impose its presence on the consciousness of the soldiers.

POPULAR CULTURE IN NORTHERN IRELAND

Northern Ireland is a bicultural society. There are two popular cultures, the Catholic-Nationalist one and the Protestant-Unionist one.[1] The division between Catholic-Nationalists and Protestant-Unionists is not just a religious or political one; it is a cultural divide—and that is why I consider the conflict in Northern Ireland to be an ethnic conflict rather than a political or sectarian one. At root, it is basically a conflict between two ethnic-national identities, arising from the fact that they are arranged in a hierarchical relationship of dominance and subordination (Rolston 1987:7) (see table 10.1). The Protestant-Unionist culture has always been dominant in Northern Ireland. The Protestant-Unionist ruling class controlled the Northern Ireland state that was created by the partition of Ireland in 1921, and Protestant-Unionist cultural hegemony dominated almost every aspect of civil society as well. For their part, the Catholic-Nationalist minority were offered subordination. This subordination, and their responses to it, have had a profound affect on Catholic-Nationalist cultural expression (Rolston 1987:7).

An example of the division between the two popular cultures in Northern Ireland that illustrates how they have developed not only separately but in fact in dialectical opposition to each other, is the contrast between Protestant-Unionist political marches and Catholic-Nationalist ones. Both communities have a calendar of annual marches. Nationalist and Unionist marches are in many ways similar, but while most Unionist marches are triumphant displays of political dominance over the Nationalist minority, the majority of Nationalist marches are displays of alienation, protest, and resistance against that domination.

TABLE 10.1   Catholics and Protestants in Northern Ireland

	Catholic	*Protestant*
Identity	Irish	British-Ulster
Politics	Nationalist-Republican	Unionist-Loyalist
History	Descendants of natives	Descendants of settlers

The high point of Protestant-Unionist cultural celebration is the Twelfth of July, when they commemorate the victory of the Protestant forces of William of Orange over the Catholic forces of James II in 1690 at the Battle of the Boyne. After partition and the establishment of the Northern Ireland statelet in 1921, "the Twelfth" became a state ritual in Northern Ireland. Every year on the Twelfth of July, the Protestant Orange Order marches in strength in cities and towns throughout Northern Ireland. For example, in Belfast the annual march on the Twelfth has always had at least 30,000 participants. The Orange marchers demand "the right to march where they will, even—or especially—if Catholics protest" (Rolston 1987:8). For the Catholic-Nationalist minority, the cultural events and artifacts surrounding the Twelfth were—and still are—perceived as domineering, threatening, and exclusionary.

The high point of Catholic-Nationalist cultural celebration is the annual Easter parade on the Falls Road. Whereas the Protestant march on the Twelfth of July celebrates Unionist domination, the Catholic march on Easter Day commemorates the 1916 Rising and celebrates Nationalist resistance to Unionist domination.

THE PROTESTANT MURAL TRADITION

In the Protestant districts of Belfast there has been a long-standing tradition, going back to at least the turn of the century, of painting murals as part of the Twelfth of July celebrations. These murals were in many ways equivalent to national monuments in other societies (Rolston 1987:7). The Unionist murals associated with the Twelfth bore all the signs of triumphalism, and they excluded the large Nationalist minority. The most common theme represented in Unionist murals was, and still is, William of Orange at the Battle of the Boyne. He is always mounted on a white horse, and the usual caption is "Remember 1690." (This standardized image of King Billy can be traced back to Benjamin West's painting of the Battle of the Boyne, done in 1780.)

Historically, not all Protestant murals were associated with the Twelfth.

Pl. 3. The annual Orange (Protestant) parade on July 12th.

In fact, the heyday of Protestant mural painting was during the years between World Wars I and II. Themes included the sinking of the *Titanic* (built by Protestant workers at the Harland and Wolff shipyard in Belfast), the Battle of the Somme (where the Ulster Division was decimated), and the coronation of King George VI in 1937. But the two oldest surviving murals in Northern Ireland both depict William of Orange at the Battle of the Boyne. They are over sixty years old, and one is in Belfast and the other in Derry.

More important than the origin of these murals is their ritual significance. In preparation for the massive Orange Order marches on the Twelfth, curbstones are painted red, white, and blue, brightly painted arches are erected over main thoroughfares in Protestant districts, Orange Lodge banners carried and Lambeg drums played during the march are painted or repainted, and material is gathered for the huge three- or four-story-high bonfires burned during the evening of the Twelfth. Many of the cultural artifacts of Protestant-Unionism displayed during the Twelfth are associated with the Orange Order, such as the bower hats, sashes, banners, and pipe and drum bands. The content of these Unionist murals, as well as these other Protestant-Unionist cultural artifacts, is intricately linked to their function as part of the ritualistic celebration of an event that has mythic proportions in Protestant-

Pl. 4. The annual Easter parade on Falls Road.

Unionist culture in Northern Ireland. The content of these murals, while anchored in the specific historical event of the Battle of the Boyne, transcends both time and history. In some ways, King Billy became an equivalent on the Protestant side of representations of the saints in Catholic ritual. For Protestants, he represents a timeless savior (Rolston 1987:9).

THE CATHOLIC MURAL TRADITION

In contrast to the long-standing mural tradition in Protestant communities, there was no mural tradition in Catholic districts until the 1980s. Before that, only two Nationalist murals are known to have existed, both of them in the Catholic Ardoyne district of Belfast. One depicted Robert Emmet, a nineteenth-century revolutionary Irish nationalist, and the other James Connolly, an early twentieth-century Irish socialist revolutionary (Rolston 1987:8).

The fact that mural painting was a tradition in Unionist areas but not in Nationalist ones was not an accident. It reflects the relationship between popular culture and the Northern Irish state. In Protestant working-class districts painting murals was regarded as a civic right and duty, but it was not a right extended to Catholics. Catholics who painted political themes on walls faced police harassment and even prosecution. For example, in 1954 the Unionist regime passed the Flags and Emblems Act, which prohibited the public display of the Irish tricolor on the grounds that it might offend people. This law was still in effect until 1986, and it was still a punishable offense to fly a tricolor or paint one on a wall during the hunger strike in 1981—when the "murals boom" began in the Catholic ghettos.

One illustration of the relationship of the two popular cultures to the state in Northern Ireland is that when urban redevelopment occurred in the Catholic Ardoyne district in Belfast in the early 1970s, the two murals of Robert Emmet and James Connolly were torn down by the Housing Executive. But when urban redevelopment occurred about the same time in the Protestant Fountain area of Derry, a mural of King Billy was preserved at great expense. The Housing Executive moved the whole wall to the new Fountain estate, where it still stands today (Rolston 1987:12). Certainly no nationalist mural would ever be accorded such status by the authorities in Northern Ireland.

NATIONALIST MURALS—THE NEW WAVE

Since the outbreak of the current "troubles" in 1969, Nationalist culture has thrived in the Catholic ghettos. There has been a cultural revival or renaissance in Catholic-Nationalist identity. Most notably, there has been a revival of interest in the Irish language. For example, today almost all of the Catholic schoolchildren in Belfast learn at least some Gaelic at school, and all of the local community centers offer evening classes in Gaelic. Other examples include revived interest in Irish folk music, Irish dancing, and Gaelic sports.

One important aspect of this cultural revival originated not in the Catholic ghettos, but rather in the prisons—especially in Long Kesh (the political prison in Northern Ireland where those convicted of "terrorist" offenses are held, and which has been renamed the Maze). There was an Irish cultural revival among Republican prisoners, who spent their time in jail learning Gaelic and Irish folk music and making cultural crafts or artifacts. These included handkerchiefs painted with felt-tip pens, woodcarving, and leatherwork exhibiting Celtic designs. Commonly used symbols included the Irish tricolor, the harp, and the mythical bird the Phoenix. By the end of the 1970s, in the majority of working-class Catholic homes you could find a wooden harp, a painted handkerchief, or a leather wallet made by a relative or friend in Long Kesh. This contributed at least indirectly to the "explosion" of visual popular culture in Nationalist areas during the hunger strike in 1981, because at least one message people got from these prison artifacts was that one did not have to have any artistic training to produce political art.

Another thing that may have contributed at least indirectly to the explosion of political murals in the Catholic ghettos in 1981 was that between 1977 and 1981 the Belfast City Council sponsored a Community Arts scheme that produced over forty murals in different working-class districts. So even though Nationalist areas did not have a tradition of mural painting as working-class Unionist districts did, murals were being produced in some of these communities. People had watched them being painted, and so there was some community experience with this form of art.

The development of Catholic-Nationalist murals can be traced through four stages. These gradually fade into each other and are not really discrete, but by identifying them we gain a clearer picture of their evolution. The first or "preliminary" phase can be identified as the pre-hunger strike (pre-1981) period. This includes the two political murals in Ardoyne and the murals painted in Catholic districts as part of the community arts scheme. The second phase is the hunger strike period. The third phase I call the "armed struggle period," and the fourth and current phase is the "party-political period" (see table 10.2).

The Second Phase of Nationalist Murals—
the Hunger Strike in 1981

I have already discussed the first or preliminary phase when I briefly described the Catholic mural tradition. But the event that triggered the "explosion" of mural painting in the Catholic ghettos in 1981 was the Republican hunger strike in which seven IRA and three INLA hunger strikers died. Support groups, called "H-Blocks/Armagh Committees," were formed in all of the Catholic districts in Northern Ireland. Their objectives included propaganda and mobilizing support for the hunger strikers, and they attracted large numbers of youths—some still in school, others recent school-leavers who were unemployed (and most school-leavers in the Catholic ghettos are unemployed). These young people were organized in youth sections of their local H-Blocks/Armagh Committee, but also sometimes independently, and they wanted to contribute to the struggle in some way other than rioting (although they did this, too).

TABLE 10.2   The Evolution of Nationalist Murals

Phase I: Pre-1981 (preliminary phase), two political murals in Ardoyne Community Arts Scheme murals

Phase II: 1981/82, hunger strike murals

Phase III: 1983/84, armed struggle murals

Phase IV: 1985-present, party-political murals

First, they began to write graffiti in support of the hunger strike. At this early stage in the murals, one technique was to change the messages on billboard advertisements. For example, a Bass beer advertisement on Falls Road that read "Great Stuff This Bass," was modified by crossing out the "Bass" and replacing it with "IRA" (Rolston 1987:27). The graffiti then became increasingly complex and ornate, including, for example, slogans and excerpts from poems, usually prison poems written by Bobby Sands.

These Catholic youths who wanted to do something to support the hunger strikers not only rioted and put graffiti on the walls but were also willing to try painting murals. Between the death of the first hunger striker, Bobby Sands, on May 5, 1981 and the end of the hunger strike five months later, at least a hundred Nationalist murals appeared in Belfast, about fifty in Derry, and many others in other towns around Northern Ireland (Rolston 1987:15). Few of these young people had more than a minimum of artistic training, but they made up for it in enthusiasm and commitment. Also, once the ball started rolling it carried its own momentum. You could copy what others did. For example, you did not have to paint something new—you could copy a photograph. The existence of one mural inspired others. You saw what someone else did, and this gave you an idea for one of your own.

The major theme in these murals was, of course, the hunger strike. A common way to present the topic was to paint a portrait of one or more of the hunger strikers and add a catchy slogan to it. For example, there was one of Bobby Sands with the slogan "You can't put a rope around the neck of an idea."

Among the secular images, the most common was the lark in barbed wire. Before Bobby Sands went on hunger strike he had written for the Republican newspaper *An Phoblact/Republican News* under two pseudonyms, one of which was "The Lark." One of the pieces he wrote was an article titled "The Lark and the Freedom Fighter," in which he drew an analogy between a trapped bird and an imprisoned man. It contained what came to be the most quoted text in murals: "I have been starved, beaten, and tortured, and like the lark, I fear I may eventually be murdered. But, dare I say it, similar to my little friend, I have the spirit of freedom that cannot be quenched." (Bobby Sands was an amateur ornithologist. From his prison cell he could hear and occasionally see birds, and these came to represent freedom for him.)

Another common image was a firing party giving the "final salute" over Bobby Sands's coffin. This originally appeared as a photograph in *An Phoblact/Republican News* and was copied by many muralists (Rolston 1987:18). The "H" in H-Blocks also appeared frequently, often as a brick or concrete structure being broken apart. This reflects another more general theme found in many of the murals, that out of seeming defeat comes triumph. This notion is portrayed in the common use of the phoenix. The phoenix was first used by the mid-nineteenth-century precursors of the IRA, the Fenians. As a symbol of hope and rebirth, the phoenix represents not only the hunger strike but also the IRA and the whole Republican movement, which proclaims that they were "born out of the flames of August 1969 in Belfast and Derry." "Out of the ashes rose the provisionals" is a common slogan (e.g., on IRA buttons). In one mural an IRA volunteer rises from the flames, rather than a phoenix.

Many different symbolic representations emerged—like the "H" from H-Blocks, the Irish tricolor, the Starry Plough (the flag of James Connolly's Irish Citizens Army of 1916), and the Fianna[2] flag (an orange sun on a yellow background). These might be described as "quasimurals." Many of these murals depict a single symbol—for example, a blanket man, hunger striker, IRA guerrilla, or a flag, and a slogan—perhaps a chorus from a song or stanza from a poem. One very common theme was memorial murals, with depictions of Celtic crosses and the names and/or pictures of dead hunger strikers.

Occasionally, a religious allusion was made. The hunger strikers were portrayed as victims of repression, they might be kneeling, and the slogan might be one like "Lord, may their sacrifice like yours not be in vain." In one an angel stands by a dying hunger striker while an armed IRA volunteer prays by his bedside. In another a dying hunger striker clasps a rosary, with the Blessed Virgin in the background. Sometimes the religious allusion was more subtle. For example, one depicts the parents of a dead hunger striker carrying his body, and I believe there is an allusion being made to removing Christ from the cross prior to burial.

Yet, what is perhaps surprising is the relative paucity of directly

Pl. 5. "The final salute."

Pl. 6. Prison struggle: Dove in barbed wire (prisoners) and an "H" (prison blocks) being broken by a Phoenix (IRA).

Pl. 7. Hunger strike: religious allusions are rare,
but not entirely absent.

religious imagery and the preference for more secular images. The
Republican movement is avowedly secular and antisectarian. It is not
anti-clerical, but has been struggling with the hierarchy of the Catholic
church—part of the battle for hearts and minds in the Catholic ghettos.
This supports the point that the conflict should be viewed as an ethnic
rather than religious one. If it were a religious conflict, there would be
more use of religious symbols in the murals. There are always important
"sacred" elements present in guerrilla struggles, and there are with respect to Republican semiotics. But these are not "Catholic" elements
per se. In the few murals that did include religious symbols, it is clear
that the political function of this was to lend legitimacy (what Dolf
Sternberger [1968] calls "numinous" or sacred legitimacy) to the Republican movement. So given that the ethnic division is in part a religious
division, and given the power of sacred symbols to enhance political
legitimacy, it is perhaps surprising that religious symbols are so rare in
Catholic-Nationalist murals. But it is not really surprising if one bears
in mind two things: (1) that the conflict is not basically a religious one
but rather an ethnic-national one and (2) the political dynamics of the
conflict between the hierarchy of the Catholic Church (who are opposed

to political violence) and the Republican movement (who endorse political violence).

During this phase, as in subsequent ones, a number of remarkable murals were painted. One was copied from a linocut by Jeff Perks titled "The Training Ground," depicting in linear fashion the whole "conveyor-belt" justice system for the arrest, interrogation, prosecution, and finally imprisonment of those involved in the armed struggle. It is remarkable in its scope, and you can basically "read" it by walking along the wall from left to right. Another, called "The Shape of Things to Come," depicts IRA guerrillas in battle against the British army, who are shown lowering the Union Jack in defeat. Yet another uses a stark, "skeletal" style in white on black and depicts an emaciated Bobby Sands. It includes a crucifixion-like figure, probably intended as a religious allusion. (This mural was also used as a prominent backdrop for a riot in the British film "Harry's Game.") Finally, some murals reflect the particular artistic ingenuity of the painters, such as an eerie, stylized depiction of Britain consuming Ireland.

The Third Phase of Nationalist Murals—The Armed Struggle Period

With the end of the hunger strike in October 1981, the original raison d'etre for the murals ended. But by then people had learned the effectiveness of political murals as propaganda, and new ones continued to be painted, although at a reduced rate. During the immediate post-hunger strike period, a number of the more talented muralists began to work directly for Sinn Fein—the Republican political party associated with the IRA. During this period, from approximately 1982 until 1984, we see a gradual process of "professionalization" occurring. Increasingly the new murals were being painted by Sinn Fein artists who had training in the arts and were not amateurs, rather than being painted spontaneously by groups of young people. The main topic treated in the new murals emerging during this period was the armed struggle. A common theme was, and still is, to depict armed IRA volunteers with a simple statement like "Provisional IRA" or "We are here to stay."

Sometimes the historical roots of the present struggle were emphasized. Often, this was done by depicting important historical Republican figures such as Patrick Pearse or by juxtaposing IRA volunteers from 1919 and the present. But like religious imagery, one is struck by how relatively unimportant historical images are in Belfast murals. It is the current struggle that is given priority. During this third or "armed struggle" phase, the emphasis is primarily on the armed struggle and repression—such as the use of plastic bullets and depictions of guerrillas

Pl. 8. The most consistent theme in Republican murals
is the armed struggle.

Pl. 9. Historical allusions are a common theme, as well as cultural symbols
such as the use of Gaelic—*oglaigh na heireann* (IRA) and *saoirse* (freedom).

killed while in active service. One mural carried the message "Warning! Irish Republican Army-occupied territory. British forces enter at own risk." Another is an almost cinematographic depiction of an IRA ambush in Crossmaglen. Yet another depicts an IRA guerrilla firing an RPG-7 rocket launcher. These murals often depict armed guerrillas firing weapons, and they are often painted in direct response to contemporary events.

The Fourth (Current) Phase—The Period of Party-Political Murals

The fourth or current phase, I call the period of party-political murals. The highly skilled mural painters who joined Sinn Fein have become party "cultural workers" (Rolston 1987). They have used their skills directly on behalf of the party, and they are primarily responsible for the murals that have emerged since 1985. These murals are directly party-political murals, as opposed to the more spontaneous "popular" murals of the preceding periods. (Other Sinn Fein party cultural workers produce a constant stream of posters, postcards, Christmas cards, buttons, rebel music tapes, and cartoons.)

There is a good deal of continuity with some of the themes from the earlier phases. The armed struggle remains a major theme. For example, one new Falls Road mural depicts eleven IRA guerrillas (male and female) in ranks and the caption "Victory to the IRA." Historical continuity between the current armed struggle and those of the past is still a common theme. For example, another new mural depicts seven of the executed leaders of the 1916 rising and a quotation (in Gaelic) from Patrick Pearse. And the mural painters continue to paint murals in response to specific contemporary events, such as the assassination by the Special Air Services (SAS) of IRA volunteers Mairead Farrell, Dan McCann, and Sean Savage in Gibraltar.

These party-professional muralists have stressed four general themes of immediate concern to the Republican movement—repression, resistance, armed struggle, and political action (Rolston 1987:23). While repression, resistance, and armed struggle were common themes in the third or "armed struggle" phase, the emphasis on the political role of Sinn Fein is new and unique to the current "party-political murals" phase. Perhaps the first of the party-political murals is one advertising the movement's newspaper—*An Phoblact/Republican News*—painted on the wall of the Sinn Fein headquarters on the Falls Road. With the closer incorporation of mural production into Sinn Fein, or the organized Republican movement, however, religious allusions, which were always rare, have become even less common. For example, even the memorial-

Pl. 10. Cinematographic depiction of an IRA ambush in
"bandit country"—Crossmaglen.

Pl. 11. Contemporary events are common themes, in this case
the execution of three IRA volunteers in Gibraltar by the SAS.
Note security force's vandalism.

Pl. 12. Party-political advertisement for Republican media—the newspaper
An Phoblact/Republican News.

style murals with their Celtic crosses have virtually disappeared. One re-markable new mural pays tribute to "Cormac"—the Republican car-toonist. It is a huge, brightly colored, eight-frame cartoon encouraging people to become involved in Sinn Fein.

The emergence of the new party-political or Sinn Fein murals reflects the growing importance of Sinn Fein that has occurred steadily ever since the hunger strike. For example, one of the spinoffs from the hunger strike was the emergence of Sinn Fein electoral politics, and this theme is depicted in some of the new party-political murals. For exam-ple, one bold red mural reads "For a New Ireland—Vote Sinn Fein." Another new theme is international solidarity with other national liber-ation movements. For example, one depicts a PLO and an IRA guerrilla, together holding up an RPG-7 rocket launcher, and reads "PLO-IRA—One Struggle." The newest solidarity mural was painted on Falls Road in June 1988, to celebrate jailed African National Congress (ANC) leader Nelson Mandela's seventieth birthday. It depicts Mandela against the background of the black, green, and gold ANC flag and the Irish tricolor, and the captions read "Mandela—Father of Freedom. The fu-ture belongs to you! Happy Birthday, Comrade." The mural is signed "Sinn Fein Youth."

Another theme in the new party-political murals is the role of women in the Nationalist struggle. The Republican movement's position is that the struggle for women's liberation and the struggle for national libera-tion are the same, although primacy is given to the national struggle (they argue that Ireland must achieve national liberation before a com-prehensive women's liberation is possible).[3] A number of murals have been painted specifically depicting the role of women in the struggle, and most of the new murals include both men and women.

As with murals in the previous phase, the new party-political murals also sometimes combined more than one of these themes. For example, there is one depicting solidarity with women involved in armed struggle in other countries. It portrays armed women guerrillas from the IRA, South-West African People's Organization (SWAPO), and Asia inside the circle of a women's symbol.

THE PROTESTANT REACTION—
THE NEW UNIONIST-LOYALIST MURALS

During the Republican hunger strike, Protestants did not respond with murals of their own. The only visual response was in the form of reac-tionary anti-H-Blocks graffiti in Unionist areas. In fact, Loyalists have a long tradition of reactionary graffiti. For example, in September 1942,

Pl. 13. Political cartoons make good murals. This one is by the Republican cartoonist "Cormac." Note security force's vandalism.

Pl. 14. International solidarity with other national liberation movements is a common theme.

Pl. 15. Mural for the seventieth birthday of African National Congress leader Nelson Mandela.

Pl. 16. Armed struggle murals now generally depict both male and female IRA volunteers.

IRA volunteer Tom Williams was hanged in Belfast for the killing of a
police constable. Conroy (1987:139) notes that while Catholics on the
Falls Road wept and prayed for him, "Shankill Protestants drew hang-
man's nooses on gable walls." During the hunger strike this occurred
again, when graffiti with slogans such as "Let Bobby Sands Die," "Let
Bobby Sands Rot in Hell," and "Don't Be Vague, Starve a Taig" appeared in Protestant districts. "Taig" is a derogatory term for Catholics,
and Rolston (1987:27) notes that this is a takeoff on a whiskey advertisement—"Don't Be Vague, Ask for Haig."

Given this history of reactionary graffiti, it should not be surprising
that Loyalists have now responded to the murals in Catholic districts
with reactionary murals of their own. This new mural tradition has
emerged over the last few years, concurrently with the latest "party-
political" phase of Republican murals. This began on a very small scale
by borrowing the idea from Catholic districts of painting simple "quasimurals" combining the Union Jack and simple slogans like "Remember
1690" or "We will not forsake the blue skies of Ulster for the misty
clouds of an Irish Republic." However, this did not really catch on as a
popular activity as it had in Catholic districts, and the new Protestant-
Unionist murals basically skipped the phase of spontaneous mural painting by youths and went directly to the "party-political" phase. These new
Protestant-Unionist murals are produced by the Loyalist paramilitary
organizations. They are clearly reactionary,[4] and they generally center
on two broad areas. The first is "traditional" Protestant-Unionist themes
like King Billy, flags (the Union Jack or the "Red Hand" flag of Ulster),
the crown, and old Unionist shibboleths such as "No Surrender" and
"Remember 1690." The second major theme is the Loyalist paramili-
taries, and this is a new development in Protestant-Unionist murals. For
example, now there are some Ulster Defense Association (UDA) and
Ulster Volunteer Force (UVF) murals depicting many of the same
themes seen in Republican ones, such as armed Loyalist paramilitants,
support for Loyalist prisoners, and honoring their dead.

Like Republican murals, the new Loyalist murals also sometimes
make historical connections with the past. For example, one mural commemorates the old (1913–1923) UVF and the Ulster Division (which was
largely recruited from that organization), which was decimated at the
Battle of the Somme in World War I. (The major contemporary symbolic significance of this battle is that Loyalists believe that they have paid
in blood for their right to remain a part of the United Kingdom.) The
conspicuous absence of gender and solidarity themes in the new Loyalist
murals is worth noting, however. Religious themes are sometimes de-

Pl. 17. Loyalists have reacted with traditional themes, such as "King Billy"—William of Orange at the Battle of the Boyne.

Pl. 18. Unionist shibboleths such as "No Surrender" are a common theme in Loyalist murals.

picted in Unionist murals, but, again like Republican murals, they are relatively rare. They usually have simple slogans like "In God We Trust," "For God and Ulster," or "One Faith—One Crown."

THE MURALS BATTLE

While it is clear that contemporary Protestant murals are a reaction to the success of the Catholic murals that emerged during and after the 1981 hunger strike, there is no direct competition between the mural painters in Catholic and Protestant districts. There is no "war of the murals" going on between them. But there is one going on between the Catholic muralists and the security forces. Protestant-Unionist murals are unspoiled by vandalism, while most of the murals in the Catholic ghettos have been repeatedly vandalized by the British army. There is a running battle going on between the muralists and the soldiers. The soldiers generally deface the murals while on patrol at night. Foot patrols write their own "countergraffiti" on murals, and motorized patrols throw paint bombs at them. These are often long-running battles, with the muralists repairing the murals each time the army vandalizes them.

For example, I followed one long-running battle involving a mural on the Falls Road protesting the use of plastic bullets. It was painted on a corner where a thirty-three-year-old mother of three, Nora McCabe, was killed during the hunger strike. She was walking to a shop to buy cigarettes when a policeman shot her in the head with a plastic bullet from a distance of about six feet. The mural included a picture of a soldier firing a plastic bullet and a caption reading "Civil Order—Plastic Death." For several months the mural was repeatedly vandalized and repaired. Then the IRA blew up the Royal Marine Commandos headquarters in Britain, severely injuring their commanding officer—Major-General Pringle—who lost a leg in the explosion. In a good example of "everyday resistance" (Scott 1985), the young muralists took the opportunity to both repair the mural again and also get in a dig at the Marines. They painted a wooden leg on the soldier in the mural, and painted the Marine general's name next to him. The mural was immediately destroyed by soldiers. After that, it was left in disrepair, until Easter.

Generally, the army wins these battles, at least in the short run. Eventually the muralists get tired of repairing them, and stop doing so. The result is that by Easter almost all of the murals are in pretty bad shape. However, it has now become part of the traditional preparations for the Easter parade to repaint damaged murals. One reason for this is because this is the largest Nationalist parade of the year and always attracts a large number of journalists. The murals are repaired so that they will have the greatest propaganda value.

There is also some evidence that British army vandalism of political murals has been systematic rather than just the result of isolated incidents by individual soldiers. At least one scholar, Faligot (1983), who has written the best book to date about counterinsurgency in Northern Ireland, claims that the army has destroyed murals and graffiti as part of the "psychological operations" aspect of their counterinsurgency effort. For example, he says that the two murals in Ardoyne, mentioned earlier as being the only Catholic-Nationalist political murals before the hunger strike and that were destroyed during redevelopment in the early 1970s, were in fact whitewashed over by the British army in an effort to "depoliticize" the urban environment of the Catholic ghettos. (Faligot also claims that in 1976 the Security Forces painted over political graffiti with nonpolitical graffiti such as "Jane Loves Seamus.")

CONCLUSION

Since 1981, political murals have clearly emerged as an important element of popular political culture in Northern Ireland, particularly in the Catholic-Nationalist ghettos. They have now become so ubiquitous and "normal" a part of the environment that some have virtually become landmarks. For example, Sally Belfrage (1987:249) notes that during her research in Belfast she learned to use the murals in this way:

> I thought I'd take some time out from the Twelfth and go to Andersonstown [on the Catholic Falls Road]. It had taken a dozen trips for me to find my way around there, so identical are the houses and the Crescents, Gardens, Parks, Parades and Drives. The knack lay in following the murals. Turn left at YOU ARE NOW ENTERING FREE A-TOWN past FOUR GREEN FIELDS and FREE OUR COUNTRY, along by VICTORY IS OURS and PROVOS RULE, and two roads past KEEP IRELAND TIDY—BRITS OUT is the Ryans'.

Not only have they become normal features of the urban landscape of the ghettos, but as the product of repetitive organized group activity for a specific purpose, they have become a political and cultural institution. Because of the political functions they effectively fulfill, both internally (e.g., as a form of political socialization) and externally (e.g., as a form of political propaganda), the painting of these murals has largely been "coopted" by Sinn Fein. This cooption does not, however, mean that those who want to cannot go out and paint a mural themselves on their own initiative—perhaps inspired by some contemporary event. Anyone can paint a mural, and no one needs permission from Sinn Fein, the IRA, or anyone else to do so. Despite having their own party muralists, Sinn Fein continues to encourage people outside the party to paint murals. For example, in July and August 1988, Sinn Fein, through *An Phoblact/Republican News* (AP/RN), sponsored a mural competition:

> Following the recent upsurge of mural painting, AP/RN is pleased to announce that it will be sponsoring a mural competition to encourage this highly developed art form and to give added incentive to those young (and not so young) people whose creative work has brightened many a dull environment. The competition is being incorporated into the [new] West Belfast festival, whose organizers have welcomed the AP/RN sponsorship of the competition judged by Robert Ballagh, the renowned Irish artist who will announce the winning entries during the West Belfast festival which runs from August 7th to August 14th.

In order to be eligible for the competition, murals had to have "a connection with some aspect of the cultural, social, political or national struggle for the reconquest of Ireland," and first prize was £100.

Today, the Republican movement is stronger and more confident than ever before. This is clearly expressed in a mural in Derry that shows a cluster of hands holding a brush, a wrench, pencils, and a placard that reads (in Gaelic) "Our day will come." Above that, a single hand holds a rifle. Thus, the mural does not challenge the primacy of the armed struggle, but does emphasize the importance of other tasks in the movement. This is also indicated by an accompanying quotation from Bobby Sands: "Everyone, Republican or otherwise, has his or her own particular part to play. No part is too great or too small, no one is too old or too young to do something."

Catholic-Nationalist murals are an expression of both political impotence and a kind of power. It is because the Catholic minority is powerless within the formal political system in Northern Ireland that they have had to develop informal means of mobilizing power, like painting political murals. Arising from powerlessness, the murals represent a form of informal political power in their own right. As a form of power, they are a step toward countering the image of stability and acceptance generated by the "normal" appearance of much of the urban landscape in Belfast, and they are an effective means of resistance, political socialization, education, and communication. I would argue that these murals initially represented an expression of political frustration and impotence, but have now evolved into the well-developed form of political power that they represent today.

There is a guerrilla war going on in Northern Ireland, and one of the most important "fronts" in any guerrilla war is the propaganda front. In such a war a paintbrush can be as important a weapon as a gun or a bomb. Indeed, the pen—or in this case the paintbrush—can be mightier than the sword. But not always: in 1981, a sixteen-year-old, Michael McCartan, was killed by a policeman in Belfast. He was shot in the back from a distance of ten yards while painting a slogan on a wall. The constable said he thought the paintbrush in the young man's hand was a gun. The constable was acquitted, and the case was dismissed. To my mind, this tragic incident is symbolic of how important a political role murals in Northern Ireland have come to play.

NOTES

1. The best characterization of the two cultures would be "Irish-Catholic-Nationalists" and "British/Ulster-Protestant-Unionists." The combination of British and Ulster identities in Protestant ethnicity reflects the fact that their identity has become ambiguous. It is usually presented as British, but there is a growing sense of a separate and distinct Ulster identity. This ambiguity was noted as early as 1971 by Richard Rose, whose research indicated that among Catholics 76 percent identified themselves as Irish and 15 percent as British, and that among Protestants 39 percent identified themselves as British, 32 percent as Ulster, and 20 percent as Irish (1971:208). Since the suspension of the Northern Irish parliament in 1973, there have been growing fears among some sections of the Protestant community that Britain might eventually "sell them out" to a united Ireland. This has produced the ethnogenesis of an increasing sense of a separate Ulster identity, as the foundation for a potential claim for an independent Ulster. Rolston (1987:26) argues that Protestants are suffering from a "crisis of identity involved in opposing Britain in the name of British identity," and that their identity has become "extremely confused." In this chapter, I will simplify the labels for the two ethnic groups and refer to them as "Catholic-Nationalists" and "Protestant-Unionists."

2. Na Fianna Eireann is the Republican youth organization.

3. See Kelley (1982:319–322) for a brief but concise overview of the relationship between Republicanism and feminism.

4. The term *reactionary* is used here in its neutral or objective sense, and not as a critical labeling or "name-calling" exercise. A "reactionary" political action is one that is undertaken in order to oppose or resist another previously occurring political action. The political use of the term emerged in nineteenth-century France, to describe attitudes and actions opposing the Revolution. It also refers to opposing or resisting reform, wishing to go back to some previous sociopolitical condition, extreme conservatism, and/or supporting a particular right-wing version of society (Williams 1976:214–216). In all of these senses, the term applies to militant Ulster Loyalism.

REFERENCES

Belfrage, Sally
　1987　　*The Crack: A Belfast Year*. London: Andre Deutsch.
Conroy, John
　1987　　*War as a Way of Life: A Belfast Diary*. London: Heinemann.
Faligot, Roger
　1983　　*Britain's Military Strategy in Ireland: The Kitson Experiment*. London: Zed Books.
Kelley, Kevin
　1982　　*The Longest War: Northern Ireland and the IRA*. London: Zed Books.
Republican Movement
　1982　　*Notes for Revolutionaries*. Dublin: Republican Movement.
Rolston, Bill
　1987　　"Politics, Painting and Popular Culture: The Political Wall Murals of Northern Ireland." *Media, Culture and Society*, 9:5–28.
Rose, Richard
　1971　　*Governing without Consensus: An Irish Perspective*. Boston: Beacon Press.
Scott, James C.
　1985　　*Weapons of the Weak: Everyday Forms of Peasant Resistance*. New Haven, Conn.: Yale University Press.
Sternberger, Dolf
　1968　　"Legitimacy." In *The Encyclopedia of the Social Sciences*, pp. 244–248, D. Sills, ed. New York: Crowell, Collier & Macmillan.
Williams, R.
　1976　　*Keywords*. Glasgow: Fontana.

PART THREE

Terror

Pl. 19. Victims of Mozambique's dirty war. Joel Chizigne, photographer.

ELEVEN

A Grammar of Terror: Psychocultural Responses to State Terrorism in Dirty War and Post-Dirty War Argentina

Marcelo Suárez-Orozco

INTRODUCTION

This chapter explores the grammar of terror during the dirty war and post-dirty war years in the Argentine Republic. The study will dissect the contention that the system induced by the political terror that flourished in the Argentine landscape in the 1970s and early 1980s, like other cultural systems, possessed its own formal structures or "grammar." Applying a psychocultural mode of analysis, I shall attempt to relate responses to state terror and universal human psychological coping mechanisms to a puzzling ethnographic fact. During the peak of terror following the military takeover of civilian institutions in early 1976 the great majority of Argentines, not unlike other peoples facing similar extreme circumstances, developed conscious and unconscious strategies of knowing what not to know about events in their immediate environment.

There is now widespread evidence that during 1976 and 1977, at a time when hundreds of people were made to "disappear," tortured and executed without any pretense at due process of law, Argentines largely refused to believe the extent of the atrocities committed in their country (e.g., Corradi 1987:113–129; Corradi et al. 1989; Fagen 1985; Kordon and Edelman 1988:33–40; Kusnetzoff 1986:95–114; Pelento and Braun de Dunayevich 1986:229–237; Simpson and Bennet 1985; Suárez-Orozco 1987b:227–246). I have called this period the phase of denials (Suárez-Orozco 1987b:227–246), the epoch when knowing what not to know was the model coping response to a state of "terror as usual" (Taussig 1988).

On return to democratic rule under Raúl Alfonsín in December 1983, following the military's disastrous adventure in the South Atlantic Malvinas-Falklands Islands, yet another seemingly puzzling complex developed in Argentina. Suddenly now there was a flood of the unspeakable into public discourse (e.g., Abuelas de Plaza de Mayo, *Informaciones* vols. 1–24; Bonafini 1985; Bonasso 1984; Buda 1988; CONADEP 1984; Duhalde 1983; *El Diario del Juicio* vols. 1–15; Gelman and Bayer 1984; Graham-Yooll 1986; Gregorich 1983; Hagelin 1984; Madres de Plaza de Mayo, *Diarios*, vols. 1–44; Paoletti 1987; Seoane and Ruiz Nuñez 1987; Timerman 1981).

What had been previously denied and banished from consciousness returned in the form of an almost exaggerated need to read and talk about the atrocities committed in the name of "national security." As the father of a *desaparecido* (disappeared) told me, Argentina had suffered "a major wound and a wound only festers if left all covered up." A wound, he said, "heals only properly if it ventilates in the open, with plenty of light and fresh air to cure it." "Curing," he continued, "would be possible only after the country assumes [*asumir*] the terror inflicted on the population during the years of dictatorship." This study, then, analyzes the sociocultural contexts in which the psychological processes of denial and elaboration flourished. We will explore the Argentine versions of denial and elaboration, two sides of the same coin, isomorphs in a logic of terror to contribute to our understanding of human behavior under most extreme circumstances of terror.[1]

EATING CANNIBALS AND OTHER APPROACHES TO TERROR

There is surprisingly little critical work on the terror systems that engulfed Latin America in recent decades. The important work by human rights groups such as Amnesty International (1973, 1980, 1984) and America's Watch (Brown 1985), tends to be of an applied nature. Such groups are generally not concerned with problematizing the political, social, and psychological meanings of the terror systems they combat. Rather, these groups typically tend to be interested in publicizing how many people disappear, where they are kept, the methods by which prisoners are tortured, and, most importantly, applying pressure on the states that sponsor terror to release the victims.

Conversely, the Latin Americans who actively participate in combatting political terror most often do so out of deeply personal experiences with the repressive systems they wish to dismantle (Anzorena 1988;

Duhalde 1983; Mignone 1986; Vázquez 1985). They often are themselves survivors of clandestine imprisonment, torture and/or exile (Buda
1988; Gelman and Bayer 1984; Timerman 1981), or relatives of victims
who vanished (Bonafini 1985; Hagelin 1984; Herrera 1987). All have
had personal experiences with the terror (Abuelas de Plaza de Mayo,
Informaciones vols. 1–24; Madres de Plaza de Mayo, *Diarios* vols. 1–44).

Some Latin Americans who write about terror tend to be reluctant to
scrutinize the materials beyond their testimonial value (see, e.g., the critical literary essays in Balderston et al. [1987] and Jara and Vidal [1986]).
They let the testimonials speak for themselves. They seem to follow the
rule that understanding, as the French say, inevitably leads to forgive-
ness. And, they say, we must not forgive or forget. This led some to take
an antiintellectual stance, noting that the terror, the atrocious tortures
and immense pain, cannot be understood the way we can attempt to
understand a neurosis, a descent system, or a religious ritual.

The materials are simply too sinister for any form of detached analysis. Any attempt at analyzing the materials would invariably do violence
to an immensely complex and delicate subject. In the end, analysis simply reproduces the discourse of violence, albeit in another idiom. Note
the kinship of this stance with current postmodern critiques in the social sciences that see (Western) anthropological analysis as "essentially
fraudulent . . . [and] as a deliberate attempt to dominate and eliminate
other traditions . . . [as] a kind of intellectual colonialism" (Bailey 1989:4).
Hence, some argue, the point of the testimonials and other materials is
not so much to understand what has occurred, but to simply inscribe
the terror and human pain into the historical record. [For a similar
debate over representations of Nazi terror, see Wiesel (1989).]

Others such as the Mothers of Plaza de Mayo believe that the materials they produce and their activities (newspapers, lectures, books,
videos, marches, press releases, manifestations, vigils, and their emble-
matic ritual walk every Thursday afternoon around the Plaza de Mayo)
is to resist the terror, injustice, and to prevent the rewriting of history.
Their work is primarily in the service of remembering their *desaparecidos*
and achieving social justice. The Mothers' aims include bringing *all* responsible for the atrocities to court, publicizing the nature and extent
of the atrocities committed during the nightmare years, the release of
political prisoners and the like.

Yet others offer their testimony in the hope that psychologists,
political scientists, anthropologists, sociologists, humanists, and others
would use the materials to help make sense of what has happened in
Latin America (e.g., Buda 1988). All agree about the importance of

inscribing their experiences and those of their missing loved ones into recorded history and popular culture. This is part of a central feature in the survivor's syndrome: trying to make sense and to teleologize the senseless pain inflicted on themselves and on less fortunate relatives and friends who did not survive (Bettelheim 1952; Suárez-Orozco 1987a, 1988b, 1989).

Most, if not all, of the Latin Americans working on the sequelae of terror do not claim any scholarly or scientific detachment from their materials. Indeed, they claim the nature of the materials they deal with is so unnerving that no distancing from the terror can ever be truly achieved.[2] The terror for these intellectuals is not a subject to be mastered but a process yet to be dismantled. They note that the survivors' pains *still* haunt them, that the children of the *desaparecidos* are *still* missing, that the great majority of the alleged torturers are free, some even in active duty in the Armed Forces (*The New York Times* 1989:8). And, of course, the *desaparecidos* are *still* missing. In short terror is part of the everydayness of life.

In mid-1988, over five years after Raúl Alfonsín, a democratically elected president, took over the government, a psychiatrist working on the psychological sequelae of terror among the relatives of the *desaparecidos* calmly and convincingly tells me to be careful what I tell him when I call him over the telephone. He noted that his telephone has been bugged (*está pinchado*, literally meaning "it has holes in it") for at least two years. A few days later, a Mother of Plaza de Mayo tells me as I am chatting with her in their official house across the street from the Plaza Congreso that they no longer receive much of their overseas mail because they are under surveillance by security forces who want to subvert their international human rights campaigns. In early 1989 *The New York Times* reports that the president of the Mothers of Plaza de Mayo, Hebe Bonafini, was almost killed as a car chased her down a sidewalk in her native city of La Plata in Buenos Aires. In October 1989, when military officers who had been awaiting trial for human rights abuses during the dirty war are pardoned by the newly elected Peronist President Menem (*The New York Times* 1989:8), many rebellious officers make combative statements about their righteous "antisubversive campaign" during the dirty war. The terror continues (Abuelas de Plaza de Mayo, *Informaciones* vols. 1–24; Christian 1988a, 1988b; Madres de Plaza de Mayo, *Diarios* vols. 1–44).

The Latin Americans's intellectual work on terror must be seen first and foremost as part of an overall *political* project of resistance to terror. They discourse on justice, imperialism, and economic and cultural independence. They see themselves as the Brechtian intellectuals for the late twentieth century, consciously committed to intellectual work in the periphery in the service of "alleviating the misery of human life." (Brecht, quoted in Kordon et al. [1988:13].)

These Latin American intellectuals almost universally frame the dirty war in the context of the East-West conflict (Anzorena 1988; Santucho 1988; Walsh 1985). More specifically, they see the dirty war terror years as the implementation of the cold war hypothesis (Anzorena 1988; CONADEP 1984; Duhalde 1983; Madres de Plaza de Mayo, *Diarios* vols. 1–44; Paoletti 1987). Some have argued that the system of collective terror that was unleashed in Argentina and elsewhere in Latin America in the 1950s, 1960s, 1970s, and 1980s is a result of the interpretation by the Latin Armed Forces of the United States-inspired "Doctrine of National Security" (CONADEP 1984:442–445; Duhalde 1983:32–44; Langguth 1978; Weschler 1990).

The Latin American intellectuals argue that the leading Latin American military personnel since World War II has been trained in U.S. installations to operate largely within the "Doctrine of National Security" paradigm. This doctrine, they note, argues that since the end of World War II, there has been more or less a permanent state of war (Rock 1985:376), mostly "low-intensity warfare," between the capitalist or free world and its allies (under U.S. leadership), and the communist world and its allies (under Soviet and Cuban leadership).

According to these Latin American leftist intellectuals, in the 1960s and 1970s the local oppressive and morally bankrupt dictatorships of Latin America and the Cuban revolution combined to fuel the project of various Latin American leftist revolutionary movements. In this context, they argue, the Latin American armed forces assumed their U.S.-assigned responsibility in the context of the larger East-West framework. A key aspect of the East-West conflict hypothesis, they argue, is the mandate given by the United States to various Latin American militaries to act as internal police forces to contain and crash any leftist revolutionary movements (Anzorena 1988; Duhalde 1983; Santucho 1988; Walsh 1985). These Latin American leftist intellectuals emphasize the dependence of various Latin American security forces on massive U.S. aid, supplies, and training. According to the Doctrine of National Security, the enemy of the Latin American Armed Forces is the internal version of international communism. It is worth noting that leftist intellectuals and armed forces personnel by and large agree that the primary task of local armed forces has become eliminating internal communist projects.

Many Latin American intellectuals note that the ideational framework

for the Doctrine of National Security was articulated in the 1950s and
1960s at various U.S. military and intelligence installations (Duhalde
1983:32–44; Walsh 1985:13–118). This program, they argue, is implemented at the various training institutions where thousands of Latin
American security personnel have been receiving training since the
1950s in anticommunist theory (in the form of the Doctrine of National
Security), counterinsurgency warfare, police crowd control, special interrogation techniques, and the like (see, e.g., Anzorena 1988; Duhalde
1983:37–43; Langguth 1978; Walsh 1985). These Latin American intellectuals regularly quote from the leading U.S. architects of foreign policy. For example, they quote from Robert MacNamara's speeches on
military aid to Latin America in the 1960s. In a presentation to the U.S.
Congress in his capacity as President Kennedy's Secretary of Defense
in 1963, MacNamara said:

> The best return on our investment in military aid probably comes from
> the training of selected Army officers and key specialists in our military
> academies and training centers in the US and abroad. These students are
> carefully selected by their countries so that they in turn become instruc-
> tors when they go home. They are the leaders of the future, the men who
> have the skills and will instruct their own Armed Forces. . . . For us having
> these people as friends is invaluable. . . . Our primary objective in Latin
> America is to aid, wherever necessary, the continual growth of the mili-
> tary and paramilitary forces, so that together with the police and other se-
> curity forces, they may provide the necessary internal security. (Robert
> MacNamara, quoted in CONADEP 1984:443–444.)

The National Security project, Latin American leftist intellectuals argue, is driven by an hegemonic project of domination (Anzorena 1988;
Duhalde 1983; Vázquez 1985; Walsh 1985). The Latin American National Security regimes, it has been widely argued, have aimed to implement, through terror-achieved social consensus, harsh economic plans.
These plans attempted to guarantee a disciplined and docile labor force,
giving transnational interests free and unrestricted access to cheap raw
products. They note that the National Security regime that ruled Argentina during the dirty war tried to establish a free capitalist economic
program, opening local markets to transnational interests and products (thus destroying the highly inadequate and traditionally rigorously
protected local industry and driving up unemployment). This, known
throughout Latin America as *liberal capitalism,* it has been argued, was
accompanied by massive cutbacks in social programs, which, combined
with high inflation rates, consumed the standard of living of vast sectors

of the work force. During the dirty war, the architect of the liberal capitalist project in Argentina was Martinez de Hoz and his team of University of Chicago-trained conservative economists. The team was widely known throughout Latin America as the "Chicago Boys." Finally, some noted that terror insured impunity for those de facto, if not de jure, in government positions to line their pockets with unimaginably large sums of money.

To recapitulate, Latin American intellectuals interested in the terror tend to be leftist in political orientation. They approach the problem of terror and its inscription and representation as a political and collective act of resistance, most often in the context of wider political work on justice, antiimperialism, and economic and cultural liberation. They tend to frame the dirty war terror as being a part of a much larger stage. The dirty war is seen as the local application of the Doctrine of National Security which accompanied a project of economic domination. The terror is not a subject of inquiry but rather an ongoing process yet to be dismantled.

A handful of U.S.-based Latin Americanists have recently begun to consider the nature of the regimes of terror that swept the region (see, e.g., Adams [n.d.], Bourque and Warren [1989], Corradi [1987], Corradi et al. [1989], Taussig [1987, 1988]; for journalistic accounts, see Langguth [1978], Weschler [1990]). The considerations of these scholars tend to be more analytical and less driven by personal investment. Although Michael Taussig does say that he writes "against terror" (1987), his writings hardly convey the concrete urgency of the writings of, for example, the Mothers of Plaza de Mayo or the Abuelas of Plaza de Mayo when they write to locate still missing children or to prosecute alleged torturers. Curiously, these United States-based authors generally fail to consider the Latin Americans' working hypothesis, that is, the Doctrine of National Security. By and large these scholars are outsiders looking in.

Michael Taussig, for example, is an Australian who explores the nature of terror that flourished in the Peruvian-British rubber plantations in the Putumayo districts of southwestern Colombia at the turn of the century. Taussig relates terror to the political economy of the colonial "encounter" between capitalism and what he sees as precapitalist forms of production. Terror, Taussig argues, was employed to "recruit" the Indians through debt, into an economic system of commodity fetishism that they resisted as most foreign to their hearts. According to Taussig, the capitalist process of ever-expanding commodification is so destruc-

tive and inhuman that "a culture of terror" emerged where torture and
other obscene rituals of depreciation became the idiom mediating the
encounter of two worlds during the colonial enterprise:

> The creation of the colonial reality that occurred in the New World will
> remain a subject of immense curiosity and study—the New World where
> the Indian and African *irracionales* became compliant to the reason of a
> small number of white Christians. Whatever the conclusions [*sic*] we draw
> about how that hegemony was so speedily effected, we would be unwise
> to overlook the role of terror. (1987:7)

In South America, Taussig argues, a culture of terror was beat out
of the Indian body and was fed with ever more delirious Spanish colonial fantasies of savagery, cannibalism, and the wildness inspired by the
steamy jungle. According to Taussig, it was sheer terror that brought
the *irracionales* into the newly emerging order of capitalist commodification. Taussig's aims are, indeed, ambitious. The Putumayo (Colombia)
atrocities of the rubber boom are not unique to that part of the world,
nor are they derivative of the peculiarities of a conqueror, in this specific
case inquisitional Spanish culture in its most paranoid form. For Taussig
terror is inevitable in the "[G]lobal stage of development of the commodity fetish; think also of the Congo with its rubber and ivory, of the en-
slavement of the Yaquis for the sisal plantations of the Yucatan in
Mexico, of the genocidal bloodletting in tragic Patagonia—all around
the same time" (1987:129).

Taussig's chapters on the "culture of terror" are largely based on his
reading of Roger Casement's report on the atrocities committed by the
Anglo-Peruvian company headed by the infamous Julio C. Arana on the
native Indians "employed" in the collection of rubber in the Putumayo
districts of southwestern Colombia.

The conquest, the act of overcoming the other, was brutal. Taussig's
writing makes the point that the devil, too, dwells in the details. Taussig
dissects the very inhumanity of a voracious economic system that can
never quite satiate its frenzied hunger for profits. The Peruvian Arana's
main problem was, simply, inducing the Indians to gather rubber for
him, Taussig tells us. And inducing Indians to gather rubber was only
half of the story. The second half of the story was to keep them, to recruit the Indians through debt into an economic system most foreign to
their ways. As Arana eventually testified in 1913 to a British House of
Commons Select Committee investigating the atrocities committed in his
rubber plantations, *conquistar* really meant doing business.

But as Taussig tells us, the Indians would not do business with the whites. And the problem was not one of labor scarcity. There were plenty of Indians. The problem was, and Taussig returns to this point again and again, that the Indians resisted adopting the white man's *way* of doing business. Recruiting Indians into the white man's ways was brutally messy, as the British House of Commons Select Committee Report noted:

> They [rubber station managers] force the Pacific Indians of the Putumayo to work day and night at the extraction of rubber, without the slightest remuneration. . . . They give them nothing to eat. . . . They keep them in complete nakedness. . . . They rob them of their crops, their women, and their children to satisfy the voracity, lasciviousness and avarice of themselves and their employees, for they live on the Indian's food, keep harems and concubines, and sell these people at wholesale and retail in Iquitos. . . . They flog them inhumanely until their bones are visible. . . . They give them no medical treatment, but let them die, eaten up by maggots, or to serve as foods for the chiefs' [i.e. rubber station managers'] dogs. . . . They castrated them, cut off their ears, fingers, arms and legs. . . . And they also tortured the Indians with fire, water and upside-down crucifixion. Company employees cut the Indians to pieces with machetes and dashed out the brains of small children by hurling them against trees and walls. The elderly were killed when they could no longer work, and to amuse themselves company officials practiced their marksmanship using Indians as targets. On special occasions such as Easter Sunday, Saturday of Glory, they shot them down in groups or, in preference, doused them with kerosene and set them on fire to enjoy their agony. (1987:34)

The bonfires of the vanities of evil, indeed. Terror, according to Taussig, was fed by capitalist hunger: the exploitation of the Indians was attempted as if to solve the bosses instrumental need for labor and the conduct of business in the peripheries. Yet instrumental exploitation is only half of the story. By "privileging" an analysis of terror based on the instrumental aspects of incorporating Indians into a profit-driven mode of production, Taussig fails to pay sufficient attention to the irrational and expressive aspects of terror. The other half of terror's coin was the white man's own paranoid fear of the steamy jungle and, particularly, of the dark powers imputed on the *indios salvages*. The nervous colonialists had, indeed, imputed awesome, mysterious, and, of course, "natural," powers to the *indios salvages*. And because the paranoid's maxim is to attack before being attacked, the colonial mirror of terror reflected the white man's worst fear in inverted form. Jorge Luis Borges's brilliant summary of the Argentine military's brutal assault on dissent during the dirty war applies well to the colonial case considered by Taussig. Borges eventually said of the Argentine generals, "They eat the cannibals."

Taussig's corpus has been welcomed in some circles as representing a new seductive "experimental" blending of political economy and interpretative traditions in anthropology. Yet Taussig's treatment of terror is not without problems. Latin American intellectuals with whom I shared Taussig's theory of terror, at once demand to know how Taussig approaches the more recent regimes of terror throughout Latin America: 10,000 to 30,000 politically motivated disappearances in Argentina during the dirty war, close to 100,000 politically motivated killings in Guatemala in the last fifteen years, close to 70,000 political deaths in El Salvador in the last ten years, and close to 50,000 political killings in Nicaragua during the war against Somoza, to name but the best-known cases (Suárez-Orozco 1989). Taussig's theory does not systematically address the more contemporary regimes of terror. The point is that terror, if not quite endemic, remains an epidemic in the South American world long after the conquest. Surely in some fundamental respects the new dirty wars and the terror they spawn are autonomous of the Spanish conquest. Yet Taussig's book although briefly discussing Jacobo Timerman's Argentine calvary (Timerman 1981), is unexplainably mute on this key and pressing issue.

In a more recent essay, "Terror as Usual," Taussig (1988) does attempt to speak of the current wave of terror in modern-day Colombia. In this essay Taussig is not directly concerned with the much-publicized wave of cocaine-related terror in that bleeding country. Rather, Taussig is interested in the "everydayness" of terror as Colombian death squads and paramilitary units implement in their country the so-called Argentine model: an assault on civil society and dissent through torture, disappearances, and terror. Taussig says of modern-day Colombian terror:

> Today, in a population of some 27 million, being the third largest in Latin America, with widespread assassinations striking, so it is said, some thirty people a day, with 500 members of the only viable opposition party, the *Union Patriotica*, [sic] gunned down in the streets over the past two years, with an estimated 11,000 assassinations carried out by the more than 149 death squads recently named in the National Congress over roughly the same time-period, and with over 1,000 named people disappeared (surely but a small fraction of the actual number)—there can be no doubt that a situation exists which is no less violent than it is sinister, and that its sinister quality depends on the strategic use of uncertainty and mystery around which terror's talk circulates and to which it always returns. (Taussig 1988:6)

Theoretically, the new piece more or less rehashes the thesis of the earlier and more ambitious work. In Colombia, Taussig argues, death squads and paramilitary units fight their low-intensity warfare in the service of a murky power structure that thrives in "uncertainty," "mystery," and "disordered order" (Taussig 1988:6). The new Colombian terror, according to Taussig, feeds on a "tropical version of the Hobbesian world, nasty, brutish and short" (ibid., 17). Like the nervous Spanish *conquistadores* of yesteryear, today's death squad and paramilitary bosses in Colombia *depend* on this fabrication of a "tropical Hobbesian world" of, alas, leftist subversives, drug traffickers, deviants, and Antichrists, to spawn their own forms of arbitrary power through terror.

Richard Adams (n.d.), in a much less ambitious project than Taussig's, approaches the problem of the reproduction of state terrorism in recent Central American history (1950s through 1980s). According to Adams, the Central American horrors must also be seen in the context of the Spanish conquest. Specifically, Adams considers the legacy of the Spanish subjugation of various indigenous groups in the New World. According to Adams, terror is an inevitable sequela of an imperfectly achieved colonial hegemony. It is based in a "conquest-based" relationship of ethnic hatred (a landed Hispanic elite versus poor, mostly landless indian and mestizo peasants). He writes, "The roots of this fear lie in the fact that the failure to exterminate or assimilate a conquered people inevitably leaves a population with divided identities" (Adams n.d.:5). Yet, surely there is some functional autonomy between the conquest (initiated over 400 years ago!), brutal and hateful as it was, and modern-day death-squad operations in Guatemala. Yet, Adams is mute on this point. He does not refer to Taussig's model, nor does he refer to the Latin Americans' working hypothesis on terror, the so-called Doctrine of National Security.

Disparate though they are in theoretical approach and emphasis, it is interesting to note that both Richard Adams and Michael Taussig "privilege" an analysis of the colonial encounter as the primary culprit in the subsequent establishment of what they call a "culture of terror." Adams and Taussig agree that the colonial "encounter" in the New World was brutally messy. The subjugation of *irracionales* to the will of the white Europeans, they both argue, was achieved by terror (Adams n.d.:1–13; Taussig 1987:5).

This historical context is, of course, important—almost self-evidently so—but surely does not begin to cover the complexities of the *new* regimes of terror. The various dirty wars that raged from the Isthmus of Tehuantepec to the Tierra del Fuego in the 1950s, 1960s, 1970s, and early 1980s can only in the most general of terms be traced to the brutal colonial encounter. The conquest background offers a necessary but hardly sufficient point of departure to analyze the various Latin American dirty wars. What, then, of the more recent background to the Argentine case under consideration in this chapter?

OLD WARS, NEW WARS, DIRTY WARS: PATHS TO THE DIRTY WAR

In the Argentine case we must pay close attention to the significant role of the more immediate developments setting the stage for the military takeover of March 1976 and the subsequent growth of the state-operated dirty war apparatus. The birth and growth of the dirty war apparatus cannot be understood without full reference to the devouring of political space for dissent which intensified during the 1960s and early 1970s.

In Argentina, by the late 1960s, following the revolts known in Argentine folk speech as the *Cordobazo* (massive revolts in the province of Cordoba), and taking inspiration from the Cuban experience, particularly its Argentine embodiment in the figure of Ché Guevara, a small but viable student-led leftist urban guerrilla movement was operational in Buenos Aires and other important centers (Anzorena 1988; Gillespie 1982; Rock 1985:320–366; Santucho 1988). The generals under Juan Carlos Ongania's command responded to the revolts in the province of Cordoba and elsewhere brutally and inefficiently. The *onganiato* repression not only further fueled the urban guerrilla project for a revolutionary Argentina but also commenced the first important wave of professional and university brain-drain from the country: the political room for debate in Argentina was shrinking.

The first half of the 1970s in Argentina was, indeed, characterized by unprecedented levels of political violence. The security forces and privileged classes were victimized by the armed left and the armed right victimized the left, armed and otherwise. Attacks against military and police officers, government officials, diplomats, journalists, industrialists, and intellectuals became daily events (Anzorena 1988; Simpson and Bennett 1985). At the same time the Argentine economy was collapsing. Extreme inflation rates made the Argentine peso a worthless currency. During the first quarter of 1976 inflation reached an annual rate of nearly 800 percent. Unemployment soared. Labor unrest and strikes were almost daily occurrences (Rock 1985:320–366).

During the early 1970s high-ranking members of the military and police hierarchies were kidnapped and/or assassinated in ultraleftist guerrilla operations on a regular basis. For example, the ex-president of Argentina, General Aramburu, was kidnapped and executed by a guerrilla group, the *Montoneros,* a seemingly peculiar blend of leftist internationalism and nationalist Peronism. The heads of major international companies in Buenos Aires were also targets of ultraleftist guerrilla attacks. In one such case the head of Fiat Buenos Aires, an Italian executive, was kidnapped in a dramatic operation. He was held for ransom for months and was eventually killed. The *Montoneros* also kidnapped members of one of Argentina's most influential agroindustrial families, the Born brothers, and extracted a reported sixty million dollars for their freedom, evidently the highest ransom ever collected in a kidnapping (Graham-Yooll 1986; Rock 1985:363).

By the 1970s ultrarightist paramilitary organizations such as the "Asociación Anticomunista Argentina" (AAA), began to systematically produce their own brand of terror. Union leaders were executed at midday in downtown Buenos Aires (Anzorena 1988; Duhalde 1983). Leftist politicians were assassinated in one spectacular operation after another. The leftist-Peronist National Deputy, Rodolfo Ortega Peña, was assassinated on July 31, 1974, reportedly the first acknowledged victim of the AAA's emerging war on dissent (Duhalde 1983). Renowned academics were also targets, such as Professor Silvio Frondizi, brother of the constitutional ex-president of the Republic, Arturo Frondizi. Professor Frondizi, a Marxist intellectual, was kidnapped and executed in public.

In brief, members of all sectors of the society were vulnerable to random flying bullets. It seemed as if the state could no longer monopolize the use of violence. The atmosphere of fear was like a thick fog. No one could feel safe, exempted. Bodyguards were in high demand. Paying bribes to terrorist groups for immunity became common practice in the industrial sector (Timerman 1981:19). Policemen supplemented their incomes by guarding homes at night in the better neighborhoods.

I must note an important difference between the Argentine case prior to the dirty war and the recent Colombian experience as portrayed by Michael Taussig (1988). Taussig argues that in Colombia the violence that led to systematic death-squad terror was "created by the press," and "not only were the accounts in the newspapers extraordinarily exaggerated, but it was as if they were designed to create and reproduce a tropical version of the 'Hobbesian world'" (Taussig 1988:17). Taussig tells us that the press created the "extraordinarily exaggerated" reports of violence prior to the emergence of the fully operational death-squad approach to social consensus in Colombia. This scenario fits Taussig's model rather well: the press, the mouth piece of the murky but nervous power structure, created an *illusion* of chaos that in turn demanded "unusual measures" (read "state-mandated terror") to restore arbitrary order through "terror as usual" (Taussig 1988).

Yet, the violence that predated the state operation we now call the "dirty war" in Argentina was no illusion. It would be irresponsible and otherwise inaccurate to suggest that the Argentine press manufactured the chaos predating the dirty war (e.g., Anzorena 1988; Graham-Yooll 1986; Rock 1985:320–366; Timerman 1981). The Argentine press did act irresponsibly, but this was mostly *during* the peak of the dirty war terror, when it largely refused, with only a few heroic exceptions, to print the horrors of disappearances and torture (Simpson and Bennett 1985; Verbitsky 1985). In pre-dirty war Argentina, the chaos, the daily bombings, kidnappings, and assassinations by the armed left and armed right were quite real. In fact, it is widely known that the armed left had consciously calculated that its own campaign of terror, kidnappings, bombings and other *atentados* (attacks), would unleash the asphyxiating repressive horror of the armed forces. The logic behind this maneuver was to try to create massive dissatisfaction in the population, thereby feeding the "revolutionary process" (Santucho 1988). Indeed, various armed leftist organizations such as the *Ejercito Revolucionario del Pueblo* (ERP) (The People's Revolutionary Army), and the *Montoneros* had *hoped* that a particularly repressive military coup would take over the government. The idea was that the new military dictatorship set on vengeance for all their dead would be so asphyxiating that the masses of oppressed workers would in turn join the elite revolutionary "vanguard," and that together they would overwhelm the corrupt bourgeois capitalist power structures and achieve the revolution (Anzorena 1988; Santucho 1988; Walsh 1985).

As it turns out, the two terrors needed one another to feed their own perverse aims: the armed left needed the repressive right in its fantastic plan for a popular uprising. The armed forces, following the coup of 1976 that ushered in the dirty war terror, perpetuated and carefully fed the myth of a subversive threat, *even after the armed left had been virtually annihilated in the field.* Even years after the threat of the armed left had been crushed, innocent civilians continued to be haunted in the name of "national security."

The armed left turned out to be only half right in its analysis: it did awaken the repressive sleeping monster, which turned out to be more repressive and monstrous than anyone had dreamed of, but the masses

failed to take arms and join the vanguard in toppling the power structures. Not unlike other youth-based intellectual revolutionary movements, the Argentine armed leftists of the 1960s and 1970s turned out
to be more suicidal than Machiavellian.

I do not mean to imply, as some have, that the terror of the armed
left in any way excuses the immensely more monstrous and devastating
state-operated terror of the dirty war years. I simply wish to point out
how the two terrors dialectically fed on each other. The armed left
needed the terrorist right to fan its own revolutionary project and the
terrorist right needed the leftist guerrillas for its own hegemonic purposes. Having said this, I must note that a state in the business of
systematically terrorizing its citizens represents a qualitatively different
syndrome than bands of armed leftists spreading terror in the name of
their own somewhat megalomaniac, and in the Argentine case ultimately
suicidal, plan for saving mankind.

The chaos predating the dirty war climaxed in early 1976 during the
last days of the regime of Maria Estela ("Isabelita") Martinez de Perón,
who was then the constitutional president of Argentina. Terrorist attacks by highly dedicated and efficient groups of both ultraleftist and
ultrarightist persuasion now became daily events. The increasing discontent of the great majority of Argentines set the stage for a military
takeover of civilian institutions. When the military, promising "order,"
finally removed "Isabelita" Perón from the Casa Rosada, the Argentine
government house, in March 1976, as Timerman put it (exaggerating
only a little bit), "the entire country, including the Peronists, breathed
a sigh of relief" (Timerman 1981:26). I would add that even the armed
left welcomed the military takeover as congruous with its own plans: the
armed forces, they predicted would be incompetent and repressive, and
would inevitably bring about massive discontent and thus fan the revolution (Santucho 1988). Embarrassing as it now seems, it was, indeed,
"the welcome revolution" (Simpson and Bennett 1985:33) among vast
sectors of Argentine society. As the blind Don of Argentine letters, Jorge
Luis Borges, put it the country would finally be ruled "by gentlemen."
Never had Borges been so blind.

Instead, of "order" what ensued was one of the most savage regimes
known in a continent already noted for a long history of brutality. The
state rapidly underwent a metamorphosis from seeming unable to
monopolize the use of violence to fully (and almost exclusively) relying
on a new kind of political terror for social consensus (Duhalde 1983;
Rock 1985:367–403; Vázquez 1985). A new state grew within the state
to spread terror. Soon terror was rediscovered as the principal idiom for

social consensus. An unprecedented system for disappearing, torment-ing, and ultimately eliminating dissenters grew to envelop the Argentine landscape (CONADEP 1984; Duhalde 1983; Vázquez 1985). The end justified all means. As the doctrine of National Security had taught them, and as the leftist guerrillas had reminded them, Argentina was finally embarked in a righteous, unconventional *war*.

The new war would be an uncommon war; hence it required uncom-mon means. According to the military's discourse, this was an internal, low-intensity conflict ignited by international, "godless," and "country-less" (*apátrida*), leftist "subversives." The atrocities committed during the dirty war depended on a new definition of the enemy. It soon became clear that to the military, the enemy was by no means just the armed left but all substantial dissent. "Subversives," as the emerging totalizing discourse had it, came in many forms. Those who actually pull the trig-ger are only the tip of the iceberg. Beneath the surface, were their ideological allies and other "idiotas útiles" (useful idiots). A key aim was to remove all subversives and their ideological allies, to induce passivity in the population and to subvert any project of collective resistance. Hence from day one the decision was made not to make martyrs by pub-lic executions or trials. Rather, this would be the war by banishment. People simply began to disappear. The relatives of the *desaparecidos* were kept in check by hope: rumors thrived. The message was clear: do not act if you want your relative back; if you make waves, that person will be hurt, badly. A massive and unparalleled social centrifugal force was set in motion. People no longer trusted one another, not even close friends. The terror induced silence and, perhaps more importantly, social isolationism.

The Argentine Armed Forces had not fought a war during this century. The Malvinas-Falklands conflict was after the "dirty war." Ar-gentina was sympathetic to Germany throughout World War II and de-clared war on Germany only on the eve of the German surrender to the Allies. Historically modeled after Prussian ideals, the military has tradi-tionally seen itself as an institution of superior men entrusted with a his-torical duty to protect the "fatherland" from foreign and, particularly, domestic enemies. The implications of a reported *castelike segregation* of the military from the civilian order is critical to understand the military's brutal assault on civil society. For example, some have noted an en-dogamous pattern where military men tend to marry women from mili-tary families (Timerman 1981). Clearly, more basic research in this area is needed.

In the 1960s and 1970s, for the first time in its modern history, the military caste came under systematic and vicious attacks from highly efficient leftist guerrilla groups. There is now evidence that both active and retired members of the armed forces organized, equipped, and directed the ultraright paramilitary groups that began to operate prior to the military takeover of March 1976 (Duhalde 1983). After the March coup, paramilitary gangs, known in the new vocabulary of terror as *patotas*, began to operate much more visibly under the direct control of the security forces.

On March 24, 1976 the Argentine military installed a junta composed of the chiefs of its three branches: the Army, the Navy, and the Air Force. The head of the Argentine Army, General Jorge Rafael Videla, became president of the Republic. Thus *El Proceso de Reorganización Nacional* (The Process of National Reorganization) began. The stated objective of the junta was to "reorganize" the Argentine nation.

Technically what most Argentines refer to as the dirty war originated as a counterinsurgency campaign against leftist guerrillas initiated under the constitutional government of "Isabelita" Perón. As president of the Republic, it was she who signed the orders to unleash military might against the armed leftists. *There is now some evidence to suggest that this initial military operation against the armed guerrillas was very successful.* In fact, according to some observers, soon after the March military takeover leftist guerrilla organizations no longer posed any serious threat to the state (Cabeza 1985:170; Vázquez 1985). Indeed, by 1978, "The Army had crushed the guerrillas" (Rock 1985:368). The armed left had been defeated in the field. Yet the state-controlled terror continued for years, now haunting largely innocent civilians and even children (Abuelas de Plaza de Mayo, *Informaciones*; CONADEP 1984; Nosiglia 1985; Suárez-Orozco 1987*b*, 1987*c*).[3]

As the military grip on civilian institutions became increasingly formalized, a new repressive terror descended on the Argentine landscape. The generals' capacity for method in terror should impress all social scientists. As General Iberico Saint-Jean, governor of Buenos Aires during the first junta regime, put it, "first we will kill all the subversives; then we will kill their collaborators; then . . . their sympathizers, then . . . those who remain indifferent; and finally we will kill the timid" (Simpson and Bennett 1985:66). What ensued was an unpredictable deployment of terror by the security forces and those working for them. Anyone thought to be sympathizing with the left, or in any way dissenting with the regime became a possible target for kidnapping, torture, and disappearance (Rock 1985:363). The discharge of terror was unpredictable but not decentralized. Indeed, there is now widespread evidence that the campaign of terror was carefully planned from the top downward, with a most eerie sense of organization and purpose (Duhalde 1983; Paoletti 1987; Vázquez 1985).

On return to democratic rule in 1983, following the disastrous adventure of the Argentine military in its attempt to take over the Malvinas-Falkland Islands, the Argentine people began to be more fully conscious of the crimes committed in the name of "saving" the fatherland from the "subversives." Indeed, a new genre of survivor's literature is now a sad but permanent fixture in the Argentine cultural landscape.[4]

In December 1983 the democratically elected government of Rául Alfonsín responded to public pressure by creating the Comisión Nacional sobre la Desparición de Personas (CONADEP). President Alfonsín had won the election largely on a human rights platform. He promised to repudiate the military's autoamnesty law for any crimes committed during the dirty war. President Alfonsín also promised to order the investigation of all crimes and the punishment of all those responsible. The CONADEP was established to investigate the crimes committed during the dirty war.

The CONADEP's objective was to document the nature and extent of the repression unleashed following the military takeover. For months the Commission received and recorded the testimony of those who had survived clandestine imprisonment. On September 20, 1985 the Commission presented its report, *Nunca Mas* (never again), to President Alfonsín.

The CONADEP report concluded that at least 8,960 citizens remain disappeared (CONADEP 1984:16). That is not counting those who were kidnapped, systematically abused, and then freed. I should point out that many regard the CONADEP estimate of 8,960 as much too conservative. Indeed, some argue that close to 30,000 persons were made to disappear during the dirty war (Duhalde 1983; Madres de Plaza de Mayo, *Diarios* vols. 1–44; Paoletti 1987; Vázquez 1985). The assault on children was so systematic that the *Abuelas de la Plaza de Mayo* (grandmothers of the Plaza de Mayo) formed to find out and make public the pain inflicted on children of "subversives" and to help locate some 400 children still missing (Abuelas de Plaza de Mayo, *Informaciones*; Guthmann 1986; Nosiglia 1985; Slavin 1985).

The restitution of some kidnapped children to their biological families has created a new wave of painful debate in post-dirty war Argentina (Bianchedi et al. 1990; Herrera and Tenembaum 1989). In some cases, children taken as "war booty" were adopted by members of the death squads (Herrera and Tenembaum 1989). In other cases, infertile couples close to the regime, but perhaps not directly involved in the reproduction of state terror, adopted children of *desaparecidos*. Yet in other cases, well-meaning families, who were in no way allied with those responsible for the terror, innocently adopted children of *desaparecidos*. Should the restituted children continue contact with their adoptive parents (with whom they spent years prior to the restitution), even in cases where the adoptive parents were allied to those who victimized the children's parents? What about those cases in which families adopted children in good faith? The questions are profound and all solutions seem unsettling.

Many of the victims of the dirty war machinery were professionals from "suspected occupations" such as psychologists, psychiatrists, sociologists, teachers and students, welfare workers, labor organizers, union leaders, and journalists judged to be "critical" of the regime (CONADEP 1984:293–441; Duhalde 1983; Simpson and Bennett 1985; Timerman 1981:93–99). It is worth noting that the security forces specifically sought out these professionals whom Foucault (1979) considers to be the modern "social regulators" who replaced jailers and torturers as the agents of consensus in post-nineteenth-century Europe. Evidently, Foucault's model of the evolution of "discipline" and "punishment" may explain the historical shift in European social control from seizing upon the "body" to the "soul," but it obviously fails to account for the recurrence of torture in the postcolonial world (Suárez-Orozco 1988*b*; Taussig 1987).

Indeed, during the dirty war attorneys who were working on behalf of disappeared persons, themselves were made to disappear as were members of human rights groups working on behalf of disappeared persons (CONADEP 1984:416–426; Duhalde 1983). University students, faculty, and labor organizers were made to disappear. Even high school students were made to disappear (Seoane and Ruiz Nuñez 1987). Others were kidnapped simply by mistake. Dagmar Ingrid Hagelin, a seventeen-year-old Swedish-Argentine binational, was mistaken for a "subversive." She was kidnapped by security officers, tortured, and then was made to disappear (Hagelin 1984). Others were picked up, tortured, and made to disappear after an anonymous call to the security forces identified them as "subversive." No questions were asked. One such call could mean a death sentence. The randomness characterizing the dirty war became a key to the establishment of social control through collective terror.

The discharge of terror was highly patterned. Women were routinely raped and men's and women's genitals were routinely assaulted with the infamous *picana* (electrical prod). The castration metaphor is unmistakable. It was as if the obscene rituals of torture conveyed the body politic the agents of the terrorist state wished to create: a state of passive, desexualized, infantile, and obedient subjects. The Devil, too, dwells in the details: the specifics of such rituals of the unspeakable sheds light on the agenda of the new consensus builders.

THE WAR BEYOND DEATH: THE "PARANOID ETHOS" IN THE SOUTHERN CONE WARS OF IDEOLOGICAL INQUISITION

An overlooked feature of the dirty war is the "paranoid" ethos (Schwartz 1976:191–197) that permeated the military's operation. By concentrating on the instrumental aspects of the repression, such as the context of implementing an exploitative and unpopular economic plan, some researchers have not paid sufficient attention to the psychological and expressive aspects of the terror system (Duhalde 1983; Vázquez 1985).

According to those responsible for the atrocities, Argentina was the epicenter of a global attack on the Western way of life. The dirty war was the war beyond death, as Admiral Massera of the first junta put it in a particularly sinister statement. "We won't fight to death, we will fight to victory even if victory is beyond death" (quoted in Duhalde [1983:79] [my trans.]). Argentina became a world strategic center for the imminent outbreak of World War III. As Jacobo Timerman noted in his controversial book, "The Argentine military tapped their vast reservoir of hatred and fantasy so as to synthesize their action into one basic concept: World War III had begun; the enemy was left-wing terrorism; and Argentina was the initial battleground chosen by the enemy" (1981: 101). Terrorist attacks were not seen in a regional frame, but were written in a grander script. A historical pattern was sketched out. For example, according to General Viola, the second president of the *Proceso,* the country was the victim of an "international Marxist aggression which began to [concentrate on Argentina] at the end of the second world war." (*El Diario del Juicio* 1985, 15:349 [my trans.].)

The security forces framed the dirty war operation in the context of saving Argentina from the evils of an alien infiltration. The military appropriated a univocal discourse identifying itself as keepers of things Argentine. All dissenters came to be framed as pathological outsiders to be removed. The raw antisemitic nature of the crusade has been treated in some detail by Timerman (1981). In a Kafkaesque dialogue between Timerman and his torturers we get a glance at "political hallucinations" (Timerman 1981:96) afflicting members of the security forces. The final plot against Argentina was headed by an improbable mixture of Zionist-Marxists working under the guidance of the Soviet KGB and Washington power brokers. The first part of the international plan was to take over Patagonia to create the "Republic of Andina."

Timerman's torturers asked him: "We'd like to know further details on the Andina Plan. How many troops would the State of Israel be prepared to send?" (1981:73) to invade Argentina! As the jailers told Timerman, the communist attack on Argentina was orchestrated by three power centers unified by international Jewish solidarity. Israel, in collaboration with "the United States, where Jewish power is evident," and "The Kremlin [which] is still dominated by the same sectors that staged the Bolshevik Revolution, in which Jews played the principal role" (1981:73–74) were operating together to invade southern Argentina, which would eventually function as the food and oil basket in World War III.

In this paranoid atmosphere, terror became an intrinsic part of the military's political mission. Prisoners were routinely terrorized with tortures before and during interrogation, before execution, or before regaining freedom. In other cases people were tortured and released without ever being interrogated. The human body, indeed, became the canvas in which Foucault's "anatomists of pain" (Foucault 1979:11) dramatized anew an ancient discourse on power and orthodoxy. A new inquisition was unleashed. The Occidental way of life was to be saved by finally removing the "subversives" from the fatherland. All means were prudent in this momentous crusade. The perverse medical—hygienic and surgical—imagery that gave the operation a surreal twist again point to the paranoid ethos that engulfed dirty war Argentina. Argentina was "diseased" and "contaminated." An infection had penetrated and was growing, spreading throughout the "fatherland." As the Argentine Minister of Foreign Affairs, Admiral C. Guzetti, put it, "When the social body of the country has been contaminated by disease which eats away at its entrails, it forms antibodies. These antibodies (death squads) cannot be considered in the same way as the microbes. As the government controls and destroys the guerrillas, the actions of the antibodies will disappear. This is already happening. It is only a reaction of a sick body" (Simpson and Bennett 1985:82). As if by homeopathic magic death and terror would cure the "disease" and "contamination" in the body politic.

Indeed, a "dirty" war was required to "cleanse" the country of ideological contamination. I must note that the killings were commonly referred to as "cleanings." "*Los vamos a limpiar*" (We will clean you), was a common phrase out of the lips of the torturers. In fact, *limpiar* (to clean) means to kill in Argentine slang, just as "to waste" does in American English slang. It took a "dirty" war to *limpiar* Argentina of ideological contamination.

The "disease" required radical surgical and hygienic intervention. The new inquisition was thus framed in medical and sanitary symbolism over ideological orthodoxy. This metaphorical logic helps explain the prominent role physicians played during the dirty war. In fact, many survivors reported that often during torture sessions, a military or police physician would come in, take their vital signs and proceed to inform the torturers whether to continue torturing, or whether to give the "patient" a break (CONADAP 1984). In fact, the torture room proper was known as the *quirofano* (operating room). I must emphasize that the operation took a very specific—indeed, patterned—tone.

A GRAMMAR OF TERROR: TOWARD A THEORY OF PSYCHOCULTURAL RESPONSES TO STATE TERROR

Thus was forged what Patricia Fagen, Guillermo O'Donnell, Michael Taussig, and others have termed a "culture of terror" (Corradi et al. 1989; Fagen 1985; Suárez-Orozco 1987*b*, 1987*c*, 1987*d*, 1987*f*; Taussig 1987:3–135). A culture with its own vocabulary and grammar, cultural facts, and artifacts ("disappeareds," *picanas* [electrical prods], *chupaderos* [torture centers], *quirofanos* [lit. "operating room," meaning torture rooms], etc.). The vocabulary of terror emerging out of the generals' monomaniacal war on dissent is highly contested territory in post-dirty war Argentina. Terms such as *guerra sucia* (dirty war) or *desaparecido* (as opposed to *detenido-desaparecido*, meaning detained-disappeared) are not only idioms for representing the epoch of the unspeakable but are themselves contested in the post-dirty war battle over just what did happen in Argentina during the dirty war. During an interview, an otherwise unassuming Mother of Plaza de Mayo launched into a lecture on why I should never refer to the dirty war again. A "war," she noted, presupposed at least two armies in place. What occurred in Argentina, as far as the Mothers are concerned, was not a war in any Clausewitzian sense of the term, but rather a unilateral assault on civil society by the armed forces set on crushing, literally, all meaningful political dissent (Madres de Plaza de Mayo, *Diarios* vols. 1–44).

The term *desaparecido* still captures the power of collective terror as social control. During the years of terror, introducing the word *desaparecido* even in the security of a family discussion produced a chilling effect. The relatives of *desaparecidos* soon found themselves abandoned by many friends and even relatives afraid of being associated with them. It was as if a plague had hit Argentina. The centrifugal forces set in motion by the terror were overwhelming.

The relatives of *desaparecidos* most often knew that a loved one had been kidnapped by the security forces. The very term *desaparecido* encouraged a form of prerational thinking: just as a son or daughter "disappeared" one day, they could so "reappear" another. Families of *desaparecidos* most commonly waited for their return. Some still do. Bedrooms and offices are kept as they were at the time of the disappearance, waiting for their "return" (Simpson and Bennett 1985). Indeed, Gorer's idea of "mummification," the mourning task of keeping the dead person's possessions intact and ready to use on their return, has taken epidemic proportions in Argentina (Gorer 1965). I relate this pattern to the problem of mourning and grieving without a corpse (see below). Magical realism was thus reborn in Argentina. The magic of thoughts now tormenting the relatives of the disappeared: What could I have done differently to prevent what occurred? What can I do to bring them back? And, of course, the unstated but ever present survivor's dilemma: What can I now do to make their senseless suffering meaningful? The psychocultural logic of the Mothers' resistance to terror in their ritual weekly walks in never-ending circles around the Plaza de Mayo, symbolizes the interminable search for their loved ones. Their chants demand *reaparición con vida y castigo a los culpables* (we want them back alive and punishment to those responsible).

In post–dirty war Argentina there is a great deal of literature about the difficulties of mourning without a corpse (Abudara et al. 1986; Freud 1955a:243–258; Kalish 1972; Kamerman 1988; Kersner 1988; Kordon et al. 1988; Kusnetzoff 1986; Movimiento Solidario de Salud Mental 1987; Nicoletti 1988:57–61; Pelento and Braun de Dunayevich 1986:229–237; Pincus 1975; Rosenblatt et al. 1976; Suárez-Orozco 1987b:227–246; Worden 1982). These psychological difficulties found a cultural idiom of expression in the Mothers of Plaza de Mayo. The very uncertainty of the disappeareds' state (alive? dead?) encourages magical thinking and hope against all hope. The mother's cry *aparición con vida* (lit. "reappearance with life," meaning "we want them back alive") captures both hope and is a paradigm of the sinister or the "uncanny" in Freud's sense of the term (Freud 1955b:219–252). The uncanny feeds on uncertainty. (Is the person alive? Or dead?)

Specifically, I argue that the Mothers of Plaza de Mayo have turned an interrupted mourning process (no bodies to ritually mourn and bury feeding a sense of uncertainty and hope) around and articulated out of their maternal pain and rage (their words), and survivor's guilt (my words, following Bettelheim [1952]), one of the most visible political discourses of resistance to terror in recent Latin American history (Bousquet 1980; Fisher 1989; Simpson and Bennett 1985). The mothers, by *coming together* to find out what was done to their children, subverted the silence and the centrifugal isolationism imposed during the years of terror by forcing public debate over the years of terror.

The dynamics of this social movement of a group of elderly, and heretofore largely apolitical *women* (not men), coming together in their pain and rage to articulate a combative political discourse, cannot be understood in its complexities without specific reference to the psychology of mourning. Nor can we fully understand, without reference to psychocultural processes, the fact that it was the mothers of the *desaparecidos* who turned private pain, rage, and terror into a *collective* project of resistance (each mother says she is searching for *all* the *desaparecidos*, not just her own child), while fathers of the disappeared turned inward, often *isolating* themselves from any collective projects, often going into major narcissistic depressive states and developing high morbidity and death rates (Daniel Kersner, personal communication).

This very important gender bifurcation, which, because of space constraints I cannot possibly do justice to in this chapter, must be related to (1) Argentine patriarchal family structure and dynamics (where the word of the father, the source of familial law was crushed by the terrorist state); (2) the image of mothers in Argentine society (as quietly suffering for their children's well-being) (Suárez-Orozco and Dundes 1984:111–133); (3) the mothers' appropriation and subversion of shared cultural expectations regarding fate, shame, and resignation. Their loud struggle for justice is, after all, in the most public space of Argentina, with the Plaza de Mayo as the symbolic center of the republic. It is worth briefly mentioning here that the mothers see their own project as being fed, rather directly, by maternal rage: as a mother put it, "We gave them (their *desaparecidos* children) birth, by taking them they have left a hole in our own bodies."

How, then, did Argentines psychologically respond to the terror? There is now substantial evidence that during 1976 and 1977, at a time when hundreds of people were disappearing daily, Argentines—even relatives of those missing—refused to believe the extent of the atrocities committed around them (Corradi 1987:113–129; Kordon et al. 1988; Kusnetzoff 1986:95–114; Pelento and Braun de Dunayevich 1986:229–237; Simpson and Bennett 1985; Suárez-Orozco 1987b:227–246). Carlos

Waisman has rightly observed that at the peak of the terror most Argentines coped, "by practicing denial . . . and rationalization on a large scale" (Waisman 1987:xiii). Indeed, as the psychoanalyst Juan Carlos Kusnetzoff brilliantly put it, the terror produced widespread "percepticide" in Argentina: the perceptual organs, too, soon became a causality of the engulfing terror (Kusnetzoff 1986:95–114).

Why was denial the first coping strategy? Denial has been singled out as a common first response to death and terror (Kordon et al. 1988; Kren and Rappoport 1980:2; Kusnetzoff 1986). In its most primitive form denial effects perception in the service of internal needs for security (Freud 1966; Haan 1977; Vaillant 1986). The ego's reality testing capacities are affected. There is a "failure to recognize" (Vaillant 1986: 128) certain aspects of the environment and of the self. An upper-status Anglo-Argentine mother of a *desaparecido* said of her first responses to her son's disappearance, "I couldn't believe it. You always think it won't happen to you, though I know it seems silly to say; it was happening to other people maybe, but not to us. And it is still a mystery to us" (Simpson and Bennett 1985:71). And her husband, "like the great majority of well-to-do Anglo-Argentines, refused to believe what she (wife) told him. . . . He didn't want to know anything about what was going on in Argentina then" (Simpson and Bennett 1985:72–73). Daniel Kersner, a psychiatrist working on the psychological problems facing the relatives of the disappeared, related to me the case of a young woman with disappeared siblings who in the midst of the terror was convinced that there were in fact no *desaparecidos* in Argentina! In brief, Argentines, as Juan Corradi has aptly put it, developed a "passion for ignorance" about the atrocities around them (Corradi 1987:119).[5]

I must emphasize that the denial mode in Argentina fed upon the novel feature of the new dirty wars—disappearances. The fact that in the Argentine case thousands of people simply vanished without bodies ever appearing in large numbers in the streets, left some critical psychological sequelae (CONADEP 1984). In Argentina, as noted above, the disappearances subverted the mourning process (Kordon et al. 1988; Pelento and Braun de Dunayevich 1986) and added further fuel to the tendency to deny: without a corpse to ritually mourn there is always the fantasy that the person is not really dead, the atrocities not real. The culture of terror thrived on ambiguities: reports of savage tortures circulated in an atmosphere of eerie calmness; reports of widespread massacres circulated even though there were no corpses to confirm them.

In the face of continued reports of widespread abuses denial eventually gave way to *rationalization* as the modal psychological pattern of defending. The Argentine modal form of rationalization during the infamous dirty war was captured in the widely used sinister phrase that a *desaparecido* disappeared only because that person "*estaría metido en algo*" (must have been involved in something, i.e., in subversive activities). I argue that *estaría metido en algo* became a formulaic response to defensively guard against the persistent reports (mostly in the foreign press, in the English-language newspaper *The Buenos Aires Herald,* in Jacobo Timerman's *La Opinión,* and in Rodolfo Walsh's *Prensa Clandestina* [Clandestine Press] [Walsh 1985]), and rumors of systematic disappearances and torture.

If the first response to the unspeakable in Argentina was "no, it cannot be happening," in the face of continued information and rumors to the effect that it *was* happening; the modal response became, "it cannot happen to me or my family, it can only happen to those involved in something." An alternative modal rationalization in the face of continued reports of the terror was that the whole thing was part of an elaborate, invented, left-wing propaganda campaign. Indeed, many in Argentina were at one point rather convinced that the reports of gross human rights violations that flourished in the international press were simply part of an infamous "anti-Argentine" campaign orchestrated by troublemakers who escaped to Europe and Mexico to "discredit" the fatherland. There is an inescapable "blame-the-victim" quality to such rationalizations: The atrocities cannot really be happening; they must be made up by the supposed victims who are enjoying refugee status in Mexico and Europe.

According to Vaillant, rationalization involves the "substitution of a plausible reason" (1986:133) for some self-serving motive. The plausible reason that people who had *not* been involved in any subversive activities were nevertheless tormented and made to disappear is substituted by the *desaparecido estaría metido en algo* formula. Such rationalization gives some sense of false security by invoking the theorem that *only those who are involved in subversive activities shall be punished, I am not involved in any subversive activity; therefore, I shall not be punished, I need not fear the reports.* The fallacy of the theorem is (1) even those who were involved in "subversive activities" should have been given trials and due process of law (which they most often were not [CONADEP 1984]) and not treated brutally and then made to disappear, and (2) many who disappeared were beyond even the remotest suspicion of subversion such as, among others, two French nuns (Simpson and Bennett 1985), a Swedish girl kidnapped and killed by "mistake" (Hagelin 1984), and the hundreds of babies who were born in captivity and then made to disappear (Suárez-Orozco 1987b, 1987c).

Denial and rationalizations were followed by widespread anger, another common response to loss. Anger was directed primarily at the authorities responsible for the disappearances and for the Malvinas-Falklands fiasco. Among those most closely touched by the terror, such as the relatives and friends of the *desaparecidos*, anger was also turned inward. ("What should I have done differently?") Anger turned inward typically leads to depression. I must emphasize an important gender bifurcation here: fathers tended to turn anger inward, whereas mothers generally turned anger to the authorities responsible for the disappearances and acted accordingly. Bargaining is another common response to death. In the case of dirty war terror, it took the form of hoping against hope that the loved one was not dead, after all. Or, as the Mothers still chant today, *"Aparición con vida"* (We want them [*desaparecidos*] to reappear, alive).

Postdisappearance magical rituals of bargaining flourished in Argentina. People tried everything from selling their houses in order to bribe the authorities for mercy (Duhalde 1983), to talking to a son's tormentors over the telephone "with an extra nice voice," as a desperate father put it to me, to better his son's chances for survival.

Depression and acceptance have been also described as basic responses to death. But many of the relatives of the disappeared cannot psychologically accept the deaths as final: without a corpse to mourn and to ritually signify death, there is always the powerful fantasy that somehow, somewhere, one's loved one is not really dead. A mother of a *desaparecido* who has been missing since 1979 told me in 1988, almost a full decade after the disappearance, that she could not come to accept the remarriage of her daughter-in-law (surviving wife of the *desaparecido*) to another man. The unstated point of this mother was, "She must wait for him, she has no final proof he is dead. What happens if he returns?" Psychologically, she was turning her rage for her son's disappearance toward her daughter-in-law, as if accusing her, unconsciously, of finally burying any hopes that her *desaparecido* is still alive and will in due time reappear. I am told by psychiatrists and psychologists working on the psychological problems of the parents of the *desaparecidos* that this is not an uncommon pattern: anger at those who attempt to move on with life, either by remarriage or by moving away.

In addition to anger as those seen as less loyal, there is, as noted above, mummification (Gorer 1965). Most often, relatives of the *desaparecidos* keep their rooms, offices, clothes, and other belongings in the exact manner they were when the person was taken away. In some cases rooms have been kept untouched for almost a decade. These rooms develop a quasi-religious atmosphere. School photographs, a childhood soccer ball, or a favorite doll become sacred mementos. Psychodynamically speaking, this pattern points toward perhaps the key aspect of living with a disappeared: the ultimate uncertainty as to their relative's fate induced by an incomplete mourning process.

Related to this complex is the seemingly paradoxical fact that one of the key groups of the Mothers of Plaza de Mayo has manifested its vocal opposition to the exhumations of cadavers under the direction of Clyde Snow and his team of young Argentine forensic anthropologists (Madres de Plaza de Mayo, *Diarios* 1:2). This is now, in addition to bringing torturers to court and publicizing the terror their children suffered during the dirty war years, one of the Mothers' projects of resistance. The Mothers have said that these "foreigners" (Clyde Snow, for example, is a U.S. forensic anthropologist), "want to make us mothers of dead people, we are mothers of disappeared," as Hebe de Bonafini, president of the Mothers of Plaza de Mayo, put it.

Confronting the exhumed corpses is, of course, psychologically complex: the *desaparecidos* were most often young and healthy when they were taken and they now return in the form of an unrecognizable mass of bones. Yet a skeleton is psychologically quite different from a recently deceased corpse. Among other things, except perhaps to the trained eye of professional forensic anthropologists and forensic physicians, all skeletons look alike. A recently deceased corpse can be unmistakably recognized as being a relative or a loved one. A skeleton is almost an abstraction of death. Incidentally, the forensic anthropologists working on the exhumations have noted how they would much rather "work" with skeletons than with more recently deceased bodies. The great divide for them is remains with "soft tissue" versus remains without soft tissue. For the anthropologists, it is much harder to exhumate more recently deceased, soft-tissue remains than dried bones. Psychologically coping with "soft-tissue" cases requires much more energy. A forensic anthropologist working on the exhumation of *desaparecidos* noted that they deal with such cases by distancing themselves from the tasks at hand, making light of the enterprise, using as she put it, *humor negro*, (lit. "black humor" or "sick humor"). Humor researchers have, of course, long noted that humor is commonly used, among other reasons, to ventilate psychologically threatening materials.

The Mothers' attitude of rejecting the exhumations has cost them further victimization. Some Mothers have reported receiving in the mail large anonymous packages containing bones. This grisly spectacle, evidently perpetrated by those who wish the entire *desaparecidos* issue to be buried and no longer publicly debated, further fuels the Mothers' battle.

Related to their opposition to the exhumations, the Madres de Plaza de Mayo also worked against the laws classifying the *desaparecidos* as legally dead (see Madres de Plaza de Mayo, *Diarios* vols. 1–44). The legal sequelae of having some 10,000 to 30,000 *desaparecidos* is monumentally complex. In the case related above, can the spouse of a *desaparecido* legally remarry? What must she do before this? Must she first divorce her *desaparecido* husband before remarrying? Can she argue, for legal purposes, that she has been legally abandoned or deserted and thereby petition a divorce before she can remarry? Or, should the spouse of a *desaparecido* be classified as a widow before she can remarry? Can the property of a *desaparecido* be distributed among that person's heirs? Can their relatives collect *pension*, the Argentine social security help to relatives of a deceased head of household?

In a Catholic country where definitions such as *viuda* (widow), *soltera* (single), *abandonada* (abandoned by spouse), and *divorciada* (divorced) carry potential social stigma, all of these are extremely delicate considerations. The law now makes it possible for a relative to have a *desaparecido* be declared legally dead by a court.

Yet, the Mothers are opposed to these legal declarations (Madres de Plaza de Mayo, *Diarios* vols. 1–44). The Mothers of Plaza de Mayo have also lobbied against attempts by the state at economic remuneration on behalf of the *desaparecido*. The Mothers are opposed to the state giving them a sum of money, or a *pension*, or any other form of monetary remuneration for the disappearance. To do so, they argue, would be to acknowledge death. As the Mothers say, *con vida los llevaron, con vida los queremos* (They took them away alive, we want them back alive). Furthermore, the Mothers argue that any such bureaucratic intervention requires them to psychologically become their children's executioners: they would first need to psychologically kill and bury their children before proceeding with the legal route. And this is too costly, too guilt-inducing. It is as if giving up hope is betraying their children.

The Mothers have turned an interrupted mourning process, their psychological inability to bury their loved *desaparecidos* into a political discourse of resistance. The mourning was subverted by the very means utilized to spread terror by disappearances (i.e., no bodies to mourn, no cultural rituals to signify the loss). The mourning process was also subverted by the collective hysterical denial that permeated the atmosphere at the peak of the terror. As already noted in the midst of the dirty war, many people firmly believed that there were some minor "abuses," but only of those who were *metidos en algo* (involved in something). After all, as the propaganda machinery had it, *Los Argentinos somos Derechos y Humanos* (We Argentines are both humans and right [a pun implying that there were plenty of human rights in Argentina]). The paradox is that the very method of repression (by disappearance) fueled the Mothers' project of resistance. I am suggesting that taking up their children's ideological cause in their very self-conscious crusade for justice is perhaps the only way the Mothers could internalize the loss.

As already noted, during the elaboration of terror, that which had been previously forbidden but vaguely known, the death and unspeakable torments of thousands of people taken with impunity from their homes returned in the form of a flood into *public* discourse of images and events previously denied. The psychological dam constructed during years of repression could no longer contain the building terror. In post–dirty war Argentina, this became known as "the horror show" period. This epoch peaked in 1984/85, soon after the return to democratic rule under President Raúl Alfonsín. During this time torture victims and torturers made daily appearances on the mass media. Magazines that had been previously conspicuously silent about the epidemic of torture and disappearances now devoted entire issues to the unspeakable. The magazine *El Periodista,* of wide circulation in Buenos Aires, devoted a special issue to the legacy of the terror, including a detailed list of all the names of the accused torturers collected by the Alfonsín-appointed National Commission on Disappeared People (CONADEP 1984).

In December 1984 the Mothers began publishing a monthly newspaper to make public the savagery inflicted on their children during those years (Madres of Plaza de Mayo, *Diarios* vols. 1–44; Simpson and Bennett 1985). Likewise, the Abuelas de Plaza de Mayo began publishing their own report, *Informaciones,* to make public their efforts to locate the children of *desaparecidos* taken as "war booty" during the years of terror (Chavez 1985a:18–19; Guthmann 1986; Slavin 1985). During this time, the gory remains of exhumed corpses regularly appeared in midday TV news reports, and neighbors suddenly dared to swap stories of terror that they would have never dared to tell before.

Books such as *Yo secuestré, maté y vi torturar en la Escuela de Mecánica de la Armada* (I kidnapped, killed, and saw torture in the Navy's Mechanic School) by a "former torturer" (Vilarino [1984]; see also Victor [1981], and *Nunca Más* (Never Again), the eerie report on state terrorism by the Alfonsín-appointed National Commission on Disappeared

People (CONADEP 1984) were widely debated in post-dirty war Argentina. In fact, *Nunca Más* became an instant best-seller in Argentina when it appeared in print (over 200,000 copies of *Nunca Más* were sold in the months after it appeared in print [see Madres de Plaza de Mayo, *Diarios* 4:4]). Films such as the Oscar-winning *La Historia Oficial* (The official story), *La República Perdida* (The lost republic), and the Spanish production written by the Argentine historian Osvaldo Bayer, *Todo es Ausencia* (All that is missing), touching on the terror years and the legacy of the disappearances and torture, grabbed the Argentine attention like no domestic films have ever done before. *La historia oficial,* for example, relates the experiences of a middle-class woman in her journey from denying the atrocities committed during the dirty war to fully immersing herself in the terror during a quest for the true story of her adopted daughter. As the dramatis persona eventually finds out, her adopted daughter was in fact born to a couple of *desaparecidos.*

When, in 1985, the heads of the military juntas that had ruled Argentina during the years of state-mandated terror were finally tried by a civilian court (Chavez 1985*b*; Montalbano 1985; *The Economist* 1985), there were not only hourly television and radio updates of the proceedings but also a special publication, *El Diario del Juicio* (The trial's daily) and other publications (Ciancaglini and Granovsky 1986) were produced to cover all major aspects of the trial. *El Diario del Juicio* published the testimonies of the surviving torture victims and relatives of the *desaparecidos,* the expert witness testimony of foreign jurists, human rights activists, and forensic scientists (*El Diario del Juicio* vols. 1–15). *El Diario del Juicio* was sold out almost as soon as it appeared in newspaper stands throughout the country. I have called this phase of involution with the horrible, the elaboration of terror (Suárez-Orozco 1987*b*, 1987*c*, 1987*d*, 1987*e*, n.d.).[6]

Suddenly a compulsion to speak of the unspeakable seemed to consume the Argentine imagination. The cathartic aspects of speaking of the unspeakable that psychologists discovered almost a century earlier were rediscovered in Argentina, the center of psychoanalytic thinking in Latin America.

In this study I have advocated a psychocultural approach to the analysis of some very difficult issues emerging out of the recent Argentine experience. The scope of the study is by necessity limited to a specific set of concerns. I explored certain key psychocultural aspects of political terror and resistance. The psychological dialectic between knowing and not knowing, between denial and involution, help us explore responses and resistance to terror under extreme circumstances.

Just as many Argentines first dealt with the terror around them by individually knowing what not to know, almost predictably they eventually fully immersed themselves into the depths of the unspeakable to come to terms, collectively, with that infamous period of their history. As Daniel Kersner, a psychiatrist working with the Mothers in their pain, put it, "To think and accept is not different from assuming and being responsible for the pains of the (social) body. In order to be healed, one must understand" (1988:148). And even if many Argentines remain unable to accept what happened to them, I hope this study will help us all to understand.

ACKNOWLEDGMENTS

Funding for the research reported in this chapter was provided by generous grants from the Tinker Foundation, the Center for Iberian and Latin American Studies and the Committee on Research of the Academic Senate, University of California, San Diego. An earlier version of this chapter benefitted substantially from critical comments and suggestions made by Roy D'Andrade, JoAnn Martin, Laura Nader, Bob Nemiroff, Carolyn Nordstrom, Melford Spiro, and Carola Suárez-Orozco. I wish to express my sincere gratitude to them. I would also like to thank the staff of the Benson Latin American Collection of the University of Texas, Austin (Argentine "Dirty War" Archives) for their kindness during my research at that institution. The efficient staff of the Benson Collection made my study of over 10,000 pages of typewritten testimony of torture victims as pleasant as the task could be. The Mothers of Plaza de Mayo generously invited me into their homes in Buenos Aires and gave me an abundance of their printed documents, books, newspapers, press releases, poetry, songs and the like. My friend Daniel Kersner, a psychiatrist working with the relatives of the disappeared, also shared with me countless publications, books, and clinical materials relating to the dirty war. Needless to say, without these materials the essay could not have been written. I wish to express my sincere gratitude to them.

NOTES

1. For an introduction to the topic of human behavior under extreme circumstances of terror, see Odic (1972), Lifton (1967, 1986), Luel and Marcus (1984), Kren and Rappoport (1980), Wiesel (1960, 1989), Levi (1973), and Bettelheim (1952). These references are largely to literature dealing with the

much larger problem of Nazi terror. I do not mean to imply that the dirty war paradigm under consideration in this study is in the same realm as the Nazi death machine. However, it is important to keep in mind the pertinent literature emerging from the Nazi holocaust, and for that matter from the Cambodian experience (Pran 1989) and the Stalinist years of terror (Fein 1989; Taubman and Taubman 1989) to explore, comparatively, psychological responses to extreme circumstances. For a report on the "banality" of Nazi terror, see Arendt (1963). For an anthropological approach to the problem of terror as a cultural system, see Taussig (1987, 1988). For a critique of Taussig, see Suárez-Orozco (1988*a*). For a consideration of psychological aspects of political terror in Latin America, see Kordon et al. (1988) and Movimiento Solidario de Salud Mental (1987). For an introduction to the topic of terror and political violence, see Walter (1969). For a consideration of the cultural politics of terror in Peru, see Bourque and Warren (1989).

2. For a series of engaging essays on literary representations of terror, see Jara and Vigal (1986) and Balderston et al. (1987).

3. For a general consideration of the dynamics of terror growth, see Mellor (1961), Vidal-Naquet (1963), Tomas y Valiente (1973), Amnesty International (1973, 1984), Ruthven (1978), Bacry and Ternisien (1980), and Scarry (1985).

4. For examples, see Timerman (1981), Bonasso (1984), Hagelin (1984), Bonafini (1985), Jara and Vidal (1986), Seoane and Ruiz Nuñez (1987), Ulla and Echave (1986), Balderston et al. (1987), Paoletti (1987), and Buda (1988).

5. Note that this pattern of shared hysterical denials is not unlike that afflicting large numbers of Germans who professed ignorance about the extermination camps in their backyards (Kren and Rappoport 1980; Lifton 1986). Note that even today sectors of German society continue to hysterically deny the Nazi terror. For example, Linke and Dundes have recently (1988) written, "With the construction of the death camps, the Nazis created a world so horrible that it became difficult to confront. For many years after the war, countless Germans pleaded ignorance or claimed that the atrocities never happened at all. While this hesitation to face the historical facts might be understood as an attempt to escape or resolve the problem of guilt, such repression of memories seems to have left Germans unable to feel compassion for the tormented victims or unable to grieve for the dead. The denial of the past continues, although with the modern twist of mockery: In 1987, at a demonstration of right-wing extremists in Hamburg, the participants gathered, dressed in black leather suits, wearing "donkey masks" over their faces, carrying large signs strapped to their bodies that read "Ich Esel glaube immer noch, dass in deutschen KZs Juden vergast wurden" (What an ass I am for still believing that Jews were gassed in German concentration camps!) (Linke and Dundes 1988:3–4). Note that here Linke and Dundes refer to the hysterical denials afflicting the victimizers, not the victims. The victimizers may wish to deny the past to avoid guilt feelings, to rewrite history, or both. Note that the Argentine victimizers (security forces) may also refuse to believe any atrocities were committed during the reign of terror (Suárez-

Orozco 1987*b*:227–246). Although the structure of the mechanism of denial may be similar, I would argue for the need to differentiate victimizer denials from victim denials. Note that during the European holocaust potential victims also denied the extent of the atrocities committed around them: the moving film *The Garden of the Finzi-Continis* makes this point well. The film tells the story of a family of upper-status Italian Jews, all of whom refuse to see, up to the very moment they are deported to concentration camps, the nature of the terror then consuming Europe.

6. Note the current internalization and elaboration of Stalinist terror sweeping the Soviet Union (Fein 1989; Taubman and Taubman 1989) and the elaboration of terror during the genocidal regime of Pol Pot in Cambodia such as now found in the Museum of the Genocidal Crimes (Pran 1989). Also witness the emergence of the so-called literature of scars elaborating the terrors of the Chinese cultural revolution. And the *destape* (literally meaning to reveal or to uncover) that swept over Paraguay after thirty-five years of repressive dictatorship under General Alfredo Stroessner (Brooke 1989:6). The frenzy of cultural and artistic representation following the repression years in these various settings must also be seen in the context of elaborating past traumas. By "opening the window," people can publicly confront and elaborate the terrors of the past.

REFERENCES

Abudara, Oscar, et al., eds.
    1986   *Argentina Psicoanalisis Represion Politica*. Buenos Aires: Ediciones Kargieman.
Abuelas de Plaza de Mayo
    N.d.   *Informaciones*, vols. 1–25. Buenos Aires.
Adams, Richard N.
    N.d.   "The Reproduction of State Terrorism in Central America." Prepublication Working Papers of the Institute of Latin American Studies, University of Texas at Austin.
Amnesty International
    1973   *Amnesty International Report on Torture*. London: Gerald Duckworth & Co. Ltd.
    1980   *Testimony on Secret Detention Camps in Argentina*. London: Amnesty International Publications.
    1984   *Torture in the Eighties: An Amnesty International Report*. London: Amnesty International Publications.
Anzorena, Oscar R.
    1988   *Tiempo de Violencia y Utopia (1966–1976)*. Buenos Aires: Contrapunto.
Arendt, Hannah
    1963   *Eichmann in Jerusalem: A Report on the Banality of Evil*. New York: Viking Press.

Bacry, Daniel, and Michel Ternisien
1980   *La Torture: La nouvelle inquisition.* Paris: Fayard.
Bailey, F. G.
1989   "Anthropology." Unpublished manuscript.
Balderston, Daniel, D. W. Foster, T. H. Donghi, F. Masiello, M. Morello-Frosch, and B. Sarlo
1987   *Ficción y política: La Narrative argentina durante el proceso militar.* Buenos Aires: Alianza Editorial.
Bettelheim, Bruno
1952   *Surviving and Other Essays.* New York: Vintage Books.
Bianchedi, E. T., M. Bianchedi, J. Braun, M. Pelento, and J. Puget
1990   "Kidnapped Children in Argentina: Methodology of Restitution to Their Original Families (Some Reflections about Their Identity)." Paper read at the Children in War Conference, Hebrew University of Jerusalem, June 25–29.
Bonafini, Hebe de
1985   *Historias de vida.* Buenos Aires: Fraterna/del Nuevo Extremo.
Bonasso, Miguel
1984   *Recuerdo de la muerte.* Mexico, D.F.: Era.
Bourque, Susan C., and Kay B. Warren
1989   "Democracy without Peace: The Cultural Politics of Terror in Peru." *Latin American Research Review* 24:7–34.
Bousquet, Jean-Pierre
1980   *Las Locas de la Plaza de Mayo.* Buenos Aires: El Cid Editor.
Brooke, James
1989   "It's Almost Winter in Paraguay, but for Many It Seems Like Spring." *The New York Times,* May 14, p. 6.
Brown, Cynthia, ed.
1985   *With Friends Like These: The Americas Watch Report on Human Rights & U.S. Policy in Latin America.* New York: Pantheon Books.
Buda, Blanca
1988   *Cuerpo I—Zona IV (El infierno de Suárez Mason).* Buenos Aires: Contrapunto.
Cabeza, Carlos
1985   "Entrevista a José Deheza, Ex Ministro de Defensa." *El Diario del Juicio,* July 9, I(7):170–171.
Chavez, Lydia
1985a   "Argentine Children Who Became 'War Booty.'" *The San Francisco Chronicle,* September 10, pp. 18–19.
1985b   "Five from Juntas are Found Guilty in Argentine Trial." *The New York Times,* December 10, pp. 1–2.
Christian, Shirley
1988a   "Rebellious Argentine Troops Still Hold Base Despite Reports that Mutiny has Ended." *The New York Times,* December 6, p. A8.

1988b "Argentine Uprising Tied to Economics." *The New York Times,* December 7, p. A3.

Ciancaglini, Sergio, and Martín Granovsky
1986   *Cronicas del Apocalipsis.* Buenos Aires: Editorial Contrapunto.

CONADEP (Comisión Nacional Sobre la Desaparicin de Personas)
1984   *Nunca Más: Informe de la Comisión Nacional Sobre la Desaparición de Personas.* Buenos Aires: Editorial Universitaria de Buenos Aires.

Corradi, Juan E.
1987   "The Culture of Fear in Civil Society." In *From Military Rule to Liberal Democracy in Argentina,* pp. 113–129, M. Peralta-Ramos and Carlos H. Waisman, eds. Boulder, Colo., and London: Westview Press.

Corradi, Juan E., Patricia W. Fagen, and M. A. Garreton, eds.
1989   "Fear and Society: The Culture of Fear in the Authoritarian Regimes of the Southern Cone." Manuscript in preparation.

Duhalde, Eduardo L.
1983   *El estado terrorista argentino.* Buenos Aires: El Caballito.

El Diario del Juicio
1985   Vols. 1–15. Buenos Aires.

Fagen, Patricia W.
1985   "The Culture of Fear: Responses to State Terrorism in the Southern Cone." Paper presented at the Center for Latin American Studies, University of California, Berkeley, October 28.

Fein, Esther
1989   "Designers Vie to Honor Stalin Victims." *The New York Times,* September 17, p. 3.

Fisher, Jo
1989   *Mothers of the Disappeared.* Boston: South End Press.

Foucault, Michel
1979   *Discipline & Punish: The Birth of the Prison.* Trans. (from French) Alan Sheridan. New York: Vintage Books.

Freud, Anna
1966   *The Ego and the Mechanisms of Defense.* The Writings of Anna Freud, Vol. II, rev. ed. New York: International Universities Press.

Freud, Sigmund
1955a   Mourning and Melancholia. [Orig. 1917.] *The Standard Edition of the Complete Psychological Works of Sigmund Freud,* Vol. XIV. Trans. James Strachey. London: Hogarth Press.
1955b   The 'Uncanny.' [Orig. 1919.] *The Standard Edition of the Complete Psychological Works of Sigmund Freud,* Vol. XVII. Trans. James Strachey. London: Hogarth Press.

Gelman, Juan, and Osvaldo Bayer
1984   *Exilio.* Buenos Aires: Editorial Legasa.

Gillespie, Richard
1982   *Soldiers of Peron: Argentina's Montoneros.* Oxford: Oxford University Press.

Gorer, Geoffrey
    1965   *Death, Grief, and Mourning in Contemporary Britain.* London: Cresset.
Graham-Yooll, Andrew
    1986   *A State of Fear: Memories of Argentina's Nightmare.* London: Elan.
Gregorich, Luis
    1983   *La República Perdida.* Buenos Aires: Sudamericana-Planeta.
Guthmann, Edward
    1986   "My Child is Missing." *The San Francisco Examiner,* January 12, pp. 23–24.
Hann, Norma
    1977   *Coping and Defending: Process of Self-Environment Organization.* New York: Academic Press.
Hagelin, Ragnar
    1984   *Mi hija Dagmar.* Buenos Aires: Sudamericana-Planeta.
Herrera, Matilde
    1987   *José.* Buenos Aires: Editorial Contrapunto.
Herrera, Matilde, and Ernesto Tenembaum
    1989   *Identidad: Despojo y Restitución.* Buenos Aires: Editorial Contrapunto.
Jara, René, and Hernán Vidal, eds.
    1986   *Testimonio y Literatura.* Minneapolis, Minnesota: Monographic Series of the Society for the Study of Contemporary Hispanic and Lusophone Revolutionary Literatures, no. 3.
Kalish, Richard A., ed.
    1972   *Death and Dying: Views from Many Cultures.* New York: Baywood Publishing Co.
Kamerman, Jack B.
    1988   *Death in the Midst of Life: Social and Cultural Influences on Death, Grief and Mourning.* Englewood Cliffs, N.J.: Prentice-Hall.
Kersner, Daniel
    1988   "The Mythological Model as a Recourse for Social and Historical Inscription." In *Psychological Effects of Political Repression,* pp. 143–149, Diana R. Kordon et al., eds. Buenos Aires: Sudamericana-Planeta.
Kordon, Diana R., Lucila I. Edelman, D. M. Lagos, E. Nicoletti, R. C. Bozzolo, D. Siaky, M. L'Hoste, O. Bonano, and D. Kersner, eds.
    1988   *Psychological Effects of Political Repression* Trans. Dominique Kliagine. Buenos Aires: Sudamericana-Planeta.
Kordon, Diana R., and Lucila I. Edelman
    1988   "Psychological Effects of Political Repression." In *Psychological Effects of Political Repression,* pp. 33–40, Diana R. Kordon et al., eds. Buenos Aires: Sudamericana-Planeta.
Kren, George, and Leon Rappoport
    1980   *The Holocaust and the Crisis of Human Behavior.* New York: Holmes and Meier.

Krystal, Henry, ed.
    1968   *Massive Psychic Trauma.* New York: International Universities Press.
Kubler-Ross, Elisabeth
    1969   *On Death and Dying.* New York: Macmillan.
Kusnetzoff, Juan Carlos
    1986   "Renegación, desmentida, desaparición y percepticido como técnicas psicopáticas de la salvación de la patria (Una visión psicoanalítica del informe de la Conadep)." In *Argentina Psicoanalisis Represión Política,* pp. 95–114, Oscar Abudara et al., eds. Buenos Aires: Ediciones Kargieman.
Langguth, A. J.
    1978   *Hidden Terrors.* New York: Pantheon Books.
Levi, Primo
    1973   *Survival in Auschwitz.* Trans. S. Woolf. New York: Collier Books.
Lifton, Robert J.
    1967   *Death in Life: Survivors of Hiroshima.* New York: Basic Books.
    1986   *The Nazi Doctors: Medical Killing and the Psychology of Genocide.* New York: Basic Books.
Linke, Uli, and Alan Dundes
    1988   "More on Auschwitz Jokes." *Folklore* 99(1):3–10.
Luel, Steven A., and Paul Marcus, eds.
    1984   *Psychoanalytic Reflexions on the Holocaust: Selected Essays.* New York: KTAV Publishing.
Madres de Plaza de Mayo
    1984–   *Diarios,* vols. 1–44. Buenos Aires.
    1988
Mellor, Alec
    1961   *La torture: Son histoire, son abolition, sa reapparition au XXe siecle.* Paris: Mame.
Mignone, Emilio F.
    1986   *Iglesia y dictadura: el papel de la iglesia a la luz de sus relaciones con el régimen militar.* Buenos Aires: Ediciones del pensamiento nacional.
Montalbano, William
    1985   "Argentina's Ex-Leader Gets Life." *The Los Angeles Times,* December 10, pp. 1–2.
Movimiento Solidario de Salud Mental
    1987   *Terrorismo de estado: Efectos psicologicos en los niños.* Buenos Aires: Paidós.
Nicoletti, Elena
    1988   "Some Reflections on Clinical Work with Relatives of Missing People: A Particular Elaboration of Loss." In *Psychological Effects of Political Repression,* pp. 57–62, Diana R. Kordon et al., eds. Buenos Aires: Sudamericana-Planeta.
Nosiglia, Julio E.
    1985   *Botin de guerra.* Buenos Aires: Tierra Fertil.

Odic, C. J.
  1972   *Demain a Buchenwald.* Paris: Buchet Castel.
Paoletti, Alipio
  1987   *Como los Nazis, como en Vietnam: Los campos de concentración en la Argentina.* Buenos Aires: Contrapunto.
Pelento, Maria Lucila, and Julia Braun de Dunayevich
  1986   "La desaparición: Su repercusión en el individuo y en la sociedad." In *Argentina Psicoanalisis Represion Politica*, pp. 229–237, Oscar Abudara et al., eds. Buenos Aires: Ediciones Kargieman.
Pincus, Lily
  1975   *Death and the Family: The Importance of Mourning.* New York: Pantheon Books.
Pran, Dith
  1989   "Return to the Killing Fields." *The New York Times Magazine*, September 24, pp. 30–54.
Rock, David
  1985   *Argentina, 1516–1987: From Spanish Colonization to Alfonsin.* Berkeley, Los Angeles, London: University of California Press.
Rosenblatt, Paul, R. P. Walsh, and Douglas A. Jackson
  1976   *Grief and Mourning in Cross-Cultural Perspective.* New Haven, Conn.: HRAF Press.
Ruthven, Malise
  1978   *Torture: The Grand Conspiracy.* London: Weidenfeld and Nicolson.
Santucho, Julio
  1988   *Los Ultimos Guevaristas: Surgimiento y Eclipse del Ejército Revolucionario del Pueblo.* Buenos Aires: Puntosur.
Scarry, Elaine
  1985   *The Body in Pain: The Making and Unmaking of the World.* New York and Oxford: Oxford University Press.
Schwartz, Theodore
  1976   "The Cargo Cult: A Melanesian Type Response to Change." In *Responses to Change: Society, Culture and Personality*, pp. 157–206, George A. De Vos, ed. New York: Van Nostrand.
Seoane, Maria, and Hector Ruiz Nuñez
  1987   *La noche de los lapices.* Buenos Aires: Contrapunto.
Simpson, John, and Jana Bennett
  1985   *The Disappeared and the Mothers of the Plaza: The Story of the 11,000 Argentinians Who Vanished.* New York: St. Martin's Press.
Slavin, J. P.
  1985   "Argentine Grandmothers Seek Lost Kids." *The Daily Californian* XVII(112), Monday, July 15th, pp. 1–7.
Suárez-Orozco, Marcelo M.
  1987a   "'Becoming Somebody': Central American Immigrants in U.S. Inner City Schools." *Anthropology and Education Quarterly* 18:287–298.

1987*b* "The Treatment of Children in the 'Dirty War': Ideology, State Terrorism and the Abuse of Children in Argentina." In *Child Survival,* pp. 227–246, Nancy Scheper-Hughes, ed. Dordrecht, The Netherlands: D. Reidel Publishing Co.

1987*c* "The War to End All Worlds: Children and the Family in the Dirty Side of the 'Dirty War.'" Paper presented to an invited session of the American Ethnological Society, San Antonio, Texas, May 1.

1987*d* "Culture and Terror in Argentina's 'Dirty War.'" Paper presented at the annual meeting of the International Psychohistorical Association. New York City, June 12.

1987*e* "Fear as a Cultural System in the Argentine 'Dirty War.'" Paper presented to a seminar of Peace and Conflict Studies, University of California, Berkeley, September 28.

1988*a* "Review of *Shamanism, Colonialism and the Wild Man: A Study of Terror and Healing* by Michael Taussig." *The Journal of Ritual Studies* 2(2): 272–275.

1988*b* "Survivors' Teleology and the Psycho-Cultural Exegesis of Human Motivation." Paper presented to a seminar of the Department of Anthropology, Princeton University. February 5.

1989 *Central American Refugees and U.S. High Schools: A Psychosocial Study of Motivation and Achievement.* Stanford, Calif.: Stanford University Press.

N.d. "Speaking of the Unspeakable: Studying Terror among Youths from War Torn Central America." Unpublished manuscript.

Suárez-Orozco, Marcelo, and Alan Dundes
1984 "The *Piropo* and the Dual Image of Women in the Spanish-Speaking World." *Journal of Latin American Lore* 10:1, 111–133.

Taubman, William, and Jane Taubman
1989 *Moscow Spring.* New York: Summit Books.

Taussig, Michael
1987 *Shamanism, Colonialism and the Wild Man: A Study of Terror and Healing.* Chicago: University of Chicago Press.

1988 "Terror as Usual." Unpublished manuscript.

The Economist (London)
1985 "Argentina Discovers Its Past, with Horror." September 28, pp. 37–38.

The New York Times
1989 "Argentina Issues Broad Pardon." October 8, p. 8.

Timerman, Jacobo
1981 *Prisoner without a Name, Cell without a Number.* New York: Alfred A. Knopf.

Tomas y Valiente, Fransisco
1973 *La Tortura en España, Estudios Historicos.* Barcelona: Editorial Ariel.

Ulla, Noemi, and Hugo Echave
  1986   *Despues de la noche: Dialogo con Graciela Fernandez Meijide.* Buenos
           Aires: Contrapunto.
Vaillant, George, ed.
  1986   *Empirical Studies of Ego Mechanisms of Defense.* Washington, D.C.:
           American Psychiatric Press.
Vázquez, Enrique
  1985   *La Ultima: Origen, apogeo y caida de la dictadura militar.* Buenos Aires:
           Editorial Universitaria de Buenos Aires.
Verbitsky, Horacio
  1985   "Una experiencia de difusión clandestina y participación popular."
           In *Rodolfo Walsh y la prensa clandestina, 1976–1978,* pp. 3–11, Ho-
           racio Verbitsky, ed. Buenos Aires: Ediciones de la Urraca.
Victor, J.
  1981   *Confesiones de un torturador.* Barcelona: Editorial Laia.
Vidal-Naquet, Pierre
  1963   *Torture: Cancer of Democracy.* Baltimore, Maryland: Penguin Books.
Vilarino, Raul D.
  1984   *Yo secuestré, maté y vi torturar en la Escuela de Mecánica de la Armada.*
           Buenos Aires: Perfil.
Waisman, Carlos
  1987   *Reversal of Development in Argentina: Postwar Counterrevolutionary Poli-
           cies and Their Structural Consequences.* Princeton: Princeton University
           Press.
Walsh, Rodolfo
  1985   *Rodolfo Walsh y la prensa clandestina, 1976–1978.* Ed. Horacio Ver-
           bitsky. Buenos Aires: Ediciones de la Urraca.
Walter, E. V.
  1969   *Terror and Resistance: A Study of Political Violence.* Oxford: Oxford
           University Press.
Weschler, Lawrence
  1990   *A Miracle, A Universe: Settling Accounts with Torturers.* New York:
           Pantheon Books.
Wiesel, Eli
  1960   *Night.* New York: Hill and Wang.
  1989   "Art and the Holocaust: Trivializing Memory." *The New York Times,*
           June 6, p. 14.
Worden, J. William
  1982   *Grief Counseling and Grief Therapy.* New York: Springer.

TWELVE

The Backyard Front

Carolyn Nordstrom

"My world is a fragile one—it is not only the hardships that have befallen me and the atrocities I have seen—it is the end of my family. They are all gone I don't know where, I don't even know who is alive and who isn't. It is the end of my community—it has been long gone after suffering the armed bandit's attack and the ravages of war . . . and this is the end of my home, my home in all that it means. I live in a fragmented world, I am no longer the person I was when I was born: a person with a home, a family, a community and a future." (Fieldnotes, Mozambique, 1989: a health care worker in his twenties who was kidnapped by the rebel group RENAMO when they overran his village. Over a year later he escaped and, although terrified of RENAMO and recapture, was preparing to return to the area of his village to provide critically needed health care.)

Research studies on conflict most frequently focus on ideology and (para)military forces as agents of rational violence directed toward changing an unjust world. Thus a common approach in the ethnography of violence is to identify the reason—if not the reasonableness—in violence and struggle. In fact, as Bibeau (1988:402) notes, "the search for logico-meaningful coherence permeates most theoretical and methodological approaches in North American general anthropology."

Rather than investigate the logic of the struggling factions, however, I want to explore the phenomenon of sociopolitical violence as experienced by average citizens, to examine how violence is played out in the larger contexts of the lives and life-worlds of civilians who find themselves on the frontlines of today's dirty wars, wars they did not start and do not control.

The term *dirty war* is most often used to describe campaigns of state-sponsored terror and repression whose goal is to suppress suspected civilian resistance (Suárez-Orozco 1987). My fieldwork in Sri Lanka and Mozambique suggests, however, that dirty war strategies can be used by all contenders for power.[1] Both states and guerrilla forces use the construction of terror and the absurd as a mechanism for gaining or maintaining sociopolitical control over a population.

The increasing reliance on dirty war tactics has escalated the equation of power and control through fear to a dangerous level.[2] Dirty wars seek victory, not through military and battlefield strategies, but through horror. Civilians, rather than soldiers, are the tactical targets, and fear, brutality, and murder are the foundation on which control is constructed.

By focusing on civilians and exploiting just-war dichotomies, dirty war tactics construct a culture of terror (Taussig 1987). This is accomplished, I suggest, by forcefully deconstructing accepted realities within daily life so as to "disabilize" fundamental meaning and knowledge systems—epistemological and ontological—that define people's life-worlds and render action comprehensible. Once the "ability" of these socially constructed systems is undermined, essential knowledge frameworks themselves can be disabled so as to be incapable of functioning with normally expected coherence. If culture grounds society, and society grounds the social construction of reality, then the disabilization of cultural frameworks simultaneously disabilizes the civilian population's sense of a viable reality and individuals' ability to act, or at least to act with meaning and definition.

Maimed bodies and ruined villages are obvious casualties of dirty wars. Maimed culture—including crucial frameworks of knowledge—and ruined social institutions are not as visible, but they are equally powerful realities and their destruction may have a much more enduring and serious impact than the more obvious gruesome casualties of war.

A WAR BY ANY OTHER NAME . . . :
MOZAMBIQUE AND SRI LANKA

Both Mozambique and Sri Lanka are currently undergoing internal conflicts that are among the most truculent occurring in the world today.

In Sri Lanka, the Tamil guerrilla war for "Eelam" (a separate state in the North of the island) continues. The conflict in the country has escalated with the introduction and dismissal of contentious Indian "peace-keeping forces" intended to control Tamil violence, and with the rise of the People's Liberation Front (JVP), a Sinhalese nationalist guerrilla group seeking to overthrow both the government and the Tamil fight for "Eelam" (Committee for Rational Development 1984; de Silva 1986; Jayawardena 1985; Kapferer 1988; Manor 1984; Rogers 1987; Tambiah 1986; Wilson 1988). These internal struggles have produced such severe state-level and community-level human rights abuses that Amnesty International (1986a, 1986b) identified Sri Lanka as one of the most serious human rights violators in the world at the time.

Mozambique, in contrast, suffers at the hands of a single opposition force, RENAMO,[3] a particularly lethal rebel movement that has virtually no ideology or popular support; Minter (1989) estimates that some 90 percent of all RENAMO recruits are kidnapped youths. More than half a million of the country's fifteen million people have died in the past decade of warfare, with Mozambicans blaming RENAMO insurgents for over 90 percent of all atrocities committed (Gersony, 1988a, 1988b).

RENAMO was formed by Rhodesia's Ian Smith in the 1970s and supported by South Africa's Military Intelligence after Rhodesia's fall (Hanlon 1984; Issacman and Issacman 1983; Johnson and Martin 1986; Legum 1988). The primary intent of these two countries was to destabilize Mozambique in order to thwart any challenge the resource-rich Marxist-Leninist country might pose to their political and economic hegemony in southern Africa.

Despite the differences between the conflicts in Sri Lanka and Mozambique, the emotional landscapes of the two countries, especially outside the capital cities, are similar. One sees the carcasses of burned-out villages and communities that got in the way of the war—that became the war. The bullet holes of the battlefields are in the houses and shops of the villages and towns; the people are frightened by any show of force, by any uniform.

The wars in Mozambique and Sri Lanka represent markedly different parameters of politicomilitary activity, but one truth seems to emerge as paramount for both countries: it is the civilian who stands at the heart—and on the frontline—of war today.

VOICES FROM THE FRONTLINES

A middle-aged Tamil woman living in Jaffna relayed the following to me in discussing the trauma of daily life in a war zone: "I never know what will happen from one day to the next, from one minute to the next.

When my husband leaves for work, I never know if he will return. . . . I am terrified everyday when I send my children off to school that something will happen to them, that they will be caught in a crossfire, that they will be taken or killed. I suppose I should worry about myself too, but I have too many other things to worry about. The [Sinhalese] soldiers always did harass and rape women, but now that the war has heated up so much here, things are much worse. The soldiers do house to house searches for information, but it is the innocent people they 'question'[4]—they can't find the guerrillas. The house just down the street, they hurt their daughter really bad, trying to find out information about the guerrillas: I guess they thought her brother was in with them, but he is just a schoolboy. The soldiers aren't the only ones, our boys [Tamil guerrillas] have done things too. The other day, maybe you saw, there was a young girl killed for supposedly talking to the Sinhalese soldiers, but I don't think she did. How can you say what is talking and what is not when the [Sinhalese] soldiers beat and even torture and kill people when they want something? Maybe it is easier to do this to women, we are at home and we don't fight. You know they came to my home, too, you know they 'interrogated' us and took my child."

The dirty war has assumed the level of spectacle in Mozambique and Sri Lanka. The rape, mutilation, and murder of civilians is often conducted as public performance to communicate dread-threat to all. In both countries the severing of civilians' ears, noses, and lips is a frequent tactic; sometimes limbs and genitals are the preferred targets. In Sri Lanka, during a trip to Jaffna, I was shown a woman whose breasts had been hacked off with a machete—her body left as a public exhibition. She was returning home from the market with her children. The same day I witnessed a man whose skull had been shot off, his brains left exposed. His crime: waiting at a bus stop. More recently, right-wing death squads in southern Sri Lanka severed the heads of scores of Sinhalese youths "suspected of left-wing collusion" and placed them around a lake in the center of a major city.

In Mozambique, the following story is not considered unusual. A woman arrived at a refugee camp in Safala province from an area under attack by RENAMO. She appeared physically unharmed, but she had been forced to watch her son being killed. Her son's murderers then chopped up the corpse, cooked it, and threatened to kill her if she refused to eat the portion they served to her. . . . "I did as they asked. I was scared. I did not know what else to do."

The mere construction of terror no longer seems sufficiently terrifying to those who wage dirty wars. The public performances become more grotesque, more aberrant; the horror rendered is sharpened by enacting violence simultaneously absurd and hyperreal (Baudrillard, 1983).

Sometimes the individual is bypassed to create a metamessage of absurd destruction: the obliteration of whole villages and towns. Water sources are polluted; crops are destroyed; hospitals, schools, and social services centers are burned, often with people still inside. In Mozambique, communities are ransacked for all useful items—food, clothing, medicines, electrical wire, railroad ties—and the rest is destroyed. Civilians are often forcibly conscripted by RENAMO to porter what has just been confiscated from them, to provide the cook for the camps, and to render sexual services for the soldiers.

An insightful narrative about the toll of terror-warfare was told to me by a middle-aged man in the Zambezia Province of Mozambique, one of the worst areas of fighting at the time I spoke with him. He had arrived at a "safe" area (ostensibly under the control of the government and not RENAMO) only the day before we spoke: "We were under RENAMO control for several years. They came in and took everything, including us. We were forced to move around a lot, carrying heavy weights for RENAMO here, being pushed there for no apparent reason. People died, people were killed, people were hurt, cut, assaulted, beaten . . . there was no medicine, no doctors, no food to help them. My family is gone, all of them. Only I am here. But the violence and the killing is not necessarily the worst of it. Worst of all is the endless hunger, the forced marches, the 'homelessness' . . . day in and day out a meager and hurting existence that seems to stretch on forever."

These stories abound in Mozambique and Sri Lanka: told, reconfirmed, retold. They become public narratives. Some become institutionalized. Lina Magaia is a well-respected government worker in Mozambique. She was so appalled by the extensive stories of RENAMO brutality told to her by peasants in the outlying districts where she worked that she collected them for publication in a book. The opening story is of a village assault by RENAMO. All the villagers are rounded up and warned not to resist in any way. The threat: the leader of the group attempts to rape an eight-year-old girl. Unable to do so because of her small size, he finishes the deed with his knife, leaving the child to bleed to death in front of her family and friends who were forced to look on (Magaia 1988:19).

The promulgation of narrative may well serve an important function. If, indeed, hegemonic ideals are imparted below the level of critical consciousness (Bourdieu 1977), and thereby maintain a powerful hold on a community until some level of critical discourse within a framework of conscious endeavor becomes possible, then narrative can come to serve as critical commentary. The same process of narration, however, can serve to reinforce the cultural inculcation of terror (Taussig 1987). Spectacle and narrative together constitute a process of construction of social action that "may serve to both consolidate existing hegemonies . . . and to give shape to resistance or reform" (Comaroff 1985:6).

From beleaguered towns and villages throughout Mozambique and Sri Lanka civilians had differing levels of knowledge of who was involved in the aggressions, and why. While the ideologues and (para)militaries waging the conflict viewed the distinction of sides and the application of right and wrong to each as lying at the core of the conflict, civilians often had difficulty distinguishing sides, especially according to ideological considerations of just and unjust. Indeed, many of the victims of war—torn from comfort and community, family, and home, too often wounded or bereaved—do not know what the conflict is about or who the contenders are.

From a refugee camp outside the Trincomalee, Sri Lanka came the following lament: "I don't know who burned my village and killed seventeen people, including my brother's son. They came at night with guns and torches as we were sleeping. They set our houses and shops on fire and shot us as we ran. Who would do such a thing? We are just farmers, we are not at war with anyone. I have heard of these people called Tigers [the most prominent Tamil political guerrilla force], and that the army [predominantly Sinhalese] can be violent and uncontrollable. . . . But I don't know, I don't know what it is all about. All I know is I want a gun to protect my home and my family—that is, when I get one. How can I get a gun when everything I own is burned and destroyed? But how can I get a home without a gun to protect it?"

These words were spoken to me by a new arrival in an abandoned schoolhouse that was serving as a makeshift refugee center. They were echoed by the nearly 200 people who came to join in the conversation. From refugee camp to refugee camp, at both Tamil and Sinhalese camps, I heard almost identical conversations taking place. For nonpolitical noncombatants, Tamil and Sinhalese alike, the conflict was a time of trial, terror, deprivation, and bereavement.

From a remote village in Zambezia, Mozambique, a similar complaint is voiced: "Mozambique what? I am from the M. people, from my father's land and the land of my ancestors—over there, beyond those hills. They came through, the armed bandits [RENAMO], I'm told. They took things and they took people, and those of us that could, ran.

Everything is destroyed, I have no home, no clothes, only the bark you see. And still these bandits circle. It is always the children who hear them first. My children, they grow up with the priority of listening for bandit armies and avoiding gunshots. And for what? I don't know. I don't know why these people fight. There is no sense to it. I don't think anyone knows."

Most civilians share these sentiments: the devastation caused by the war is undeniable, but that it has sense is another matter altogether. Possibly the most astute observation on the ideology of the violence-afflicted citizens came from a young man living in Beira, Mozambique: "the only ideology the *people* have is an anti-atrocity ideology."

THE DIRTY WAR: PRODUCTION AND REPRODUCTION

Whether overt or covert, the dirty war is essentially a message directed not toward contending militaries, but to a more amorphous "enemy": the population at large. The victims themselves become the template on which power-loaded scripts are inscribed. The message can be conveyed through the "silent space" left by the simply disappeared and by the implication, but never the verbalization, of torture so horrifying that it cannot be contained within the framework of normal social dialogue and cultural metalogue. Or the message can be grotesquely visible—a social advertisement of dread and a symbolic threat of terror—as in cases where people are routinely maimed and returned to the community as a reminder and a reinforcement of the powerlessness of the general population.

As we have seen, "sense" and the "sense organs" alike are assaulted: the world they normally perceive is rendered meaningless, chaotic. The attack is both literal and symbolic: the cutting off of sense organs (ears, noses, lips) is a powerful metamessage: the war attacks all sense, leaving the population "senseless." They are thereby left without the means to perceive and reason—and, more importantly, to criticize and resist the forces confronting them.

The processes maintaining sociopolitical ideologies and hegemonic constructs are wed to the phenomenology of the body and the experience of identity in a fusion Bourdieu (1977) labels "embodiment." Embodiment has epistemological and ontological, as well as practical, ramifications: fundamental orientations are produced and reproduced throughout many levels of personal and cultural undertaking.

The dirty war focus on "disembodiment" in this context becomes a perverse double entendre representing the social construction of a reality of "impairment": a public process cum spectacle aimed at the garnishment of conceptual as well as sociopolitical control. "Disembodiment" is thus embodied: simultaneously producing constructs of terror and the absurd in a hegemonic diatribe and, at the same time, a mechanism attempting to "sever" the body from the body politic—at least that of the opponent's.

The political identity of the body is manipulated in dirty war torture such that "at least for the duration of this obscene and pathetic drama, it is not the pain but the regime that is incontestably real, not the pain but the regime that is total, not the pain but the regime that is able to eclipse all else, not the pain but the regime that is able to dissolve the world" (Scarry 1985:56). For the victims of such assaults it is not difficult to figure out, as Scarry (1985:207) concludes, that "to be intensely embodied is the equivalent of being unrepresented and is almost always the condition of those without power."

Most scholars concerned with dirty wars, Scarry included, tend to equate the use of torture with institutionalized regimes. In Mozambique, however, the regime has remained remarkably restrained in the use of dirty war tactics; as I have pointed out, it is the opposition that has coopted them. The sociopolitical association of body and state begs the question of boundaries. Challenges to the state are contests about the parameters of who controls definitions of "right" and the ability to enforce these parameters. Severing the actual boundaries of human bodies through maiming and torture can simultaneously serve to portray an assault on the boundaries of the body politic. Both a human body and a state without boundaries are inherent paradoxes—each a conceptual as well as geopolitical absurdity.

Just as "disembodiment" is a double entrendre in the power-terror dyad, "re-membering" is also a symbolic double entrendre (Gusterson n.d.). Boundaries can be reestablished, bodies and identities reaffirmed—all as sociopolitical process. Re-membering can provide socioconceptual coherency—the identification of something rendered whole—and with this epistemological meaningfulness, can be imparted. The reverse side of the process of re-membering should also be recognized: returning the limbs to the body politic rests on the recognition of stories of immense cruelty against the bodies of average people, a process capable of inculcating the very terror it seeks to overturn.

The disruptions of war far exceed the physical casualties and material destruction. If the foundations of culture are jarred in a war turned dirty, ontology is thrown open to question and people's sense of reality itself is rendered tenuous. If we accept the premise that reality is socially constructed (Berger and Luckman 1966; Schutz 1962, 1964), then the disruption of the basis of social relations and the shared epistemological truths on which it rests necessarily imperils people's ability to continue to construct a significant reality. As a Mozambican peasant eloquently pointed out to me, identity itself is then jeopardized: "This is my third 'place' [he does not use the word for home] in several months. My home was attacked and everything destroyed, and I escaped and ran to a new area. There I started to work the land again, but this place, too, was attacked and burned out, and I was lucky to escape with my life. Not all of my family are here with me. We all ran to escape the attackers, and we lost one another in the confusion—ran different ways. I hope the others are alive, safe somewhere else. Now I am here, and I am trying to farm again, but my heart is not in it—when will they attack again? When will all my labor go up in smoke, and I find myself reduced to having nothing yet one more time? Maybe they will take even my life next time. Before this situation the majority of people had homes, animals. Now, here, they have nothing. So we are always thinking 'yesterday I was different—I had my own liberty because I had my own things; my house, my animals, my land . . . ' Now it is different. Yesterday I was a person, I had my own personality, now I have nothing. All that I feel, all that I own now, is my suffering."

Possibly the most destructive aspect of dirty war tactics is the creation of the culturally destabilized space. The disappeared, the incised body parts, the family scattered and missing, the smoking husks of burned-out towns on the landscape leave a void in sociocultural process and conception that horrifies by its senselessness as much as by its brutality.

The dirty war is enacted as a cultural metalanguage encoded on the body and the social geography of the community. In its most basic terms, it plays on a fundamental horror of the body rendered unwhole—absurdly so—that produces a concomitant horror of a cultural reality rendered unwhole. For the victims of this process, the result yields what might be termed a skeletal epistemology.

Since culture and epistemology are a naturally regenerating phenomena, the disabling of cultural knowledge per se does not represent irreconcilable devastation. There is a danger in this process, however.

Schutz and Luckman (1973) have postulated that life-worlds—socially constructed knowledge systems so essential to cultural viability they are taken to represent reality in its most fundamental sense—ground human endeavor, conceptual and actual. While knowledge systems are not inherently consummate, the reality of the life-world(s) resting on them depends on the illusion that their integrity remains unchallenged. When the viability of the life-world is challenged, the sense of reality itself is simultaneously challenged.

If one follows Schutz and Luckman's argument, the routine transmission of knowledge and thus of a sense of reality is anchored in social structure and process. In times of crisis, rather than tolerate or critically reflect on gaps in the knowledge that grounds their life-worlds, people seek to "plug" any disjunctions in such a way that the fragility of knowledge does not become apparent and demonstrate that reality is in fact simply a social construction, one among a plethora of possibilities. Thus, when people's knowledge frameworks become threatened, they uncritically reconstruct a sense of life-world reality by borrowing from other available epistemological systems that are, or can be made, compatible with the impaired one.

As we have seen, among the main casualties of the dirty war are the basic social institutions that ground everyday life, the structures that substantiate knowledge. But during a war—when families are scattered, communities destroyed, and valued life-world traditions have been bankrupt by difficulty, terror, and need—epistemological systems that would normally provide the raw material for repairing impoverished frameworks of knowledge and meaning are being seriously undermined by the viciousness of the widespread violence.

For populations in areas devastated by fighting, one of the only immediate systems of knowledge and action visibly intact and in operation is the politicomilitary one, in which force is equated with right and violence is seen as instrumental to power. Terrorized civilians thus may increasingly come to absorb and, more dangerously, accept fundamental knowledge constructs that are based on force. The average citizen then comes to "know" that politics, force, and might (and possibly even justice and right) are equal. Violence parallels power. Witness the following conversation: "Talks with the armed bandits will never work unless we can first get to a place where we can crush them militarily—show them we are stronger . . . only then will they feel the pressure to talk." When I reminded the speaker that he had previously told me the many ways his culture had for approaching conflict resolution, he violently shook his head: "I can't believe that, not now, not with things like they are. That was before, now it is different . . . I tell you, the only way to solve these problems is to be the stronger, the more forceful."

To survive, then, is to coopt the force turned against people and to reflect it back on the perpetrators. This is ultimately why the dirty war

is doomed to fail, although the violence it has inculcated may be reproduced from one conflict scenario to another across sociopolitical time
and space—now increasingly a part of the cultural repertoire for the
society at large.

The need to create a counter-life-world construct to challenge the
politicomilitary one is not lost on some civilians who, casting a critical
eye at the situation they find themselves in, recognize the need to check
the tendency of many to incorporate the dirty war paradigm as a survival
mechanism. The following is an excerpt from a conversation I had with
an eighty-year-old Mozambican traditional medical practitioner. We
spoke in a remote district in northern Mozambique, in an area recently
liberated from RENAMO control by government forces. Under government protection, supplies could get through, and streams of displaced
people came seeking food and protection. The arrival of supplies
brought further RENAMO attacks, one of which took place several
hours before this conversation: "Wounds can be easily treated," the old
man said. "That is, the physical wounds. Some of these kids have
wounds because they have seen things they shouldn't see, that no child
should have to see—like their parents being killed. They change their
behavior. This is not like being mad. That we can treat. No, this is from
what they have seen—it is a social problem, a behavioral problem, not
a mental problem. They beat each other, they are disrespectful, they tell
harsh jokes and are delinquent. You can see it in their behavior toward
each other: more violence, more harshness, less respect—more breaking
down of tradition. There is no medicine for this."

In a similar vein, several women who belong to the Organization of
Mozambican Women explained: "What you call dirty war, we call part
of our life today, and we see it tearing us apart, insinuating itself into
our lives and ways. But there is something more to us. We survived hundreds of years of barbarous oppression under the Portuguese—and we
survived by keeping the seeds of our culture, ourselves, alive. We will
do the same now, but we need to be very conscious and directed in this,
a great deal of help and work is necessary to offset the problems and
pitfalls introduced by these hard and violent times. We know we must
do this at the level of the people and the culture."

The wars in Sri Lanka and Mozambique have become more socially
entrenched over the last decade. The violence and brutality have become increasingly widespread in terms of both the (para)militaries
fighting and the civilians affected. While grievances and a tendency for
revenge run high, there is also a strong counterforce of sheer fatigue

and disgust with the violence and its attendant atrocities. There are those, like the old Mozambican indigenous medical practitioner and the members of the women's organization, who realize ending the war, repairing the damage, and restoring the peace depend not only on ameliorating hostilities but, more importantly, on reconstructing people's disabilized life-worlds in ways that do not reproduce the conditions or ideologies that fueled the conflict.

ACKNOWLEDGMENTS

Fieldwork was conducted in Sri Lanka in 1981, 1982/83, 1985, 1986, and 1988 and in Mozambique in 1988 and 1989. I would like to thank the National Science Foundation for funding my Sri Lanka research and the MacArthur Foundation and the Institute for International Studies at the University of California, Berkeley for supporting my research in Mozambique. I have also had the opportunity to do comparative cross-cultural work on three world voyages with the Institute for Shipboard Education and have benefited from the camaraderie and insights provided by the deans and faculty of this program. I would like to thank Keith Gohsler, JoAnn Martin, Elizabeth Colson, and Jeff Sluka for their thoughtful critiques and comments on this chapter.

NOTES

1. This century has shown a remarkable trend in this regard: in World War I, over 80 percent of battlefield deaths were soldiers; by World War II half of the casualties were military and half civilian, while today nearly 90 percent of all war-related deaths are civilian (Bedjaoui, 1986; SIPRI, annual). It may safely be said that the least dangerous place to be in a war today is the military. With one-third of the world's countries at war today and two-thirds routinely relying on human rights abuses to control their populations in a bid to consolidate power, generating some twenty million refugees annually—and more than half a million casualties every year (Sivard 1989)—these problems take on an immediate importance of global dimensions.

2. Studies of military governments (Sivard 1988), interventionism (Klare and Kornbluh 1988), modern war dynamics (Foster and Rubenstein, 1986; SIPRI, annual) and human rights abuses (Amnesty International and Cultural Survival records) show a global trend toward increasing civilian decimation in contemporary conflicts.

3. RENAMO is the Portuguese acronym for Resistencia Nacional Mozambicana; the English acronym MNR (Mozambique National Resistance) is also in use. In Mozambique, the group is generally referred to as *bandidos armados*

(armed bandits). RENAMO, however, is the term most widely used in the literature.

4. The words *question* here and *interrogate* below are in quotation marks to denote the inflection the speaker used to convey the irony and anger people felt at the fact that these words actually translate into terror, beating, torture, and, possibly, murder.

REFERENCES

Amnesty International
  1986a   *Sri Lanka: Disappearances.* ASA 37/08/86. New York: Amnesty International.
  1986b   *Sri Lanka: File on Torture.* ASA 37/20/86. New York: Amnesty International.
Baudrillard, Jean
  1983   *Simulations.* New York: Semiotext(e), Columbia University.
Bedjaoui, Mohammed, ed.
  1986   *Modern Wars.* London: Zed Books.
Berger, Peter, and Thomas Luckman
  1966   *The Social Construction of Reality.* Garden City: Doubleday.
Bibeau, Gilles
  1988   "A Step Toward Thick Thinking: From Webs of Significance to Connections Across Dimensions." *Medical Anthropology Quarterly* 2(4): 402–416.
Bourdieu, Pierre
  1977   *Outline of a Theory of Practice.* Cambridge: Cambridge University Press.
Committee for Rational Development, ed.
  1984   *Sri Lanka: The Ethnic Conflict.* New Delhi: Navrang.
Comaroff, Jean
  1985   *Body of Power, Spirit of Resistance.* Chicago: The University of Chicago Press.
de Silva, K. M.
  1986   *Managing Ethnic Tensions in Multi-Ethnic Societies: Sri Lanka 1880–1985.* Lanham, Md.: University Press of America.
Foster, Mary Lecron, and Robert A. Rubenstein, eds.
  1986   *Peace and War: Cross-Cultural Perspectives.* New Brunswick: Transaction Books.
Gersony, Robert
  1988a   "Rebels Create Havoc in Mozambique." *Cultural Survival Quarterly* 12(2):31–40.
  1988b   "Summary of Mozambican Refugee Accounts of Principally Conflict-Related Experience in Mozambique." Report submitted to Ambassador Jonathon Moore, Director, Bureau for Refugees Program,

and Dr. Chester Crocker, Assistant Secretary of African Affairs. April 1988.

Gusterson, Hugh
N.d. "Nuclear Weapons and the Discipline of the Body." Unpublished manuscript.

Hanlon, Joseph
1984 *Mozambique: The Revolution under Fire.* London: Zed Books.

Issacman, Allen, and Barbara Issacman
1983 *Mozambique: From Colonialism to Revolution 1900–1982.* Hampshire, U.K.: Gower.

Jayawardena, Kumari
1985 *Ethnic and Class Conflicts in Sri Lanka.* Dehiwela: Center for Social Analysis.

Johnson, Phyllis, and David Martin
1986 *Destructive Engagement.* Harare: Zimbabwe Publishing House.

Kapferer, Bruce
1988 *Legends of People, Myths of State.* Washington, D.C.: Smithsonian Institution Press.

Klare, Michael, and Peter Kornbluh, eds.
1988 *Low Intensity Warfare.* New York: Pantheon.

Legum, Colim, ed.
1988 "Mozambique: Facing up to Desperate Hardships in Post-Machel Era." In *Africa Contemporary Record,* vol. 19 (1986–1987), pp. B681– B701. New York: Africana Publishing Co.

Magaia, Lina
1988 *Dumba Nengue: Run For Your Life. Peasant Tales of Tragedy in Mozambique.* Trenton, N.J.: Africa World Press.

Manor, James, ed.
1984 *Sri Lanka in Change and Crisis.* New York: St. Martin's Press.

Minter, William
1989 "The Mozambican National Resistance (RENAMO) as Described by Ex-participants." Research Report Submitted to Ford Foundation and Swedish International Development Agency. March 1989.

Rogers, John D.
1987 "Social Mobility, Popular Ideology, and Collective Violence in Modern Sri Lanka." *The Journal of Asian Studies* 46(3):583–602.

Scarry, Elaine
1985 *The Body In Pain: The Making and Unmaking of the World.* Oxford: Oxford University Press.

Schutz, Alfred
1962 *Collected Papers I: The Problem of Social Reality.* The Hague: Martinus Nijhoff.
1964 *Collected Papers II: Studies in Social Theory.* The Hague: Martinus Nijhoff.

Schutz, Alfred, and Thomas Luckman
  1973   *The Structures of the Life-World.* Evanston, Ill.: Northwestern University Press.
Sivard, Ruth Leger
  Annual *World Military and Social Expenditures.* Leesburg, Va.: World Priori-
  (1974–) ties.
Suárez-Orozco, Marcelo
  1987   "The Treatment of Children in the 'Dirty War': Ideology, State Terrorism, and the Abuse of Children in Argentina." In *Child Survival,* pp. 227–246, N. Scheper-Hughes, ed. Boston: D. Reidel Publishing Co.
Swedish International Peace Research Institute (SIPRI)
  Annual *World Armaments and Disarmament.* Stockholm: SIPRI Yearbook.
  (1972–)
Tambiah, Stanley
  1986   *Ethnic Fratricide and the Dismantling of Democracy.* Chicago: University of Chicago Press.
Taussig, Michael
  1987   *Shamanism, Colonialism, and the Wild Man.* Chicago: University of Chicago Press.
Wilson, A. Jeyaratnam
  1988   *The Break-up of Sri Lanka: The Sinhalese-Tamil Conflict.* London: C. Hurst.

Epilogue

THIRTEEN

Conflict and Violence

Elizabeth Colson

That human beings are social animals who are formed within social environments is a basic tenet of anthropology from which much else follows. We are also large and potentially dangerous animals, a fact denied by those who regard the natural as inherently benevolent, but accepted by the philosophers who formulated the theory of the social contract (Hobbes [1651]; Locke [1690]), by Freud (1930) and his followers who traced aggression to the frustrating of innate drives when these were checked by the constraints instituted by society, and by most of the communities where I have worked whose members accepted that friends, relatives, and casual neighbors might turn violent if angered by rejection and denial of demands or when envious of the good fortune of others. Belief in the existence of aggression in others, and in oneself, and a recognition that this is dangerous if uncontrolled are fundamental elements in the dynamics of social life (Colson 1974:35–51).

Aggression is inherent in our biology. Conflict of interests is endemic to social life. This does not mean that violence is inevitable, as Hobbes and Locke also argued when they proposed that government had been instituted because of the recognition that human ends were best served by controlling the right of individuals to pursue their individual interests by any means. Hobbes and Locke wrote in the seventeenth century, having themselves—especially Hobbes—experienced the violence of disorder associated with revolution and the breakdown of government. They thought public order and restraints on violence worth sacrificing for. They assumed that the primary purpose of government is the maintenance of order within a territorial state. They also assumed that rational humans would share a consensus about the desirability of order.

Since then the powerful ideological brew of nationalism has created that explosive entity, the nation-state with its potential for ethnic mobilization and confrontation. Economic systems have emerged that create massive conflicts of interests between classes and also nations. Technologies empower those who are able to seize control of the state apparatus and enhance the stakes for which people contend. Revolutionary changes that transform social life put in question such consensus as had emerged on values and on the limits of the permissible and the impermissible. Add to such disruptive forces the further creation of technologies that enable humans to play with destructive emotions and habituate themselves to violence under conditions that give them the pleasure of terror without expectation that it will recoil upon them.

The media saturate us with violence. In the late 1980s, American parents and children celebrate Halloween with visits to "ghost houses" organized by civic groups where they can thrill to "torture" scenes and the flow of imitation blood (reported on National Public Radio, October 31, 1989). Terror, and not pity for the victims, is the point of it all, but terror is divorced from the understanding of its consequences in immediate human pain and continuing fear. Entertainment of this sort is symptomatic of the fact that we are becoming both increasingly impressed with violence and increasingly detached from an understanding of it as social phenomenon. For some, as apparently for the New York youngsters who go "wilding" in Central Park, violence becomes an end in itself and needs no further justification. Terror and violence then assume no previous social relationships between violator and violated: they arise from no conflict of interest; since no end is served beyond their own experience, no acceptable alternative is available to those who experience pleasure in such acts.

For the most part, however, violence is still justified as a means to an end and is seen as emerging from conflict of interests between those who have some kind of social bond. The end pursued may be purely personal, as among the drug dealers in Spanish Harlem described by Philippe Bourgois (1989:9), who used displays of open ruthlessness to provide themselves with security: they said they trusted no one and "were claiming . . . that they were not dependent upon trust because they were tough enough to command respect and enforce all contracts they entered into." The one who shot his brother, paralyzing him for life, found that his vendors became "awesomely disciplined." This is comparable to the terror practiced by RENAMO force in Mozambique who "appear to have no social or political goals" other than to extract labor and food from a terrorized population (Ruiz and Frelick 1989:33).

Violence and terror used as the quickest route to obtaining what one happens to want are understandable but frightening because the widespread adoption of such tactics means the end to social life as most of us have known it. They become destructive of the very notion of a common good. We are back in a Hobbesian world that identifies the hero with the gunslinger who operates outside the law, where the only defense is offense (the justification of the gun lobby), and no guarantees can be trusted. This is precisely what most humans do not want, for no matter how much they dislike restraints on themselves, they ardently desire restraints on their associates.

They are more likely to condone the use of violence as a means to some larger goal to which they themselves adhere, whether this be in defense of some set of values or in defense of a community of identification, even though the numbers injured by such violence may be enormous, far greater than where violence is a case of each against all. Violence in the interests of a larger goal feeds on itself as it becomes a policy justified by the righteousness of suppressing dissent, overcoming tyranny, creating a nation, defending religious orthodoxy, or obtaining religious freedom. Then anything and everything may become acceptable. But this involves the denial of humanity to those identified as dangerous to the noble cause, a denial that in turn dehumanizes the aggressor.

Dehumanization has its roots in our ability to make discriminations and to prioritize degrees of identification and responsibility. That ability is at the base of social order and makes social life workable. But it is also dangerous, especially when large-scale societies make most fellow humans anonymous others. When we were free to think of human progress as inevitable, progress was to be measured by the degree to which basic rights were guaranteed across the barriers of distinction and adjudication replaced self-help when rights were infringed upon.

The twentieth century has been marked by valiant attempts to extend the rule of law across international boundaries and to make peaceful resolution of conflict both at the personal level and in public policy. World government is seen as one means of outlawing warfare, and nations are asked to accede to pacts that entrench certain basic rights to which all humans are entitled. The century has seen the birth of organizations such as Amnesty International that have a mission to investigate and publicize state violence against citizens. International agencies, such as the United Nations High Commissioner for Refugees, have been instituted to provide protection for those who must flee the violence or potential violence of their own governments and find themselves without the protection of citizenship. A common obligation of charity is laid upon individuals, corporate groups, and governments to provide for the needs of those who suffer anywhere in the world from natural or human-engineered disasters. Television provides vicarious participation immediately in the suffering of others, however distant. The world is increasingly seen as a single fragile environment, and recognition grows that we are all intricately involved in the solutions that will ensure its survival.

These efforts are a denial that violence is an appropriate solution for either personal or communal conflicts. Yet much that has happened during the century puts paid to any belief that violence, including the use of torture, is alien to us as a species, and underlines how difficult it is for us to control aggression or accept compromise solutions. During this century the scale of warfare increased; cities and industrial centers have become prime military targets; genocide has been adopted as public policy by more than one country; terror formerly outlawed in many countries has again become common; assassination is used against political leaders at home and abroad, sometimes by dissidents as currently in Colombia, and sometimes by governments. The Congress of the United States debates its legitimacy as a tool of public policy.

During the last few decades, war and preparation for war have preempted ever larger proportions of the world's resources. Even adjusting for inflation, industrial countries have doubled their outlay since 1960, and in the Third World the outlay has increased more than sixfold. The amount spent in 1986 alone was $825 billion (Renner 1989:133). Much of actual warfare has taken place in the so-called Third World, where since 1945 some 120 armed conflicts have killed at least twenty million people. The prime losers have been civilians, as Nordstrom (chap. 12) points out. Civilians accounted for 52 percent of all war related deaths in the 1960s, but 85 percent in the 1980s (Renner 1989:134–135). The majority of these conflicts since 1945 have been civil wars, pitting elites against domestic opponents, and they have accounted for approximately one-half of the war dead during this period (Renner 1989:135–136). They have been exacerbated by the intervention of industrial countries who have used the Third World as an arena to pursue their own differences. Civil wars and state terror have also put millions of people into flight—in 1988, it was estimated that some fourteen million who meet the U.N. criteria for refugee status were in need of protection and/or assistance, but many go uncounted because they fear to make themselves known. The known number is equaled by the number of people who are displaced within their own countries because civil disturbance makes it impossible for them to live normal lives at home (U.S. Committee for Refugees 1989:32–36).

North America and much of Europe have been free of warfare on home ground since World War II, but they have been involved in the wars that have disrupted much of the Third World, and the possibility of war dominates public policy. In the United States war is a dominant motif, a key symbol, used to define experience and suggest appropriate action. We war on poverty, drugs, crime, child abuse, AIDS (autoimmune deficiency syndrome), and much else, however inappropriate the context may be. We speak of campaigns and battles and militarize our objectives. Ellen Goodman (1989) points to the consequences of this preoccupation, for defining programs as war "simplifies the complex. It draws sides, us and them, good and evil. War demands a human enemy, people that in time become dehumanized." The metaphor justifies recourse to violence and destruction.

It is not only in the United States that violence shapes speech and thought. It is ironic that the rise of humanitarian concerns has gone hand in hand with the rise of violence and the processes of dehumanization that label whole categories of persons, irrespective of their actions, as legitimate targets of violence. In earlier years much of anthropology was shaped by the fact that it was concerned primarily with what it viewed as small-scale face-to-face communities and the emphasis was on homogeneity and assumed consensus. Much work was also done in colonial situations where violence was a state monopoly and people did not expect to be able to gain their ends through physical violence against one another. When the old colonial systems began to disintegrate from the 1940s on, conflicts of interest became blatant and the possibilities for violence multiplied. We are only beginning to reckon with the fact that people are now part of a world system that is highly stratified, rife with contradictions, and technically capable of tearing itself apart.

This volume is one instance of the growing awareness that much that we assumed as part of the nature of things is problematic and that violence is a construct that needs investigation. The volume deals with the metaphors used to designate some people as others and so vulnerable to attack, and it deals with the consequence of vulnerability and the deployment of terror.

Winans (chap. 6) found the Sukuma on the eve of Tanzanian independence activating the belief in the hyena-witch as communities became divided on political issues: fear of the witch then justified action against those who fell under suspicion. Orozco-Suárez (chap. 11), who writes of Argentina, looks at the degradation of torture that dehumanizes those who authorize it, those authorized to inflict it, the immediate victims, and the community at large. Jakubowska (chap. 5) and Sluka (chaps. 2, 10) are concerned with the emergence of a culture of resistance against state authority in which violence becomes not only a legitimate tactic of self-protection but also a source of honor and a powerful element in the definition of self. Such violence is now a pervasive element of daily life in the Palestinian West Bank and Gaza, feeding on the processes of exclusion identified by Jakubowska as providing the context for the transformation of the political interests of the Bedouin of the Negev toward resistance to the Israeli government. Violence is also pervasive in Northern Ireland, where in Belfast, violence engenders further violence and Sluka found art, poetry, and music infused with its images and justifying its use. In both places, children have become habituated to its presence and play with violence as a game through which they demonstrate personal worth.

Under these circumstances terrorism becomes an acceptable tool and becomes more terrible because no legitimate authority exists that can contain it within limits. Yet, terrorism, with its attacks on civilian planes and gathering places such as shops and theaters, unlike state terror, can work with a premise of shared responsibilities for action—it holds civilians ultimately responsible for actions carried out by their governments and finds them guilty of what is done in their name. Nordstrom (chap. 12), however, is concerned with a situation in which terror no longer appears to have any reference to a larger social purpose in the war RENAMO forces are waging on the people of Mozambique. Rather, it is used to destroy the bases of community life and undermine trust in any social relationship. RENAMO uses children both as objects of violence and as instruments of atrocities. They will find it difficult to reenter society even if peace is eventually reestablished. Violence let loose in this fashion can destroy the future. It can also force its victims to settle for any form of government that gives them freedom from attack.

What are the alternatives to violent defense of life and property or violent challenge to discrimination? Some of the chapters in this volume are concerned with situations in which people have used other alternatives. Parnell (chap. 8) and Dumont (chap. 7) describe techniques developed by Philippine communities to defuse potential confrontations and maneuver for advantage, while Scott (chap. 4) considers the techniques for distancing used by those who would risk too much by open challenges to the system of discrimination that oppresses them, and Martin (chap. 9) finds Mexican villagers responding to the possibility of political action that might bring them piecemeal gains.

There has been much talk of the indecency of thrusting one's own values on the rest of the world and of the impossibility of finding any means whereby systems of values can be evaluated against each other. A great many people in the world, however, have looked at what is happening and do not like it. They believe that there can be some agreement about what is essential if humans are to live in decency and without fear. This lies behind the drive of the human rights movement, which is attempting to set international standards to which governments and individuals will be held. They believe that the obligation to negotiate and adjudicate should be given priority over the freedom to subjugate or use violence against one another. If this is the wave of the future, well and good. But the question remains—however good the law, who shall enforce it, and how?

REFERENCES

Bourgois, Philippe
  1989   "Crack in Spanish Harlem: Culture and Economy in the Inner City."
          Anthropology Today 5(4):6–11.
Colson, Elizabeth
  1974   *Tradition and Contract: The Problem of Order.* New York: Aldine.
Freud, Sigmund
  1930   *Civilization and Its Discontent.* London: Hogarth Press.
Goodman, Ellen
  1989   "Off to War We Go." *San Francisco Chronicle* September 12, p. 20.
Hobbes, Thomas
  [1651] *Leviathan.* Ed. C. B. MacPherson. London: Penguin Books, 1968.
Locke, John
  [1690] *Two Treatises of Government.* Ed. Peter Laslett. Cambridge: Cambridge University Press, 1963.
Renner, Michael
  1989   "Enhancing Global Security." In *State of the World 1989,* pp. 132–153, Lester R. Brown et al., eds. New York: W. W. Norton.
Ruiz, Hiram A., and Bill Frelick.
  1989   "Africa's Uprooted People: Shaping a Humanitarian Response." *Issue, a Journal of Opinion* 18(1):29–35.
U.S. Committee for Refugees
  1989   *World Refugee Survey 1988 in Review.* Washington, D.C.: U.S. Committee for Refugees.

CONTRIBUTORS

John H. Bodley is Professor of Anthropology at Washington State University. He earned a Ph.D. from the University of Oregon in 1970 and has conducted fieldwork among indigenous groups in the Peruvian Amazon. His interest in government policies and native peoples is reflected in his books *Victims of Progress* (1990) and *Tribal Peoples and Development Issues* (1988).

Elizabeth Colson is Professor Emeritus, Department of Anthropology, University of California, Berkeley. She has carried out research on the effects of forced resettlement on various populations in the United States and in Africa. In 1988/89 she was a senior research associate at the Refugee Studies Program, Queen Elizabeth House, Oxford University. In addition to numerous books and articles on other subjects, she is author of *The Social Consequences of Resettlement* (1971), based on research in Gwembe District Zambia, and is junior editor (Scott Morgan, senior editor) of *People in Upheaval* (1987).

Jean-Paul Dumont is the Clarence J. Robinson Professor of Anthropology at George Mason University. He is currently working on a book based on his ethnographic experience of the central Philippines.

Longina Jakubowska received her M.A. from Warsaw University and Ph.D. from State University of New York at Stony Brook in 1985. She is presently Assistant Professor of Anthropology at the University of the Pacific in Stockton, California. Her research among the settled Bedouin in Israel extended from 1981 to 1987. She is currently working on political symbolism in eastern Europe.

JoAnn Martin received her Ph.D. from the University of California, Berkeley in 1987. She is presently Assistant Professor of Anthropology at Earlham College and Assistant Faculty Fellow at the Kellogg Institute at the University of Notre Dame. She is currently working on a book on peasant politics and the state in Mexico.

Carolyn Nordstrom received her Ph.D. in medical anthropology from the University of California, Berkeley. She is currently a Visiting Scholar/ Research Associate in the Peace and Conflict Studies Program at the University of California, Berkeley. She has carried out extensive fieldwork in South Asia and southern Africa with a focus on Sri Lanka and Mozambique, respectively. Her current research interests include the culture of conflict, internal guerrilla and low-intensity warfare, communal conflict, resolution, and complex medical systems.

Phillip Parnell, an anthropologist who is interested in furthering both interdisciplinary and comparative research, is an associate professor in Criminal Justice, Anthropology, Latin American Studies, and at the Law and Society Center at Indiana University in Bloomington. During eleven months in 1987 and 1988, while supported by a Fulbright Senior Research Fellowship and a grant from Indiana University, he lived and conducted research in one of Manila's largest squatter settlements. Parnell's highly acclaimed ethnography, *Escalating Disputes—Social Participation and Change in the Oaxacan Highlands*, charts the interweaving of social, political, and religious movements through extended disputes.

Jim Scott researches peasant politics and specializes in Southeast Asia. He is author of *The Moral Economy of the Peasant* (1976), *Weapons of the Weak* (1985), and *Domination and the Arts of Resistance* (1990). He raises sheep in Connecticut and teaches at Yale University. He is currently trying to understand why the modern state has typically been so hostile to seminomadic peoples.

Jeffrey Sluka received his Ph.D. in anthropology from the University of California at Berkeley in 1986, based on fieldwork conducted on the Falls Road in Belfast, Northern Ireland. He is the author of *Hearts and Minds, Water and Fish: Support for the IRA and INLA in a Northern Irish Ghetto* (Greenwich: JAI Press, 1989) and is currently a lecturer in the

Department of Social Anthropology at Massey University, Palmerston North, New Zealand. He is a critic of contemporary counterinsurgency theory and practice, and is currently researching liberation theology and Republican political rituals in Northern Ireland.

Marcelo M. Suárez-Orozco was born and educated in Buenos Aires, Argentina. He received his Ph.D. in Anthropology at the University of California, Berkeley in 1986 and is currently Assistant Professor of Anthropology at the University of California, San Diego. His most recent publications include *Central American Refugees and U.S. High Schools: A Psychosocial Study of Motivation and Achievement* (Stanford University Press, 1989) and *Status Inequality: The Self in Culture* (with George A. De Vos, Sage, 1990). He is Associate Editor of *Anthropology and Education Quarterly*, a publication of the American Anthropological Association.

Edgar Winans is Professor of Anthropology and Chairman of the African Studies Committee at the University of Washington. He has taught at Washington since 1966 and at the University of California, Riverside, 1959–1965. Winans received his Ph.D. at the University of California, Los Angeles in 1959 based on fieldwork in Northern Tanzania in 1956/57. He has conducted research in Tanzania, Kenya, and Uganda since that time. He has also been Economic Adviser to the Government of Kenya; Social Science Program Officer, Ford Foundation, Nairobi; a member of visiting missions to Kenya; and a member of the Culture and Ecology in East Africa Project supported by grants from the National Science Foundation and the National Institute for Mental Health during the 1960s.

INDEX

Designer:	U.C. Press Staff
Compositor:	Prestige Typography
Text:	10/12 Baskerville
Display:	Baskerville
Printer:	Maple-Vail Book Manufacturing Group
Binder:	Maple-Vail Book Manufacturing Group